WORTHLESS

WORTHLESS

Marilyn Hardy

Some of the names in this book have been changed for legal reasons

This paperback edition first published in Great Britain in 2008 by
Virgin Books Ltd
Thames Wharf Studios
Rainville Road
London
W6 9HA

First published in hardback by Virgin Books Ltd in 2007

A catalogue record for this book is available from the British Library.

ISBN 978 0 7535 1396 5

Typeset by TW Typesetting, Plymouth, Devon
Printed and bound in Great Britain by CPI Bookmarque Ltd, Croydon, CR0 4TD

1 3 5 7 9 10 8 6 4 2

To my beloved nephew, Stuart John Douglas.
A shining star among the darkness,
Stuart was a special person
and will remain in our hearts, always.

PROLOGUE

I was thirteen years old when I decided to end my life. Though, at the time, it was probably more of a cry for attention than a deliberate suicide attempt. All my young life I felt I had been striving to win my mother's affection, yet in my heart I could only feel her bitter rejection.

The evening before I took the pills, I had been indecently assaulted by some boys outside my friend Grace's house after going out to talk to them. The assault had shocked me badly, and as soon as I got away from them I sobbed bitterly on Grace's shoulder. I should never have gone outside to even talk to the lads.

I ran home a little later, traumatised by the assault, feeling that somehow it must have been all my own fault. I was terrified my mother would find out about it; I felt she would kill me if she knew and I had not intended to tell her. Yet at the same time, I felt a need to confide in her, hoping she would be able to ease my pain and lessen my embarrassment over the incident.

It was not to be.

As I crept in the back door of our house, Mam was waiting for me. She had already been told by Grace's neighbours that something had happened to me – my screams had alerted them – though what version of the incident she was given, I never did find out.

As soon as I walked into our kitchen, I was confronted by Mam. She slapped me hard across my tear-streaked cheeks.

'You dirty little tramp,' she yelled at me, as I tried to shield my face and head from her hard hands.

'Just what do you think you've been up to?' she demanded. As she continued to rain down her blows I tried to escape by running into the sitting room but she was soon after me, continuing her attack as she called me a 'dirty little bitch'.

'You are nothing but trouble to me,' she cried, as she punctuated every word with another slap.

The curtains were open in the sitting room and I wondered briefly if anyone would witness the scene of my mother hitting me as I cowered before her.

As I tried to evade Mam's blows, she kept up with her verbal abuse, yelling at me, 'You're bloody worthless you are, our Lyn, you've always been nothing but trouble to me and now you're a dirty little tramp into the bargain. I don't know what I've done to deserve a worthless girl like you.'

In between slaps and sobs, I tried to explain to Mam what had really happened, but she was having none of it. I had brought shame to her door, she told me.

Dad was at work on a night shift at the pit, so was not there to defend me this time.

'Get yourself off to bed and out of my sight, you tramp,' cried Mam, giving me a final whack to the head as I trembled in fear and shock in front of her. Her vivid, blue eyes bore coldly down into mine with neither love nor mercy in them.

I half-crawled up the stairs to bed as tears of injustice flowed freely down my stinging cheeks. I prayed she would not tell my dad about it.

Dad held me on a pedestal and I did not want to fall from his grace – it would break my dad's heart as well as mine. I did not sleep that night as the whole incident played over in my head. It was Mam's reaction and her cruel words, still resounding in my ears, that had hurt me most of all.

It was during this sleepless night that I made the decision to end my worthless life.

ONE

I'm on a mission today.

I have been filling out the never-ending forms to apply for my state retirement pension. These forms have to be completed early and sent back to the office that deals with this kind of thing, along with my birth and marriage certificates. It's while I am searching for these documents that I come across my box of treasures, which holds keepsakes of my past 60 years.

Opening the lid, I take a look through my mementos. I have hoarded many things over the years. There is a little box that contains my babies' first milk teeth and, when I count them, I'm surprised to find there are 44 of them in total. I'm amazed they have kept so long and not rotted away.

As I look further, I come across the little wristbands two of my children wore when they were born – surely they were never that tiny! They are pinned together with old-fashioned nappy pins that I once used to pin the terry-towel nappies on my babies. There were no disposable nappies cheaply available in those faraway days of 1966. Thank goodness they had been invented by 1979, the year I gave birth to my third child, Wayne. Not like

1966 when I gave birth to two of my children during the same year, Helen in January and Paul in December.

Those terry-towel nappies! I used to rinse them then soak them in a bucket of Napisan with a lid on. Then I had to wash, rinse and boil them in a galvanised bucket over the gas stove, then rinse them out again several times before hanging them out to dry on a washing line. No tumble driers in those days.

I continue to rummage through my souvenirs and find a lock of my eldest granddaughter's fine, golden-blonde hair. I've had this for many years, as Gemma is now eighteen. Yet I remember so well the day on which she was born in 1988. She was Helen's first child and I was present at the birth.

I keep a few letters in my box, one of which is from my youngest son, Wayne. He was staying with Helen and her husband David when I was in hospital having heart-bypass surgery the same year Gemma was born.

In his letter Wayne tells me he is having a good time and hopes I am too. I have to smile to myself, though at the same time a couple of teardrops fall from the corners of my eyes. I have read his letter so many times over the years the paper is now quite fragile. Wayne had only been nine years old at the time; in later years, he would tell me he thought I had gone on some kind of holiday on my own.

There is another letter I cherish, sent to me by Tom Cookson, husband of the late Catherine Cookson. I have read many of her books and had corresponded with her over the years, complimenting her on her work, especially her autobiography *Our Kate*. She always wrote back to me in her own hand and told me in one of her letters how difficult it had been for her to write *Our Kate*, having rewritten it many times before it finally went to press. These letters from Catherine I have also kept and treasured.

The last time I had written to her was to ask her advice on writing my own story, and I received this letter from

Tom. It is a beautifully handwritten letter in which he tells me how ill Catherine is, that she is bedridden and almost totally blind. He goes on to say that even if it had been forty years earlier, Catherine would have said the same thing to me: 'It's *your* story and only *you* can finish it.' So I think to myself that maybe now will be a good time to start. If I don't do it now, perhaps I never will.

I realise it will be no easy task to write of the emotional turmoil I have endured. There have been times of poverty, heartache and hunger akin to any novel that may have been written by Catherine herself; unfortunately, my anguish and sorrows have been all too real. It has taken me many years to even be able to confide in my husband Richard about my past life. Even then, my whole sorry tale of past miseries and torment has unfolded slowly and painfully, in dribs and drabs, while his shoulder has been the sponge soaking up my endless tears. It has been Richard who has comforted me during endless nights as I suffered constant nightmares of my past.

I have also come across some photos, although most of my precious snaps are stored carefully in albums. There is one of Helen and Paul aged about two and three years old. They are hand in hand on my mother's front doorstep, dressed up in the new outfits I had bought them for my young sister Ann's wedding. Paul now has four children of his own and I notice how much his children look like him at the same age.

I have also kept two old key rings that contain photos. They are the kind where if you hold them up to the light, the photos are so real they almost bring the people in them to life. One is of my mother and father together at a Butlin's holiday camp in Skegness. It was the last holiday they spent together, one of very few holidays they ever had. When I look at this photo of Mam and Dad together they look happy, yet I still feel a yearning for my mother's love. I still remember the years of trying to win my mother's affection but never quite managing it, always trying to please her and win her love, and I wonder if she ever loved or wanted me. But it's too late now and I feel I will never know.

In the other key-ring photo, Dad is on his own. He must have been around the age I am now when it was taken. He seems to be smiling especially at me and I can still feel the love that he gave me. He seems so alive in this photo I can nearly touch him. I loved my dad so much and I still feel the sadness of his death, though he has been gone from us now for 28 years. He died when he was only 62 years old and never did get to see my youngest son, Wayne. It's a pity – he would have loved Wayne and been so proud of him. Wayne is like him in a lot of ways.

Dad always wanted a son but the only son they ever had died during birth. My Aunt Kitty had told me the tale many times.

It was during an air raid in the Second World War that Mam had gone into labour. Problems had occurred and the midwife sent my dad to fetch a doctor, who was reluctant to come out during the air raid, as his wife was nervous of being left on her own.

He had attended but, according to Aunt Kitty, he had been in so much haste to get back to his wife that he had put Mam to sleep with chloroform then proceeded to deliver the baby by forceps. Apparently the doctor was in such a rush to get the delivery over with that he had badly damaged the baby's head and the baby was stillborn. The doctor had rushed home, leaving the midwife and Aunt Kitty to sort out mother and child.

Later, as Dad was handed the baby wrapped up in a little blanket, he had gone to stroke the dark hair of his perfect baby son's head. As he caressed his son's hair lovingly, the scalp peeled back – Aunt Kitty said this had been the doctor's fault as he had been in too much haste. Had it not been for this fact, she claimed Dad would have had his son, but had been left to arrange a burial instead.

Dad had never had much faith in doctors, and following that day it shrank further.

I remember so much of him, and the things he used to say are still in my head, just old proverbs like 'Don't put off till the morrow what you can do today', 'Don't let the grass grow under your feet', 'He who hesitates is lost' and so on. They are sayings that I often use to this day, so I'm sure Dad still lives on in a way inside me. I am sure he has looked over me during my lifetime, especially in my times of stress and trouble, when one of his little sayings would often pop into my mind.

I am sure the way Dad brought me up is why I have been able to survive the hard times – and hard times have been plentiful over the years. I was not always as happy and contented as I am today.

Finally, I find my marriage certificate, take it out of its envelope and scan it lovingly. My marriage to Richard David Hardy took place at Leicester's register office in 1986.

Richard is my rock, he is my knight in shining armour, and was the man who would save me from myself. He has been with me now for over 23 years. Without him I would not have become the person I am today. He has shown me such unconditional love and given me back my sense of self-worth, which I totally lacked before we met. Without him I would have been nothing. He has been by my side faithfully through good times and bad, for better or worse.

Indeed, the night I met Richard was to be the start of my 'happy life', my life of new beginnings. Richard always called our marriage certificate 'The Rule Book'. We've had little use for it throughout our years together; no rules have ever been broken. We remain as much, if not more, in love as the day we first met. We are closely bonded together – Richard is my life.

I replace the marriage certificate in its envelope: mission accomplished.

* * *

Today I have a wonderful husband and three children, now grown up with children of their own.

I have three stepdaughters: Mandy, Wendy and Joanne. Mandy is very close to me, and I love her like a daughter.

I am also a proud grandmother of eleven grandchildren, my daughter, Helen, gave birth to a lovely, baby boy Jamie earlier this year, when she was forty. Jamie came as a delightful surprise to us all, especially as Gemma is now eighteen and James is sixteen. They delight in their new baby brother and are able to spoil him. Helen has followed in my footsteps and has graduated as a nurse. She now works as a district nurse, following her maternity leave after having the baby. It reminds me of when I was doing my nurse training and had to take maternity leave to have her. It does not seem that long ago, yet my state badges were issued in March 1967.

I had tried to write my story years ago. It took me about two years to do it in long handwriting. Richard would often come in from his bingo nights at the club and find me writing at the dining room table. I would continue to write well into the early hours of next morning. When I finally finished it and re-read it all I felt as though I had exorcised old ghosts, but I thought no publisher would even look at my work, as rough as it was, so I tore it up and threw it out. Even Richard never got to read it and I think he worried at the time that I may later regret throwing it all away. I did not regret it, yet even now I still feel the urge to write, to try to get some of my 'self' onto paper before it is too late.

I know that in order to try to tell the story of my life there are many unhappy memories to be rehashed and sorted through if I am to be truthful about events. I do not want to upset my now happy life, yet I know there is no point in me trying to tell it unless I am truthful. To tell it all, I have to go back to the beginning, the year of my birth.

TWO

I was born on 21 January 1946 when Mam and Dad were living in Delacor Street, Stanley, County Durham. I was classified as a peace baby, as the Second World War had ended in 1945. My parents were George William Bennett and Georgina Bennett, known throughout her life as Ena.

My mother had been in hospital having part of her thyroid gland removed when she met my dad. She was born and raised in Pelton, County Durham, one of two daughters of William Grey, who had been a miner. As soon as Mam had left school she was placed into service.

I don't think Mam or my Aunt Kitty, her sister, had enjoyed a happy home life but they would never go into much detail of their childhood. Mam confessed to me in later years that she had been very unhappy at home and also when she had been in service. She wanted to be out of it, but it was the only work she had been trained for. While working there, though, she developed thyrotoxicosis, which landed her in the hospital, where she met my dad.

My dad was born in Sedgefield, County Durham, one of two sons of John William Bennett.

Dad, too, had suffered an unhappy childhood as his father had been a drinker and a gambling man. My dad would tell me as I got older how when he was a child, his father would often have his friends around at their home, where they would drink, smoke and gamble well into the night. As a result, they were quite poor in those days.

It was when my paternal grandmother was taken into hospital in Darlington that my father and mother were to meet. Dad had been visiting his mother when he spotted this young girl. She never had any visitors of her own and lay in her bed with huge popping eyeballs and beanpole skinny, the result, of course, of her illness. Dad plucked up the courage to go and talk to her and was soon spending more time at Mam's bedside than his own mother's.

According to Mam, she was instantly taken by Dad's brown eyes set in a ruggedly handsome face, but what had impressed her more was his dark, wavy hair. Dad was not a large man, about five foot ten inches tall, but had been clean and smartly dressed. As Mam was a miner's daughter, though, she had been disappointed at finding out that Dad was a miner, too. She had been hoping to meet someone in a better position.

Dad himself had not wanted to be a miner either. His father made him leave school at the age of fourteen to go down the pits to provide another income for the household, so he could continue to gamble.

Dad's family lived at Broom, Ferryhill, while Mam lived at Lanes End in Pelton, about 17 miles away. Before she was discharged from hospital, Dad asked Mam to hold court with her and she agreed. Dad had an old bicycle and thought nothing of riding the few miles to be able to visit her. He used to take her to the pictures or out for walks.

Mam and Dad had a brief courtship and married on Christmas Eve 1938; he was 22 and she was 23. The Second World War broke out in 1939. As mining was a reserved occupation, Dad did not have to go to war. Their first child, Elizabeth Palmer Bennett – we always called her Betty – was born on 19 July 1940.

Then they lost their baby son, born during an air raid, and I was next to be born in 1946, when Betty was five years old. I'm told I was a huge baby, going on for ten pounds at birth. Betty always liked to tell me I had a mass of dark hair and had hairs all down my back when I was born – she thought I looked like a monkey.

When I was six years old, along came Ann, my younger sister. I was smitten by our new baby. Whereas I looked up in awe at Betty, being my older sister, Ann soon became 'my baby' and I cherished her. As she grew into a toddler, she used to follow me everywhere. From first learning to walk, she would be there behind me, holding out her little hand. Whenever I tried to play with children of my own age, Ann would be there tagging on behind me, so I would take her hand and take her everywhere with me.

This got me into trouble sometimes. We lived in South Stanley by now and my Aunt Kitty and Uncle Joe lived in Stanley. One day I decided to visit Aunt Kitty, who I adored. As I set off on my journey, there was Ann toddling along behind me and, as much as I kept telling her to go home, she persistently followed me until I just gave in, held her hand and took her with me. When we returned home later that day I was in trouble. They had been looking everywhere for our Ann, fearing she was lost, even though in those days you never seemed to hear of child abduction. When I confessed where I'd taken her, I was severely reprimanded as I'd walked her all the way up the hills by the old pithead and crossed a railway to get there.

I still took her all over the place anyway. One day, a Sunday afternoon, Mam and Dad had gone to bed for a lie down after dinner. I wanted to go to a park with friends, but I was supposed to be looking after our Ann, so I decided to take her with me. I think she was only about two years old. She had a short bob of blonde hair pinned back at one side with a bobby-clip. On our way to the park, Ann fell over. I immediately ran to pick her up and looked at her in horror. Her face was streaming blood from a small wound on her forehead where her bobby-clip had penetrated it. She bled so profusely I thought she was going to die.

I picked her up in my arms and ran all the way home with her. I was terrified. Fortunately, the next-door neighbours spotted us before I had the chance to wake up Mam and Dad. They took us in and cleaned our Ann up and stopped the bleeding, which was a great relief to me. I could have been in serious trouble had it not been for their kindness. Looking back on it now, I don't know how I managed to run all that way home with a toddler in my arms. I was only eight myself.

We lived in a prefab: prefabricated homes that had been put up before the war and were not meant to last long. We ended up living there until shortly before I was eleven years old, then the council moved us to a three-bedroomed terraced house in South Stanley, further down the hill.

By this time, Betty had her own friends and, of course, our little Ann had made friends of her own, though we shared a double bed in one bedroom while Betty had her own little bedroom. So Ann and I remained close as sisters. When we went to bed, I used to tell her stories. I made them up as I went along and especially enjoyed telling her scary tales. She remembers them to this day, although I used to scare her so much she would wet the bed some nights, as she was too frightened to get up to go to the toilet. Of course when that happened it was trouble for both of us, as I'd be soaked through too.

I did not make friends easily and always felt myself to be a lonely child. Before we moved from the prefab, I can remember the long, lonely walks up to school and then home again, where I was constantly bullied. It was always the boys who would be the worst. One day, I remember walking home being bullied and taunted by boys until my temper snapped and I lashed out with a new bag my Aunt Kitty had bought me. I managed to hit one of the boys but broke the strap of my new bag in the process. I was so upset.

While I have some vivid memories of my childhood, whole chunks seem to be missing. Mam and Dad were very wrapped up in themselves, and although our dad always worked, we stayed very poor. Dad liked a cigarette and used to smoke Woodbines and save all the dog-ends in an old Oxo tin. When he could not afford to buy a packet of ten Woodbines, he would take out his old Oxo tin and a packet of Rizla papers, open up the old fag-ends, take out the baccy and proceed to make roll-ups. Mam never smoked and neither of them drank much and certainly Dad never gambled. He was dead against drinking and gambling all his life. He had seen enough of that with his own father.

He was a good father to us, always in work, and every Friday would turn his pay packet over to my mother. She managed the household budgeting and Dad always praised her for being 'a good manager'. He would get pocket money off Mam, about ten shillings a week. He used to send me to the shop to buy him a shilling 'screw' every week. This was chewing tobacco for down the pit, as cigarettes and matches were not allowed underground for obvious reasons. Miners used to be searched in those days before getting into the 'cage', the lift that would drop them hundreds of feet underground. It was a sackable offence to carry cigarettes or matches on one's person in the pits and, as far as I know, Dad never broke the rules.

Mam always expected Dad to buy her sweets or an ice cream off the van out of his pocket money to keep in her good books. He adored her, but nothing he ever did seemed to please her enough.

He had an old bike to get to the pit and back and was always working on it and constantly mending punctures.

He was forever busy. If he wasn't at work, he would be repairing his bike, gardening or making things. He had a knack of making electrical things and I used to sit on our back steps with him, watching whatever he was doing. Dad loved going down the scrapheap as well, and most times he would take me with him. We would set off to the dump, which was Dinky Bells scrapyard, where we spent hours sifting through rubbish. Sometimes it was for something he especially wanted, like a part for his bike. Other times it was just looking for anything in general that might prove useful.

One time I found an old dripping tin and shouted to him, 'This any good, Dad?' I was ecstatic when he agreed it would 'come in for something'. We would trek home through the fields, filthy, tired and hungry, carrying our odds and ends. Mam was never pleased with us coming home so dirty and bringing all the rubbish home – we had to get cleaned up before we were allowed any tea – but I think she liked me going off with Dad, if only to keep me out from under her feet.

That old dripping tin was made into a basic electric fire with old coils and wires and a plug. It worked, though we never did use it. For one reason, Mam would not give it houseroom and made Dad put it out in his shed with the other bits and bobs he'd invented. For another, why spend good money on electricity when we could have a proper coal fire? After all, Dad received free coal from the Coal Board as part of his wages. They used to deliver it a ton at a time about four times a year. I would help Dad shovel the coal into the coal shed, which he kept bolted and under lock and key at all times. The only time it was unlocked was when we shovelled the coal in or needed to fill a bucket of it for the fire. He trailed the fields for wood for chopping up into bundles of sticks to light the fire and also to supplement the coal. I always went with him and carried back as much wood as my little arms could hold. We walked for miles and miles, my dad and I. Those long walks bonded us closely together and I remember those early years as happy times. Mind you, I'm sure Mam always felt resentful of the time Dad spent with me when he wasn't at work and we used to go off on our rambling walks.

Sometimes he would take me up to the pit when he went to collect his pay-note. Then he would show me all around the pithead, the lamp shop where the miners' lamps were stocked and the token room. Every miner was accounted for by a token, a metal disc with a number on that he would be handed before his shift. At the end of every shift that token had to be returned so they knew all the men were above ground safely. They kept these tags on hooks in the token room. Dad would stop every now and then to have a word with a workmate or two, who would usually pat my head and say, 'This your lassie then, George? By, she's a bonny one.' I was always proud to be with Dad wherever we went, but to be acknowledged as one of Dad's lasses was praise indeed. I must have glowed with pride on those occasions.

Dad would point out the pit-baths, where they all showered after finishing a shift, yet if he had anyone to see there, he made sure I stayed where I was told to and waited for him. 'They run around there bare-arsed and I don't want you seeing that,' he would say. So I would stand dutifully wherever I was told until he returned to fetch me.

Dad once took me down a drift mine in Dipton, with only a torch for light. It seemed we walked for ages in dense darkness, the walls of the mine dripping wetter the further in we got. I was glad to get back out to see daylight again and wondered how men could work down there in near total blackness, in so much wetness, for up to twelve hours at a time.

He used to tell me about the conditions he'd worked in, just eighteen-inch seams sometimes, maybe flooded with water. Then he was a coal-hewer and would have to crawl along on his belly and hew out lumps of coal with a pickaxe. In his later years in the pits he was put onto pipefitting, which was easier for him, but it was too late in his life then to escape the aches and pains in his bones caused by working in such wet and restricted areas for so long.

Sometimes at home, before a night shift began, he would have to get up out of his bed and lie on the floor in front of the fire and try to doze there awhile because of the pain in his back, legs and arms. Then he'd get up, have a cup of tea and two Anadin tablets and be off to work with his tin of jam sandwiches and bottle of water. He said no other sandwiches kept as well as jam ones down the pit, and he used to share his with the pit ponies. He had shown me these little animals and I had been told how the men treated them with kindness down the mines. Once their working lives were over they would be brought out to graze, but they were good for nothing by then and were already blinded by constant darkness. It used to worry me about those poor ponies and sometimes, if it was my turn to do Dad's sandwiches, or his 'bait' as it was called, I would do an extra round of bread for him just to make sure the ponies got some.

We never went hungry, as some of our neighbours' children had to, although at times our food was very basic in the early years. Especially if Mam was laid up bad again. Sometimes she would take to her bed and be there for weeks at a time. I realise now that she suffered gynaecological problems, but as a child I only knew Mam was bad again and we'd have to cope without her.

These were the only times Dad didn't go to work, but our old GP would visit Mam at home and tell Dad to visit the surgery where he would issue him a sick note for work. Then it would be a joint effort between Dad and us girls at running the household, cooking meals and looking after Mam with her mysterious illnesses. I was about ten years old when they first began.

While I can never quite remember her showing me much affection or telling me she loved me, I can still remember always striving to win her approval. It was always a fruitless effort. However much I tried to please her, I could never win kisses, cuddles or any nice loving words that a child always yearns for from a mother.

Although Dad was not one with words of love, I always felt his love and affection. I swelled if he praised me, and sometimes he even hugged me. I always knew he would be there for us. Our walks together came to a halt when Mam took to her bed. There just wasn't time for that sort of nonsense any more. My childhood was abruptly coming to an end.

THREE

Six years between each child was quite a long time, I suppose, and meant there was a twelve-year gap between my older sister Betty and my younger sister Ann.

I was christened Marilyn, but was always called Lyn, except if a serious situation arose or I was being chastised. Even now, at my age, if I am addressed as Marilyn, it seems to make something in me want to stand to attention.

We three girls were all different natures. Betty, being the eldest, seemed to be the most defiant, while I was the one that was quiet and wanted to avoid trouble and confrontation. Our Ann, the youngest, was a devil-may-care tomboy type who seemed to make friends easily and on the whole seemed to enjoy her childhood. I tend to think she may have been shown more affection by Mam than either Betty or I was. If this was the case then good for her, but it would still never prepare her for when she would be shunned in later life by our own mother after Dad had died.

Although I felt Dad was a good loving father, I also knew him to be strict. He liked to feel he was head of the household and had a fearsome temper if he was disobeyed.

I can remember him getting angry and shouting to try to get to the bottom of things. I knew enough to keep quiet and not to backchat. Betty, however, liked to have the last word and would sometimes answer back, especially at the dinner table when we were all having a meal. Then Dad would pound the table with his cutlery and shout with rage at her. This used to scare me and I found it easiest to keep quiet and be obedient rather than risk his wrath.

He was not the type of man to hit us, but I remember Betty being clouted on odd occasions for answering him back. If we ever got on Mam's wrong side you could be sure my dad would be notified and duly felt it his duty to shout at us to let us know who was boss of the home.

I'm sure in my writing of our childhood memories there will be discrepancies that Ann and Betty may find with it. Perhaps they will remember things quite differently to myself, but I write through the eyes of the child I was then and the feelings I had in those times as truthfully as I can.

There were happy times in our childhood. Dad always made us our very own sledge in winter and branded it with our names on with a red-hot poker so other kids could not claim it for their own. The winters up North could be cold, harsh and cruel. We would wait for a good snowfall, take our homemade sledges out to go whizzing down the banks, then drag them all the way back up the hills and start all over again. We stayed out in the snow till our feet and hands were frozen solid. Once, after sledging for ages, I had to go home to get thawed out. Mam had a raging fire going as she was baking cakes. The oven was attached to the fireside so the fire had to be blazing well to get the oven hot enough to bake in. After getting washed and cleaned, and hanging up my soaking wet coat, gloves and scarf, I went to sit by the fireside to get warm. Mam told me to make myself useful and cream a huge bowl of butter and sugar together ready for her next batch of sponge cakes. As I dutifully beat and blended the ingredients together, the heat from the fire suddenly made my nose run. I sat there blending and beating and sniffing, but suddenly a drop ran off my nose into the mixture. It was just as Mam was turning around. 'Was that something fell into that bowl?' she screamed. 'No, Mam,' I lied, and continued with my blending more vigorously than ever, making sure the snot was blended in with the butter. I was too scared to admit the truth, and felt a bit of snot in the cakes would do no harm. Wasn't it my dad who always said, 'The more the muck, the stronger the man'?

Mam could be a hard woman in a quiet, cold way. If I had not done a good enough job for her in any task I'd been set, or if I had dared to try and explain myself to her, she would give me the cold-shoulder treatment. Often I would be made to stand in the corner and face the wall for long periods of time. If neighbours came into the house, as they tended to do in those days, Mam always made a point of whispering my latest misdemeanours to them to explain why I was being punished and they were instructed not to talk to me. I always felt this was unfair as I could never remember what sin I had committed to warrant the punishment. They were nearly always handed out to me when Dad was out at work. If ever he came home while I was stood in a corner, he would look very sad and helpless, then, after a whispered conversation between my parents I was usually let out of standing in the corner and sent to bed with no tea. By this time I was glad to get into bed as my back, arms and legs would be so tired and, even though I felt hungry, I nearly always fell straight off to sleep, just glad of the rest. Before dropping off to sleep, I would rack my brain to try and remember what I had done to deserve it and always fell asleep with a great sense of injustice and sadness.

Mam always showed a great sense of disappointment in me. On the whole, she treated me with coldness and, strive as I might to win her approval or a slither of praise, it was hardly ever forthcoming. Maybe it was because she realised Dad loved me and had given me so much time with him that she resented me, or perhaps it all had to do with her upbringing.

I can now forgive her and understand that she was just being the only kind of mother she could be to me, but it stripped me of all self-confidence and it's something I can never forget.

FOUR

I can't remember how old I was when we moved into the prefabs. I know our Ann was born while we lived there. She was a beautiful baby, blue-eyed like our mam and her hair was blond like Mam's used to be; both Betty and myself shared Dad's brown eyes and dark hair.

We lived next door to the Rodham family, who had one son, Tony.

The prefabs were small, pre-constructed buildings. They were very cold in winter and winters in the Northeast were bitter. The walls of our prefab used to be damp with condensation; even in summer there was a dampness to the walls. We could never keep the house dry. There was no central heating, just a coal fire in the living room. No heat ever reached the rest of the house.

The prefab was all on one floor and consisted of living room, two small bedrooms, a tiny bathroom with inside toilet and a small kitchen. There was a little front garden that sloped down towards the lane and concrete steps that led onto the lane itself. The back garden was quite big and Dad planted potatoes, carrots and a goosegog bush. He also put a rose bush just opposite the kitchen window for Mam. We didn't have much furniture, just the basics, which was a double bed in Mam and Dad's front bedroom and a bed in the back bedroom that Betty and I shared. There was an old dark-brown, leather sofa and one chair – reserved for Dad – in the living room. There was a small table Dad had made, on which we had an old wireless that we sat and listened to on dark winter nights while Mam sat and did her knitting.

Dad liked the programme *The Man in Black*. It used to start something like, 'This is Valentine Dial and I am your man in black.' I can't remember how the stories went much after that, but I remember how scared I used to be. We had to sit quietly when Dad listened to his stories on the wireless and he was forever twitching at the knobs and dial trying to get a better reception. Sometimes Betty and I shared comics on the floor, like *Bunty*, keeping them so long they were dog-eared. We had a small table and chairs in the kitchen, which had to be moved every time someone wanted something from the pantry.

Mondays were washdays and you could hardly move in the kitchen when the washing machine was pulled out. It was the old-fashioned type. You heated up the water in an old boiler, where first clothes were boiled, then they had to go into this contraption that had an agitator fitted to its lid. Once the clothes were in there, the lid was closed and someone, often me, was given the task of turning the handle to agitate the clothes. I would turn that handle until I felt my arms would drop off, they ached so much. Then Mam used a 'poss-stick' to lift the clothes out into a bowl to be rinsed in cold water in the big square sink. After that we would turn the handle of the mangle while Mam fed the clothes between the rollers. Finally the clothes could be hung out on the line to dry outside, but if Mondays were rainy, clothes would be hung on clothes horses in front of the fire to dry. Consequently, the whole of Mondays were always taken up by helping Mam do the washing and the constant drying or airing of the clothes made the condensation even worse.

In winter, the walls ran wet throughout the prefab. The dampness got everywhere, even the cupboards in our bedrooms. Whatever clothes or linen we had in cupboards often came out covered in bits of green mould, which we just brushed off.

We used to have a cat when we first lived in the prefabs, but it came to a sorry end. One Monday washday, Mam was doing the washing and she stepped on the cat by accident. There was this sudden screeching, drowned out by Mam's screams, and when Betty and I dared to look the poor cat lay badly hurt on the floor making a terrible noise. Mam was in hysterics, howling and crying. I just didn't know what to do, but our Betty shot out of the house and disappeared up the lane.

Next thing I remember Dad was home in a fearful temper. Betty had run all the way up to Stanley Pit and sobbed and cried to the weigh-man there that Mam had killed the cat and they had to fetch my dad. Consequently, someone was sent down into the shaft where Dad was working and he was told only that there had been an accident and he had to go home straightaway. When he was brought up out of the pit, he was met by the weigh-man who was holding onto a crying, sobbing Betty, who was now quite incoherent.

Dad got his old bike, sat Betty on the crossbar and cycled home as fast as he could pedal, fearing the worst. He knew it was washday and thought perhaps I'd been scalded or Mam had got her fingers trapped between the rollers of the mangle. He was confronted at home with the sight of me screaming, the cat screeching and Mam still hysterical. He looked like a big black bat in all his coal dust, only the whites of his eyes showing through all the black coal dust.

After calming both my mam and me down, Dad put the cat in a sack and pedalled away with it. We were told later the cat had been put to sleep and gone to heaven. As we were very poor and could not have afforded a vet's fees, I suspect now that Dad probably put the poor cat out of its misery himself and buried it somewhere.

'There will be nay more bloody animals in this house,' he swore to us. We were all in the doghouse for days. Not only had Dad lost part of his shift money, he was made a laughing stock by his workmates when he relayed his tale to them next day. He was the butt of their jokes for days to come and took it out on all of us by being quiet and withdrawn at home for a while.

Dad built a 'tent' outside for me and Betty to sleep out in one some summer evening. He did this by turning his wheelbarrow upside down with the long shaft handles resting on the wall below our bedroom window, then proceeded to cover the whole wheelbarrow with a huge tarpaulin cover, held in place on the ground by stones. Another tarpaulin cover was put on the ground to keep out any wet inside the tent, then Betty and I made up a bed for ourselves out of old coats that we kept for the purpose of piling on top of our beds in wintertime when our bedcovers were inadequate for keeping out the freezing cold.

We were quite excited at the prospect of our adventure of sleeping out all night and settled ourselves in early with our torch, jam sandwiches and a comic. We must have gone to sleep eventually, but in the early morning hours I was abruptly wakened by Betty's cries. She sat bolt upright staring into the eyes of a huge toad, screaming her head off. To be fair to Betty, it was the biggest toad I had ever seen. Rather than being scared of it myself, I was more disappointed than anything as Dad came flying out the back door and made us get indoors. We had woken them up alongside all the neighbours with our 'bloody racket'. That was to be the end of our camping out days. Betty was quite traumatised by it and still has a phobia of frogs and toads to this day.

That was not the only use for Dad's wheelbarrow. It was a huge, sturdy, wooden affair with very long handles. He used to take me with him when he pushed this old wheelbarrow down to the woods. Once there, he would look for the most lush-looking grass then cut out square clods of it and pile it all into the wheelbarrow. We would then push it all the way back up the hill and Dad would carefully lay all the sods down in the front garden. I'm sure it was probably illegal to do this, but Dad didn't care about that and he ended up having one of the best lawns in the lane.

The local farmer had loads of fields and let his cows roam freely. He never did keep his fences right – or else it may have been us kids that broke them down again, as we often went out in the dark evenings, stealing his potatoes and turnips. We even dared to bring some home. Dad didn't seem to mind us doing that as long as we didn't tell him about our intentions before we did it. After all, he'd gone out at nights himself and raided the farmer's fields, coming home with a sack full of vegetables. Mam used them to cook delicious stews with suet dumplings. Sometimes Dad would take us for miles tramping through the farmer's fields to pick blackberries. We would be out for hours, returning home with our carrier bags full of fruit that Mam would turn into blackberry tarts next day.

Anyway, due to the condition of the farmer's fences, his cows tended to escape. As we had no fence around our front lawn, the cows often wandered onto it and kept the lawn grass short, saving Dad the job of mowing it. When they shit on his lawn or tapped on their bedroom window with their noses and woke Mam and Dad up, though, that was a different matter. Dad took umbrage. He had the audacity to complain to the farmer about his fences being broken and letting his cows wander the roads, after the farmer had been unknowingly supplementing our diet for years. Dad didn't want the cow shit on his lawn, yet when the store horse and cart came around, the horse shit was a different matter.

The horse and cart came around the block on a certain day each week driven by the horseman who would sell household wares from his cart. Dad acted like the horse shit on the road was coveted, though I never ever saw any of the other neighbours shovel it up. Dad wanted it for manure for his rose bush and he had his timing down to a fine art. The horse and cart always stopped dead in front of our prefab and after all the neighbours had finished their transactions, and immediately after the horse and cart had moved off farther down the lane, Dad would be out of the house in a flash, bucket and shovel at the ready to collect his prized possession. What amazed me was the horse never let Dad down – how did it know where to shit, anyway? It was funny to watch him sprinting down those steps to shovel up his manure but things took on an embarrassing turn when he decided Betty and I could be trained up to collect it for him. Betty point-blank refused but, being the timid one, I let him train me instead. I was given the bucket and shovel and Dad would be at the window waiting. As soon as the horse had the first 'giddy-up', he would shout, 'Right, quick, off you go,' and there I'd go, running down the steps to shovel up the horse shit, stinking and steaming hot. Oh, the shame of it was awful. I'm sure the neighbours must have enjoyed the pantomime. When Dad wanted me to go all around the block following the horse, spade and bucket at the ready, that's when it got too embarrassing and I refused, much to his disappointment.

Mam had heard about some twin beds that were for sale at Craghead. They were second-hand but she wanted them for mine and Betty's room. The old double bed was 'past it', she said. They must have been going very cheap as we had little money to spare in those days. When Mam wanted something and had set her heart on it, though, Dad would always do his best to keep her happy.

Dad and I set off to buy the twin beds and fetch them back on the wheelbarrow. It was quite a long way to walk, about three miles, especially as it was way up the top of Craghead on a steep hill. It was not so bad walking all the way up there, but getting back down the hill again proved to be a bit tricky, especially with the springs and bedstead of twin beds strapped and tied onto the wheelbarrow with rope. Having manoeuvred one big hill, we then had to push the wheelbarrow up another hill. I don't suppose I was of much help to Dad really, but he seemed to like me along for the company and I was more than happy to be his 'little helper'. On making it back home, Dad had several mugs of tea, smoked a Woodbine then proceeded to put the beds back together in our bedroom. I could hardly wait for him to finish – I was so tired I just wanted to crawl into my new bed and go to sleep.

Mam and Dad were constantly disturbed by me or Betty in the night by us talking in our sleep. As we got older, Mam said it got worse, as one of us would talk in her sleep and then, still asleep, the other one would answer. It's a habit I've never grown out of and my husband still complains about my talking in my sleep to this day, as well as the sleepwalking I often do.

We knew all the neighbours in the prefabs, and amongst them were the Richards. There were two sisters, Vivian and Rosie, and a brother, Geordie. They all lived in their little home along with an old granddad as well as their mam and dad. It puzzled me how they managed to all fit into a two-bedroomed prefab.

Betty made friends with Vivian and Rosie. I used to want to go with them when they roamed the lanes gossiping, but Betty would not let me. I would trail after them, jealous of Betty's new friends, but they always chased me away. Geordie, however, was a bit of a loner like myself and often let me ride on the handlebars of his bike. We would go tearing around the block, full speed ahead. Geordie did the pedalling and I just sat there on the handlebars and enjoyed the recklessness of the ride.

When their granddad died, Geordie said he would let me see the body if I wanted to. I had never seen anyone dead before, so I was well up for it. He took me behind their coal shed and told me that before he would let me into the house to see his granddad I had to show him my knickers. I was mortified. I still wore old navy-blue school bloomers I was so young. I refused to lift my skirt and show him my knickers, so I never did get to see his dead granddad.

Betty continued her friendship with Vivian and Rosie, but still found time for me some evenings when we'd stay indoors. My hair had grown long, thick and wavy and Betty used to love brushing it for me. I would wash it with water taken from the butt outside the back yard as someone had said rainwater made your hair curly. We used to heat the water up in a big saucepan. Betty told me years later that she was always envious of my hair, especially as everyone complimented me on it.

While I may have been proud of my hair, it caused me problems as I was always the first one to catch nits. When this happened, I would inevitably pass them on to Betty and sometimes Mam and Dad as well. We'd all be scratching away like mad until Mam checked our hair then brought out the dreaded bottle of Suluo lotion. I remember the horrible stink of it and when Mam put it on our hair and scalps, it would have to be left on for hours. Then we would have to stay indoors or else the other kids would know we had the nits by the smell of the lotion. Mam would then wash our hair and, while it was still damp, she would sit us on hard kitchen chairs placed over sheets of newspapers on the lino floor. She would then proceed to rake a small-toothed Derbac metal comb through our hair to clean off all the eggs (nits). Any 'dickies', as we called them, she would crack between her thumbnails with a satisfied grunt. She was on a mission with her nit comb and used it to check our hair even if we weren't scratching with the 'dickies'.

It got to the stage where we were afraid to have an innocent scratch or Mam would be straight to the bathroom cupboard, armed with her nit comb and newspapers. It was a kind of torture, especially for me as my hair was so long, but Mam showed no mercy on her nit-checking mission, and for us to moan and be ouching while it all went on would only result in clouts around the head and orders to sit still.

I swear she did it some evenings just because she was bored and had no knitting on the go. There used to be a nit nurse come to our school to check all pupils' heads, class by class. For anyone to receive a letter from the nit nurse to take home was a matter of shame, so Mam raged a constant battle with her nit comb to prevent the dreaded head lice. It was a bit of a struggle for her really, as other neighbours' kids took home their notes from the nit nurse but the families were so poor they could not afford to buy the Suluo lotion or Derbac combs. No matter how poor we were, Mam always managed to have the dreaded Suluo stocked in.

The Wilson family lived farther down the lane from us. The dad, Billy, did not go to work like our dad. He was supposed to have a bad back and was issued with sick notes from his doctor on a continuous, long-term basis. Our dad disagreed with this as he used to say that you could set your clock for the time when Billy Wilson would be seen striding up the lane, off to the pub in his best clothes. He would be gone for hours and when he finally went home he would expect a meal on the table waiting for him. The family had two daughters: Mary, who was about our Betty's age, and Susie, who was about the same age as I was. Their youngest daughter would come along later, whom they would name Connie. She was born about the same time as our Ann. Their ages being similar to ours was quite a coincidence; Dad used to say Billy's back could not have been that bad, though I never understood what he meant.

Mrs Wilson had a part-time cleaning job in the mornings at the local police station. She worked there every weekday, starting early and coming home at lunchtime. As much as she worked, the family never had a penny to share between them. Dad used to say that Billy drank every penny she ever earned and that he was 'just a long string of useless piss and a good day's work would kill him off'. If Dad ever spotted Billy walking up the lane toffed up to the nines, he would say things like 'look at the lazy bugger, nowt wrong with his back now'. He would rant on about him saying what a lazy sod he was and that he'd never worked a day in his life. He would go on and on about him so much, though none of us disagreed with him or said a word. He got so wound up when he saw Billy either going up to or coming home from the pub, his tirade would be a source of entertainment for us.

I think what upset Dad the most was that always when Billy had gone out, it would be not much later until either Susie or Mary would be knocking on our door saying, 'My mam says, have you got any crusts to spare, please?' More often than not, Mam would give them a few slices or even half a loaf of bread, then off they'd go, onto the next door, knocking and saying, 'My mam says, have you any margarine to spare, please?' They would do the rounds of the prefabs, a cup of sugar at one, a jug of milk at another or 'Two Oxos for Dad's dinner, please,' so their mam could have some gravy to go on Billy's dinner. Though Billy always had to have his dinner, the girls rarely had a good meal. People felt sorry for them and often gave them bananas or, if they were very lucky, a few biscuits to share. Sometimes, having already obtained the bread from one neighbour, it would be a knock on the door and either Susie or Mary would be there, 'Mam says, have you anything to put in some bread for my dad's tea, please?' Although this infuriated Dad, he never said a word to the two girls about their dad to their faces and he never tried to dissuade Mam from giving them one thing or another, but it all fuelled his tirade of wrath and swearwords against Billy.

Dad never used really bad language at home. It was bugger and bloody this or that, but never much worse than that. He used to say the language down the pits between the men was bad and would make your hair curl, but he believed bad language was not to be used in front of one's wife or children in the home. He still had some choice words of his own, though. If something was lost and we asked Dad if he knew where it was, if he had the mood on him he would say, 'Where the hell do you think it is? Probably sticking up my arse along with all the other things.'

In one of the fields above the prefabs were some old sheds. Now abandoned, they had been used at one time as part of people's allotments. Betty, myself, Mary and Susie used to play up there quite a lot. They had acquired an old mongrel dog by the name of Sox. It was so called because it was black all over apart from its four white legs and feet. The poor old dog was starved and skinny like a bag of bones – his ribs nearly stuck together. Sox ran after us all the time but stopped every so often to eat dog shit. I even saw it stop, do its business, then promptly eat it back again. I was both amazed and disgusted. I had never seen anything like it before and that day when we got home I told Mam and Dad about it, being careful not to say the word shit in the retelling of the tale. It was one thing for Dad to swear but it was woe betide us if we ever did.

Dad said, 'There's nowt surprising about that. Bloody dog's starving, the same as the bairns.' Then he added, 'If the girls had been a bit quicker, they should have scooped it up with a spade and taken it home to put between two slices of bread for their dad's tea.' We all laughed at that one.

One day, when we were all out playing up that very same field, we decided to play at how far we could roll ourselves down the hill. They had been pulling those old sheds down by then, and bits and pieces still lay scattered around on the ground. As I rolled over and over in the grass down the hill, I felt a sharp pain in my left knee. When I stopped rolling and had a look, I had a six-inch nail sticking in it, complete with a piece of tarred mineral felt about six inches square. It was what had been used on the roofs of the sheds. I hobbled home with this piece of roof nailed into my knee thinking I would probably have to have my leg chopped off. My dad's brother, Uncle Stan from Darlington, happened to be at our house that day on a visit. They all looked up at me in surprise as I hobbled in, then Dad just quickly pulled the whole thing out of my leg, Mam gave it a quick wash and Uncle Stan told me to 'get away out to play again'.

Susie Wilson let me into her house to show off my knee wound to her mam, one of the rare occasions I went inside their prefab. They had less furniture than us even and it wasn't very clean. Things were strewn on the floor and everywhere. Even though we hadn't much, at least Mam kept the place clean. It must have been very hard for Mrs Wilson though, as it was well known around the block that Billy had a bad temper and it was not unknown for her to be sporting black eyes. Socially, apart from letting their girls come out to play sometimes or go around on their borrowing rounds, they kept themselves pretty much to themselves.

The Martindales were another family that were neighbours of ours. No one saw much of the dad, but Mrs Martindale was quite friendly with our mam and sometimes, when Dad was at work, she would come into our prefab and share a pot of tea with Mam and they would gossip, especially about 'women's problems'. On these occasions we would be sent out to play. They had two sets of twins in their family, Carol and Sheila, who were about my age, then Malcolm and Melvin, who were a lot younger. The twin boys both had only three fingers on each hand, along with tiny little thumbs, and their fingers were webbed like little fishes. There were two other younger boys, but I can't remember their names now. They were spiritualists and, according to what Sheila and Carol told me, they had spirit guides who could be mischievous. They said they would go to bed each night leaving everywhere tidy and in the mornings, when they got up out of bed, the place would be all messed up, which they claimed their spirit guides had done. Our dad scoffed when we told him about that and said it was a 'load of bloody nonsense'.

We weren't a very religious family, being Church of England. Mam and Dad didn't go to church except for christenings, marriages and (mostly) funerals. Betty and I were sent to Sunday school, though, and I quite enjoyed it, especially the Bible stories. Dad said the only religion worth its salt was the Salvation Army, as it didn't expect half your wages and he said at least they did help the poor and the down-and-outs with their soup kitchens and such. I didn't dwell on religion much then as a young child, but did used to wonder about heaven sometimes, especially as it was supposed to be somewhere our old ginger tom had gone to after the washing-day episode.

The rag-and-bone man came around regularly with his horse and cart. We used to dash out with a pile of old rags when we heard him shouting and ringing his huge old school bell. He would give us either pennies or a balloon for our rags, but one fine day after I had raided the cupboards and put a couple of Dad's old jerseys on the pile, I was rewarded with a goldfish in a small plastic bag of water. Mam bought us a small goldfish bowl and some fish food, but the goldfish didn't last long and soon died. I put it in a wooden pencil case and buried it in the garden, believing it would go to heaven. Later on, after questioning the adults on the subject and being told it was only the soul that went up to heaven, I tried to dig the pencil case up again as I wanted to cut open the goldfish to see if its soul was still in it. If so, what would it look like? The problem was I'd forgotten what part of the garden I'd buried it in. I never did manage to find the pencil case, but I did get told off for digging little holes all over Dad's garden.

We were allowed to go out and play quite a lot, especially on the long summer holidays from school. At Easter time Mam tried to buy us a new dress and either new sandals or plimsolls. She would hard-boil eggs in onion skins, some in cochineal red food colouring, and on Easter Day we would be all excited as all the neighbourhood kids and us would take our eggs out in the farmer's fields to roll down the grassy banks, seeing whose egg lasted the longest without breaking. If they broke, we'd peel them and eat them. If they didn't crack, we'd keep them as long as we could. Our Betty once kept a paste-egg, as we called them, in a dark bedroom cupboard for years. When an unknown stink kept drifting through the prefab it was finally traced to the cupboard where Betty's prize egg had cracked and gone rotten and mouldy.

On the darker evenings after school, we would be allowed out to play until we heard Dad's whistle to go in. He used to put two fingers in his mouth and make the loudest whistle I ever heard. You could hear it miles away and, as he was strictly protective of his girls, we always went straight home when we heard its piercing sound. The other kids used to make fun of us because of it, and some of them would be left out much later.

We used to play knocky nine doors, as we called the old game of knocking on people's doors and running away. There was an old lady lived further around the block who we called Mrs Moony, though that was not her real name. She was eccentric, but all the kids thought she was mad, and she was called Mrs Moony as it was rumoured every night of the full moon, she would go out in the back garden naked and howl at the moon, though no one I knew had ever witnessed this. Anyway, we plagued that poor old woman by knocking on her door constantly, and

I was always the one that the older kids elected to knock on her door while they all held back in a group. I used to be terrified she would catch me, as the other kids could run away much faster than me. One night the inevitable happened and she did catch me – I think she must have been stood behind the door waiting for us. The kids had pushed me up her path then took shelter way back to watch.

Before I even got to rattle her knocker she had the door open and grabbed me by the front of my jersey. She had white hair that stood up on end and she shook me so much my teeth rattled while she gave me a good scolding. When she finally let me go I ran as fast as my legs could carry me to find all the other kids laughing around the corner. I never knocked on that poor woman's door again.

Another thing the older kids used to do was stuff people's drainpipes with newspapers then light them with matches until they made a roaring ghostly noise and the neighbours would come out to see what was causing the noise. I suppose it was dangerous really, as the prefabs were flimsy dwellings. When we used to have good old northeasterly gales it was not unknown for one or more of the neighbours to get up next day and find the roof had been blown clean off. It even happened to ours – Dad was forever up to the council offices complaining about the state of the properties and the damp. Nothing was ever done apart from the roofs being replaced. They were just not meant to last the thirty years that they were eventually used for before being pulled down and the ground used for new council houses.

Once in a blue moon when we were young, Mam and Dad would take Betty and me to the cinema at the Albert Hall at the top end of Stanley. We would go on a summer's evening to the first sitting so it wouldn't be too late on getting out when the film was done. Afterwards we would go to the fish shop, where you could either eat in or take food out. As a special treat, if we were flush, we would all eat our supper inside; Mam and Dad shared fish and chips, Betty and I had chips and bread-and-butter, and we had a pot of tea between us. Then we would walk home tired and happy with our full bellies, ready for bed when we got home. We felt like kings of the block after these outings. Though we never had money to spare in those days and never went on holidays or had many new clothes, we at least got fed. Dad always worked and Mam cooked cheap but nutritious meals, even if the farmer did unknowingly supplement our diet sometimes. We had clothes on our backs, shoes on our feet and, even though they may have been a bit threadbare, at least we were clean and – like children do – we never thought we were different from anyone else.

FIVE

Aunt Kitty, my mother's sister, was married to Joseph Ruddick. They lived up in Stanley in a rented house that was really a house turned into two flats. Aunt Kitty and Uncle Joe lived in the downstairs flat, which had two bedrooms, one of which had an old shop front, as it had been used as a shop before the war. Then there was Aunt Kitty's small bedroom and a living room with a huge black leaded fireplace with a combined oven and boiler, on which she used to heat their water. There was a tiny scullery with a big square sink, a bench top and small pantry. They had a small back yard with an outside lavatory which was communal and shared by the people who lived upstairs.

It even had a midden, like all the houses in that street. The middens had been used as dry toilets years before, when the midden-man would come around once a week with his horse and cart to shovel them out.

Aunt Kitty and Uncle Joe were very poor. They had no children of their own, though I later learned that Aunt Kitty had delivered a son who was stillborn. It was their little bedroom where Mam had lain in labour with her own son, delivered during a wartime air raid, also stillborn because of the botched, rushed, forceps delivery of the doctor in haste to get back to his wife at home.

I heard the tale quite a few times over my childhood years from Aunt Kitty on dark winter evenings in front of her fire. Dad had run through the streets of Stanley in the pitch-black darkness while the bombings went on all around him, lighting up the sky. It was the pits the Germans had been aiming for, as well as the Consett Iron and Steel Company and Randsome and Marles, the engineering firm that made ammunitions during the war. Although it was hard to get the tale from Dad himself, Aunt Kitty used to tell me of his heartbreak when she and the midwife wrapped the dead child in a blanket and let Dad hold him. He sobbed over the child and stroked the cheek of his perfect little face. It made me so sad to hear about the brother we could have had.

I used to be allowed to stay with Aunt Kitty overnight to keep her company when Uncle Joe was out at work on the late shifts. He worked as a bus conductor for the Northern Bus Co and was known as Smoky Joe as he chain-smoked Woodbines. Uncle Joe was quiet and never had much to say for himself, but if we ever got on a bus to go up to Stanley and Uncle Joe was conducting, I loved the fact he'd go up and down the aisle saying, 'Fares please,' coughing his lungs up, a lit Woodbine in one hand, his other on the ticket machine – and never stopped for our fare. Aunt Kitty was more refined in her taste of tabs and smoked Players. Neither of them drank alcohol yet they remained very poor. They had an old dining table in the corner of the under stairs that was always laid with an oil-cloth cover on which sat a teapot, a sugar bowl and tin of condensed milk. There was also a Singer sewing machine, on top of which sat an old wind-up gramophone with a big horn. The lid of it was always shut and never used. The only other furniture they had were two chairs set aside the big fender of the fireplace. In Aunt Kitty's bedroom was a double bed and an old-fashioned writing bureau, which our Ann later inherited and is now in Australia.

They did not have a bathroom so when I stayed at Aunt Kitty's, if I wanted a bath, she would bring in the old tin bath that hung in the yard outside. She would have a good fire blazing to heat up the water and we used jugs to fill up the tin bath – it seemed to take forever. This was on evenings when Uncle Joe would be at work on the buses and it was a treat for me to sit in the bath in front of the fire while Aunt Kitty sat smoking her Players tabs.

Sometimes I came out of the bath dirtier than when I went in as it used to be all sooty from hanging out in the yard, but Aunt Kitty would only laugh at my despair and help rub the muck off me with an old towel. All week Aunt Kitty got her provisions from a little shop down Stanley Main Street on a 'tick list', for which she would settle up the bill when Uncle Joe had his payday. I often went to the shop with her; I was fascinated by the bell over the shop door, the bacon-slicer and, best of all, the rows of glass jars stacked on high shelves behind the counter, containing various boiled sweets of all colours of the rainbow. There were bull's-eyes, black bullets and allsorts. As a special treat on Uncle Joe's payday, Aunt Kitty sometimes bought me two ounces of sweets. It took me ages to make up my mind about which sort to have, then I'd suck them slowly to make them last. Throughout the rest of the week meals were very sparse at Aunt Kitty's: slices of bread with margarine, sprinkled with sugar or spread with thick, sweet condensed milk. Though they didn't have a lot, Aunt Kitty and Uncle Joe would happily share whatever they had with us. With not having children of their own, they liked the company of having Betty and myself there, though I think I was their favourite, being the youngest at the time, and Betty was never as keen on staying there as I was.

We would have to get used to it though, as in later years

Betty and I were sent to stay with Aunt Kitty quite a lot when Mam was laid up bad or in hospital.

The first long stay we had there was in 1952 when Mam was in hospital giving birth to our Ann. Mam's blood group was rare, being rhesus negative, and with our Ann being her fourth child, Mam had accumulated antibodies in her bloodstream that were damaging to the unborn baby. Hence Ann was born a blue baby and had to have all her blood re-transfused at birth. Mam nearly lost her, so she was very special to us. She was born in Princess Mary's Hospital in Newcastle, the same as me. When Mam brought her home and I saw this little tiny baby who was our new sister I was full of love for her. She had blonde hair and blue eyes like Mam and was a little fighter right from day one.

I used to love helping Mam with Ann and became like a second mother to her. When she started walking and toddling about I was really proud of her and more so when she began to follow me about everywhere.

I was very proud to have a new baby sister. It was after having our Ann that Mam often took to her bed. 'Mam's bad again,' Dad would tell us, 'so we'll have to get on with things.'

So Mam would be laid up bad in her bed and with Dad still having to go down the pit, as the doctor would not always issue Dad a sick note, Betty and I tried to cope as best as we could. I never minded being kept off school to look after Mam and Ann when Dad was off to work. I hated school anyway and would gladly offer to stay off. Aunt Kitty and Mrs Martindale would come and visit Mam but the cooking was managed at these times mainly by Dad, who was a dab hand at frying leftover mashed potatoes and vegetables in the pan with a couple of Oxos sprinkled over it until it was crisp and brown. It was quite delicious really, served up piping hot. We used to put it on our bread and butter until the butter melted into the sandwich. I loved it but we had it so often Betty said she was sick and tired of it, and when we got older she would turn her nose up at it, whereas I always tucked in heartily.

Mam liked scrambled eggs on toast and Dad showed me how to do this so as to get the eggs to just the right consistency, not too well done and not too sloppy. She liked them done just right.

When Mam was better and up and about again, she would resume the cooking. She was a good baker and on baking days I used to help her mostly by looking after Ann while she made and rolled out pastry and turned out lovely bacon and egg pies and apple or blackberry tarts. She was a good cake maker too, and if I had been a good girl and helped her a lot, she would let me lick out the big cake bowl and wooden spoon when she'd finished. This was before I got down to the task of washing up all her pots and pans.

When Mam was laid up in bed, I was often given the task of fetching her some library books. I knew what to fetch her – romance stories – and I was warned not to bring her any she'd already read. I used to take Ann with me in her pushchair, which had a tray on the bottom, handy for putting the books in. One particular day I also had to stop off at the shops and get the groceries we needed. I had been to East Stanley Library, got her books, bought the shopping from my list, then walked back home down the big hill, Durham Road. A library book must have slipped off the pushchair somewhere along the road as there was one missing when I got home. I was in big trouble about that and was sent all the way back again to look for the missing book, but I never did find it. Mam gave me her cold treatment for a week afterwards. I hated the way she did this, it was worse than the shouting at we would occasionally be given. I could take the shouting but when she told me what a bad, naughty girl I was and would not speak to me for days, that hurt me most of all.

I used to walk to school on my own by now, all the way up to Stanley Board School, quiet and withdrawn. I didn't have many friends in school, which made me hate the place all the more. I was bullied on the way to school, bullied in school, and bullied on the way home from school. They would call me names and constantly pull my hair. I was a very shy, quiet, timid child by now, which I suppose made me a prime target for the bullying. I sometimes called in at Aunty Kitty's on the way home, giving the bullies time to disappear before I would have to resume my journey. But if I was late getting home from school, I would be in trouble again and get more of the cold treatment. We were expected to help Mam as soon as we got in. There was always plenty of chores to do: washing up pots, peeling vegetables, and our Ann to look after.

I used to walk up to school via the old pit-heap way instead of along the main Durham Road that most of the other kids used. The old pit-heap had once been a Stanley main mine and had been a working mine up until 1909, when there had been explosions underground and many men lost their lives. My dad used to tell me about it. He told me the fire raged underground for so long it was impossible for the rescuers to get in to rescue them. Later on the bodies of some of the men were found where they had been trapped, fused huddled together like rats in a trap.

It had been the West Stanley colliery, also known as the Burns pit. Dad told me how conditions down the pit had been cramped, with little health-and-safety provision. There had been hazards and dangers everywhere, he said, from explosions, fires and roof falls, to suffocating gases as well as flooding. Seams in the Burns pit had been sunk too close together and working conditions in small seams had been the cause of many miners becoming bandy-legged.

On 16 February 1909 there had been one explosion at 3.45 p.m. followed by a second one less than a minute later. The whole town stopped in its tracks and smoke was seen pouring up into the wintry sky. Dozens of people soon became hundreds, as they flocked towards the pit head. The womenfolk screamed as they feared the worst. As there was not much damage to the surface buildings of the pit, it was obvious the damage must have been below ground.

The explosions were thought to have been caused by illegal lamps – 168 men and boys lost their lives, 59 of them under the age of 20. Their kinfolk had received only minimum compensation payments. It was the worst mining disaster ever in the Durham coalfield.

In later years, as I researched the disaster, I was interested to find that a mines inspector, Frank Keegan, was praised as a hero for his part in rescuing 26 men from the mine workings. His grandson, Kevin Keegan, would go on to become a national hero in his own right as an England football legend.

As a child, I had listened to my dad's tale and found it both chilling and fascinating. It always made me feel sad and I worried constantly for our dad's safety down the mines. I knew he had been injured down the pit on several occasions from falling rocks and stones. He had several scars on his face, forehead, back and arms where the cuts had healed. They were blue scars from coal dust that had got into the cuts and never cleaned out properly.

Dad never bothered to stop work when he injured himself, even though they had a nurse on duty in the medical centre above ground. To seek medical attention for minor injuries meant losing time and money from their shifts, so he just kept working on. I heard of other men who had received bad injuries down the pits, usually by stone falls, or sometimes a coal wagon that ran along a track underground would run over some hapless man, not quick enough to get out of its way in time, and break his legs. There were other men my dad knew of who had been injured so badly they never worked again; some had their backs broken.

Dad used to visit some of his old workmates that had been injured and were off work. I used to go with him sometimes and wondered how they could be so cheerful. Of course it was all top show and on the way home Dad would be very quiet and I sensed his sadness. I used to pray that would never happen to our dad. Little did I know at this early age that a more sinister threat from the mines would have such a devastating effect on him. A quiet, stealthy deadliness – the coal dust itself – would affect Dad and many other miners and their families over the following years.

One bitter winter's day, after continuous snowfall, we were let out of school early. I called on Aunt Kitty but she was not in. She could not have been far as she only ever came to visit us or went to the shops. I felt cold and lonely and for some reason just didn't feel like going home. I can't explain properly why I did this as I never understood it myself, but I waited long enough to give the bullies time to get home then eventually started going down the pit-heap route home. Instead of walking my usual route around the heap, I decided to climb it instead. I trekked all the way to the top in knee-deep snow, then sat down in the snow to have a look around. I could just about make out our rows of prefabs through the thick, falling snowflakes. Had it not been for the fact that the snow was still falling so fast, I would have been rewarded with a wonderful view over many miles of countryside, as far as Durham and Chester-Le-Street. As it was, I could barely make out the shapes of our prefabs.

Though I felt very cold I had no desire to go home and just felt dreadfully lonely, sad and tired. I lay down in the snow and decided I would stay there. I lay there and cried for all the poor men that had died in that pit. Then I just lay there, going to sleep with ever more snow swarming around me. A long time later I was disturbed by a man walking his dog who had spotted me. He asked me where I lived and tried to get me to stand up, but my legs were so frozen they wouldn't take my weight. He ended up carrying me all the way home, explaining how he'd found me to Mam and Dad. Dad made Mam put me to bed to try and get me warmed up while he went off to fetch the doctor. The doctor came to see me, said I had mild hypothermia, and advised 'plenty of warm drinks and keep her in bed', shaking his head all the while, as I could not, or would not, explain why I had gone there. Mam gave me more of the cold-shoulder treatment, which was colder than the snow itself.

I was always a bit of a dreamer when I was a young child. I would sit on the kerbside for ages watching the other kids skipping or playing hopscotch, 'bays' as we called it. I could be quite happy watching our Ann play out while I made up stories in my head, stories I would write about at school, even making sure I'd be careful to get the description of what everyone wore down exactly, even to what colour socks they wore.

I had started suffering from pains in my belly but when I told Mam about it she just told me it was wind and would dose me up with syrup of figs. These bouts of pain kept bothering me so Mam eventually took me to the doctor. He agreed with Mam and I had to keep on with the syrup of figs.

1953 was Coronation year and Mam, Aunt Kitty and all the other women in the prefabs worked and baked cakes together while the men organised street parties. Ours was to be held up near the garages past the old farmhouse. Banners were made and bunting put up in red, white and blue. There was a whole community feel to everything.

There was only one family in all of the prefabs who owned a television set. It was an old black-and-white with a nine-inch screen and it belonged to the Chapmans – Dad was secretly envious of them. Every family in the prefabs suddenly all started being nice to the Chapmans as they all wanted to be the lucky ones to be invited to watch the Coronation on their TV set.

Eventually, it was mostly children who were invited, including Betty and me. Dad said he wasn't fussed about it but I know he would have loved to have watched it really. The street party was a jolly affair that went on for hours. All us kids were presented with a crown coin in a plastic case, which was worth five shillings in old money, 25 pence in today's money, and we were all given a Coronation mug. The jollification went on, the beer was flowing freely, the women made countless pots of tea in huge tin teapots, and sandwiches and cakes were in abundance. The local press were there taking photos of the long trestle tables with the paper cloths on and bunting decorating them all. The food seemed never-ending which was such a treat for us as food had been on ration since the war years and some of the food would stay on ration up until 1954 so all us kids made the most of it, but when some of the men started getting a bit worse for wear by all the free-flowing beer, Dad decided it was time to go home. It had gone on all afternoon and into the evening and dancing had begun. There was such a happy liberated feeling to it all I didn't want to go home. We were stuffed, and all slept well that night.

One day, when I was ten, I was coming home from school around the pit-heap as usual. They had made a new path from Stanley to South Stanley. They called it the black path and it bypassed all the old allotments and was a short cut home. Still, I went my own way, but I had got the bellyache on me real bad that day. I had felt it all afternoon in school, then it eased a bit, but while I was walking home around the old pit-heap I had to stop and sit for a while, hoping it would ease again. At home, if I got the bellyache on me, my dad told me to get down on the floor on my hands and knees and to get my bum up higher than my head. He said this would help me fart and get some of the wind out of me and sometimes it did. I had not dared to get in this position outdoors, as it would have been embarrassing if anyone was to come by and spot me with my bum up in the air trying to have a good fart to get rid of the wind.

Instead, I walked a bit, then sat down on the ground for a while to rest, then I was nearly on my hands and knees crawling to get home. Finally I made it home, but I told Mam the bellyache was really bad and she let me lie on the old brown leather settee. It gradually got worse and when Dad came home from the back shift, Mam whispered to him and he biked back up to Stanley to fetch the doctor to see me. The doctor didn't want to come out, but Dad threatened him so he did. It was very late when he came to our prefab and when the doctor examined me he again said it was just the wind.

By this time sweat was pouring off me and Dad went mad – you could smell the whisky on the doctor's breath. Dad threatened him that should anything happen to me, he'd 'sue the arse off him' and said he'd better do something for me. The doctor relented, had a think about things, then told Dad he'd go back and send for an ambulance, but he still felt sure it was just the wind on me. Mam busied herself getting me a nightdress and some toiletries together while Dad sat beside me on the settee drinking his tea and smoking his Woodbines, telling me not to worry, the hospital would have a good doctor who would be able to get rid of all that wind. Although I was in a great deal of pain, I was still worried about having to go into hospital and wondered how they would get rid of that much wind, as my belly had about blown up with it by now. The only time I'd been in hospital was to have my tonsils removed when I was only a baby and I couldn't remember that.

When the ambulance came they took me to Shotley Bridge General Hospital in Consett. Mam and Dad came with me while Betty stayed at home to look after our Ann. When the doctor at the hospital examined me, he told Mam and Dad that he needed a second opinion and that a surgeon would be out to see me directly. I was very scared as Dad looked frantic and I was thinking they may have to puncture my belly to let all the wind out.

Very quickly, it seemed, the surgeon came dashing in, looking about six and a half feet tall. He was called Mr McKenzie and towered above me with his cold hands feeling my swollen belly. Then he told Mam and Dad to step outside for a minute. He got a nurse in with him while he asked me to roll over, then proceeded to snap on gloves and put some jelly onto his gloved fingers. I did as he bid – well, I had no choice – and then Mr McKenzie slipped a finger up my bum. I was horrified, especially afterwards when he told me I could roll back and I produced a little fart. This mortified me and I said, 'Pardon me,' but he ignored me. When Mam and Dad were allowed in to see me again Mr McKenzie explained to them quietly, 'It's acute appendicitis and she'll have to go to surgery immediately.'

They gave me a quick kiss goodbye then I was whisked off within minutes. I was put in a green gown and placed on a trolley, with a porter pushing me down long, long tunnels with lights beaming down from the ceiling. I needed my dad but they wouldn't let him come with me. I was finally in a small ante-room, where another doctor came and put a needle into the back of my hand. Suddenly all noise started to recede until I fell into a dark blackness.

When I next woke up I still had pain in my belly – in fact, it was hard to move at all because of the pain. I was in the children's ward in the middle of the night, and all lights were out except one in the middle, which had been draped by a green towel, so it was very dim. I thought I'd died and woken up in hell. I was groaning in fright as much as the pain until a nurse came to roll me over to give me an injection into my bum. I tried to swat her hand away and she got very angry at this and told me she'd slap my face if I tried that again or made any noise. So I lay still until gradually the effects of the injection kicked in and I fell asleep again until morning.

When I next woke up the day-shift nurses were on duty and treated me more kindly. Mam and Dad visited me the next day – I was surprised Dad was not at work. He tried to joke and made me laugh, which hurt my stitches, but I was relieved when he reassured me that all the wind had been removed along with my appendix. I later learned from our Betty that, after the operation, Mr McKenzie had gone to have a word with Mam and Dad and told them I had got through the surgery fine and was OK, but if it had been another half an hour the appendix would have ruptured and I could have ended up with peritonitis.

I was in hospital for two weeks and missed our Ann dreadfully. I was glad to get back home but old Mr Rodham next door told me, 'That's what you get for sitting on those cold kerbsides too much.' Another neighbour told me a similar thing and added, 'You ought to wear warmer bloomers.'

Dad came up with a wonderful two-liner for me and repeated it every time he passed wind. He would fart then say, 'Let the wind go free where'er you be. In church or chapel, let it rattle.'

SIX

Dad continued to complain to the council regarding the damp conditions of the prefabs and finally we were moved to Cleveland Terrace, farther down the hills of South Stanley. This was a three-bedroomed terraced house with an upstairs bathroom and separate indoor toilet.

Downstairs we had a sitting room, rarely used except for best occasions, and a dining room, which we used for everyday. There was also a kitchen big enough to get a small kitchen table and chairs in and a pantry.

On one side of our house lived a nice Catholic family and on the other were the Wilsons, who were moved from their prefab around the same time as us. Billy still didn't go to work yet strode out every day, dressed up to the nines, off for his pint. It continued to nark Dad about him not working, especially as the borrowing continued.

One day Mam had been baking and left a batch of scones to cool on the bench by the open back door. The scones disappeared and Dad was out there like Sherlock Holmes, tracing the trail of crumbs along a path we had under the dining-room window – sure enough, the trail of crumbs led straight to the Wilsons' back door. He ranted about that but he knew the girls were just hungry and let the matter drop.

Directly opposite our house was the Thompson family, who had twin little girls, and the Johnson family, who had a boy about my age named Warren. Poor Mrs Thompson suffered from terrible depression after having her twins. She became friendly with Mam, along with Mrs Johnson, whom my dad used to say had lovely legs. He used to tease Mam about Mrs Johnson's legs trying to make her jealous, but Mam ignored him. Mrs Thompson got so depressed that she stuck her girls outside one day and locked herself in. The police had to be called and they broke into her house, having sent for her husband to be brought home from work.

Her doctor came out to see her and promptly sent her into a mental hospital, where she stayed for several weeks. After she came out she used to come over to our house sometimes in the day and Mam would make a pot of tea and they would sit there in front of the fire gossiping over their cups of tea while I strained my ears to try and catch snippets of their conversations. That's when I first heard of electric-shock treatment.

I used to play for hours on end with Warren Johnson. They were continuing to build new council houses out of the front of our house and, while the building was going on, Warren and I used to enter the houses in the evenings after the men had knocked off work. We used to play inside, jumping from beam to beam of the unfinished floors. When climbing out of one of the window frames one evening, I received the biggest whack I had ever had on my bum. It was the night watchman, who had caught us. Warren managed to get out and ran off, leaving me to face the music. He whacked me so hard I tried to stay out of his way after that and I never told my parents.

Shortly after moving to Cleveland Terrace it was time for me to sit the eleven-plus exam at the board school I still attended. On the day of the exam my mind went blank and I failed miserably. The following autumn term I had to start at Shield Row School, the school our Betty had attended. Betty had left school by then and worked in a bakery shop in Stanley.

I hated Shield Row; I couldn't make friends there and, to make matters worse, it was a longer walk.

Mam continued to give me the cold treatment and often stood me in a corner of the dining room. If the neighbours came in for a cup of tea and a chat with Mam, she would tell them I was in the doghouse and they were not to talk to me. I felt so humiliated and worthless. Betty and Dad were out at work, our Ann was playing outside with her new little friends and I was stuck there, standing in the corner facing the wall, because I'd not made a good enough job of cleaning the windows after school, or for some other minor offence.

Mam had fallen out with Aunt Kitty by this time as well. It was something to do with one of our grandparents, who had died in Chester-Le-Street. Aunt Kitty had cashed in an insurance policy and, her being the eldest sister, had not shared it with Mam, who had the hump over it and wouldn't visit Aunt Kitty any more. If we were out with Mam on Stanley Main Street shopping and saw Aunt Kitty on the street, we were ordered not to try and speak to her. Mam passed her by as if she was a stranger. This hurt me badly and I felt so sorry for my aunt, who had been so good to Mam by looking after us so many times when Mam was in hospital. Later on, as I got older, I snuck up to see Aunt Kitty, but I didn't tell Mam about this. The feud would continue up until just before our Betty got married, when she relented and invited Aunt Kitty and Uncle Joe to Betty's wedding.

On the top end of the opposite street to us lived a girl called Grace Coupling, and we made friends. She was my age and should have gone to Shield Row School as well, but her mam let her go to Bloemfontein Secondary Modern School in Craghead. I was very envious, as it was not so far to walk there. As Grace and I became firm friends I whined on and on about being allowed to go there until my parents relented and allowed me to change schools. I felt a bit happier going to school then, as I had Grace to walk with. I used to call for her every morning where she lived with her mam, her sister Margaret and three other small children, one of which was still a baby. Grace's mam and dad were divorced, which was unusual in those days, though as kids, we never thought about it.

They were very poor and some mornings Grace didn't get any breakfast, as there was no food except baby milk in the house. On a good day they would perhaps have some bread in and bananas and Grace used to make all the little ones banana sandwiches, grabbing one for herself to eat on the way to school. Our friendship flourished and we confided everything to each other. Some nights Grace had to baby-sit while her mam went out to the working men's club. I begged Mam and Dad to let me keep her company while she baby-sat and they finally agreed, though Dad was old-fashioned and didn't believe women should go out on their own. I was even allowed to stay overnight at Grace's on weekends.

Her mam had blonde hair, which she got out of a bottle, but it looked nice after she had the poker in the fire and curled her hair with the hot iron. She ended up with soft little curls all over her head. I had to sleep with Grace in her bed, which she shared with two of the younger children. Some nights the little ones wet the bed and it would go all the way up the back of our nighties as well. But I didn't care, as we usually had a good evening playing records on an old record player they owned. Grace and I tried to teach ourselves how to rock and roll after the younger children had been washed and put to bed.

Grace had to stay in school all day as she received free dinners, but as I had a dad at home who went to work I had to walk home at dinner time to have something to eat, then walk all the way back again. There was an old saying that the people who lived at Craghead used to eat their young, and I've got to say most of the kids were quite wild. The boys were the worst and played the teachers up shocking. They were always being caned, either up in front of the whole class or sent off to wait their turn outside the headmaster's office. It never seemed to do the harder boys much good, who were the ringleaders. The only one the older boys seemed to have any respect for was our science teacher, who was very strict. He would have boys up in front of the class for six of the best at the least bit of disruption in his class.

Of course, a lot of bullying went on once we had been let out of school. There was a little shop just past the school that we had to pass. It was just a wooden hut of a shop that mostly sold sweets, boxes of matches and cigarettes. The owner had no qualms about selling cigarettes and matches to the schoolchildren, who would gather around outside the old shop smoking on the sly.

It was here the boys waited to bully the girls and Grace and I were prime targets as we had no other way to get home except by passing the shop. We would find ourselves surrounded by the bullies, who would form a ring around us, then get out their twopenny Woodbines and force us to smoke, chanting 'fake it, fake it', meaning for us to inhale. They would not let us be on our way until we had accomplished it, by which time we'd be feeling sick, dizzy and looking green. It was not long, though, before Grace and myself were both hooked on Woodbines. You could say we were weaned on Wills Woodbines and were soon buying our own twopenny tabs if we were flush.

When I went to stay at Grace's house to help her baby-sit, sometimes I used to swipe some of Dad's tab-ends out of his old Oxo tin and Grace and I would smoke them. They were so small we had to hold them with a bobby-clip to get them lit.

Soon Dad started asking, 'What's that on your fingers, is it nicotine stains?'

'No, Dad, I've been peeling carrots,' I would lie and I thought I'd got away with it, but he was not daft.

After Grace and I started smoking, the boys left us alone a bit and looked for other kids to bully. Grace and I would walk home, short-cutting through the woods where we had once played when we were younger, spying on the courting couples. Dad had taken me through the very same woods to cut out his turf to make his lawn when we lived in the prefabs. He knew we sometimes played in the woods but used to warn us about the pitch and toss games that went off down there on Sunday mornings and he forbade us to go there on Sunday mornings. Apparently pitch and toss was a gambling game played by the men and was illegal.

While we lived in Cleveland Terrace Mam's bad bouts had got worse and more frequent. She would be laid up in bed and, as Dad and Betty had to go to work, it was inevitably me who stayed off school to help look after her, and do the housework, cooking and shopping. I was always willing to stay off school, but it was quite an ordeal to try and fit everything in.

I would be waiting on Mam, trying to scramble her eggs, just as she liked them, always hoping for a bit of praise, and juggling to fit all the other jobs in. There were pots to wash, clothes to be washed, dried and ironed for five of us, the house had to be cleaned, vegetables and potatoes peeled and prepared for an evening meal. It was no easy task to try and run the home at such a young age and, however hard I tried to get things just right, it seemed it was never good enough for Mam. Once I was sent off with a list to do the shopping and I was starving. I looked at the small three-penny bars of Cadbury's chocolate and my mouth was drooling. Temptation overcame me and I bought a bar and ate it on the way home. I felt very guilty about it and on arriving home found my dad was back from the fore shift at work.

I went straight to Mam's bedroom, gave her the list back along with the change, then proceeded to put the shopping away while the kettle boiled on the stove to make a pot of tea. Dad sat in the bedroom awhile talking to Mam. Next thing I knew, Dad was back downstairs putting on his bicycle clips preparing to go back to the shops, telling me they'd short-changed me by three pence. I sat at the kitchen table, put my head on my arms and sobbed my heart out. Dad put his arms around me and said, 'I know what's wrong with you, hinny, you're worn out.' In between sobs I managed to tell him what I'd done, saying how sorry I was.

'I'll have to tell your mother,' he said, with only a small look of disappointment on his face. Off he went upstairs to tell Mam, after which he came back down, took off his bike clips and said she wanted to see me. I went up, tail between my legs, and apologised to Mam, promising her I would never do it again. She shouted at me in utter contempt and told me how I was such a bad girl, sneaky and sly and always had been. Her words hurt me to the core. I was sent downstairs in disgust to make the tea and keep out of her sight. She gave me the cold treatment for a long time after that. I never did anything like that again. You could never fox Mam, especially when it came to money.

The housework, drudgery and slavery continued. The school board man was a regular visitor to our door. If Dad was in he'd sort him out, but sometimes I had to face him myself and had to lie and say it was me that was sick.

Mam was in and out of hospital and when she came out I heard her telling Mrs Thompson and Mrs Johnson about D&Cs for their heavy, menstrual periods, and wondered what they were. Then she went in to have a hysterectomy. Aunt Kitty came to see us and I strained my ears to try and hear what Dad was whispering to her. I knew it was about Mam and I saw from the worry on his face that it was serious. Mam had been in hospital for a while and I wanted to see her. Dad said children were not allowed in to visit but Aunt Kitty tried to dress me up to look older – she had me take off my white cotton socks and borrowed a pair of our Betty's Cuban-heeled shoes – then Dad took me with him to visit Mam. I had made her some little buns and a home-made card to wish her 'get well'. It took me ages to make it, sticking little flowers on out of the garden.

When we got there, Mam did look bad and I tried to cheer her up by giving her my gifts. I was proud of them but she showed no interest and let them just lie on her bed beside her. I put them on her locker and hoped she'd like them when she got a bit better. When the bell rang to announce visiting time was over, I leaned over the bed and kissed her goodbye. I realised that, though she didn't seem to like me much, I still loved her and missed her.

Dad and I were quiet on the bus home that night; as young as I was, I realised it was hard for him too. Mam didn't come home for a long time. She was sent off to Silloth to a convalescent home for six weeks. When she finally came back in a nice knitted jumper and tartan pleated skirt, she looked much better and Mrs Johnson and Mrs Thompson came over to see her. They shared pots of tea and whispered conversations. I made the tea for them and tried to be seen and not heard. Mam didn't act like she'd missed us and made no fuss over me at all. Dad was glad to have her home. It had been hard for him having to go to work and make the visits to Silloth to visit Mam.

Dad always wanted a motorbike but Mam would not let him get one. He did, however, acquire a moped scooter and rode up to Stanley on it while it putt-putted away. People laughed at him on it and he got the nickname Putt-Putt Geordie. He kept it in a lean-to shed at the side of the house, and it was his pride and joy. He loved his garden, too, especially the front one where he planted various flowers, including wallflowers, night-scented stock and carnations. The smell of them on summer evenings was delightful. He had a thorn in his side, though, in the shape of the insurance man, Billy Wright.

On doing his rounds collecting his weekly money on insurance policies, Billy always called on our house last in the street, where he took a short cut through Dad's garden. He even trampled some of the flowers down and, as much as Dad told him not to do this, Billy ignored him. One day Dad decided he'd had enough. He dug a hole at the side of the garden and covered it with loose sods of grass, making a trap to 'catch the bugger'.

Sure enough, next time Billy was short-cutting through the garden, he fell down the hole and nearly broke his legs. 'That will teach the bugger,' laughed Dad. Billy did not cut through our garden again.

Mam put weight on after her hysterectomy and got slimming pills off our old doctor. She had pills of all colours and sizes in Dad's drawer, alongside his Oxo tin of tab-ends. By this time, Grace and I had started taking an interest in boys. There was one boy I liked at school called John Winning. He was a quiet, studious boy and walked with a limp, as he had polio as a child. He was just a friend, but secretly I was hoping he'd fancy me one day.

One night I was up Grace's house helping her baby-sit, and the younger kids were in bed. Dad was on the night shift at the pit so I was not allowed to stay over with Grace that night. While we were listening to records and smoking our purloined tab-ends, there was a knock at Grace's front door. She answered it and found some of the boys from our school were out there and wanted to talk to us. She went outside first, then came in saying they wanted to talk to me. I was a bit shy and nervous but went out the front to see what they wanted. It was then that the incident happened. Two of the boys grabbed hold of me and kept my arms tightly held while two others indecently assaulted me. As my arms were pinned to my side, they put their hands up my dress and inside my knickers. They groped me in my most secret place, which both shocked and hurt me. What made it worse was that John Winning was there, though he looked all hangdog and ashamed. John did not take any part in the assault, but failed to stop his mates.

I screamed my head off until they eventually let me go, as the next-door neighbours were banging on their windows. I flew back inside Grace's house and sobbed my eyes out. Grace had been nearly as scared as me when I told her what had happened. We should never have gone outside to even talk to the lads, and feared if we were found out there would be big trouble for both of us. I felt dirty and ashamed and eventually went back home.

The assault had shocked me badly. I ran home, traumatised by the assault, feeling that somehow it must have been all my fault. I was terrified my mother would find out about it; I felt she would kill me if she knew and I had not intended to tell her. Yet at the same time, I felt a need to confide in her, hoping she would be able to ease my pain and lessen my embarrassment over the incident.

It was not to be.

As I crept in the back door of our house, Mam was waiting for me. She had already been told by Grace's neighbours that something had happened to me, though what version of the incident she was given, I never did get to find out. As soon as I walked into our kitchen, she slapped me hard across my tear-streaked cheeks.

'You dirty little tramp,' she yelled at me, as I tried to shield my face and head from her hard blows.

'Just what do you think you've been up to?' she demanded as she continued to rain down her blows. I tried to get away from her by running into the sitting room but she was soon after me, continuing her assault as she called me 'a dirty little bitch'.

'You are nothing – but trouble – to me!' she shouted, as she punctuated every word with another slap.

The curtains were open in the sitting room and I wondered briefly if anyone would witness the scene of my mother hitting me as I cowered before her.

'You're bloody worthless you are, our Lyn, you've always been nothing but trouble to me and now you're a tramp into the bargain,' she ranted, still hitting me over and over again. 'I don't know what I've done to deserve a worthless girl like you.'

In between slaps and sobs, I tried to explain to Mam what had really happened but she was having none of it. I had brought shame to her door, she told me.

Dad was at work on a night shift at the pit, so was not there to defend me this time.

'Get yourself off to bed and out of my sight, you tramp,' cried Mam, giving me a final whack to the head. Her vivid, blue eyes bore coldly down into mine with neither love nor mercy in them as she ordered me upstairs.

I half-crawled up to bed as tears of injustice flowed freely down my stinging cheeks. I prayed she would not tell my dad about it. He held me on a pedestal and I did not want to fall from his grace; it would break my dad's heart as well as mine.

I did not sleep that night as the whole incident played over in my head, yet it was Mam's reaction and her cruel words that resounded in my ears – that had hurt me most of all.

It was during this sleepless night that I made the decision to end my life.

Next morning I got up early for school before anyone else was up. I was feeling terrible about it all, especially the injustice of Mam not letting me explain what had really happened. I had no breakfast but grabbed a handful of her pills out of the Oxo tin in the kitchen drawer.

I met Grace on the way to school and told her what had happened with my mam. We were way too early for school but headed there anyway. I dreaded going into class and having to face the boys who had molested me. It was so early when Grace and I got to school that there were not many pupils about, and there were still the cockroaches running around the floor in the cloakroom. I showed Grace the pills – not many of them, but some were huge red capsules – and she tried to stop me taking them, tried to wrestle them out of my hand, but I took them anyway with huge gulps of water from the taps above the little hand basins. I don't think I really intended to kill myself – at that young age it was just a cry for attention. I was thirteen.

Grace was crying but I told her not to worry, I'd be OK and to be sure not to tell anyone about the pills. We went into assembly where all the pupils were gathered along with the teachers and headmaster and we stood in lines while we had prayers. Then we went to our science lesson, which was conducted in a Portacabin class built across the yard from the main school. Not long into the lesson I started feeling odd and next thing I knew I had fallen off my chair. The science teacher thought I'd fainted and got two of the boys to help him get me outside into the yard in the fresh air with a chair to sit on.

I must have blacked out again because the next thing I remember is being carried unceremoniously across the yard to be put on the couch in the staff room. In the fleeting moments when I came round I worried in case my dress had come up and my knickers were showing. Then I was out for the count again until they put me into an ambulance, which had been summoned to school.

I remember nothing more about it until I woke up again in a hospital bed with the screens pulled around me and Mam and Dad sat there, looking worried. Dad looked relieved when I woke up and said, 'I know what's wrong with her.' He promptly lit up a Woodbine, took a few puffs, then offered it to me.

The cat's out of the bag now, I thought, but I duly took a couple of puffs then handed it back to Dad, where he proceeded to smoke it (against all hospital policy, even back then), then he 'nipped' the Woodbine and put it in his pocket for later. Looking back on it, I think it was Dad who was craving for a smoke, but I accepted this as a great act of kindness, then went back to sleep again.

When I next woke up my parents had gone home. I was moved onto the main ward so I must have been getting better, but I felt dreadful.

I suspect some of the pills I had taken may have been sleeping pills, others probably her 'diet' pills, which were probably amphetamines, though I didn't know it then. I didn't say a word to anyone about the pills. The doctors and nurses had been so kind, even Mam seemed to have forgotten about the incident of the previous night. I wonder now if she ever told Dad about it. She always used to say to us if we were playing her up, 'I'll brain you in a minute.' Perhaps she thought she had done me a bit of damage, hitting me around the head. Regardless, she didn't mention the incident and I didn't mention the pills.

The doctors came on their rounds about ten o'clock next morning and gathered in a group around my bed. I was poked and prodded and duly discussed, then later that day they came back and proceeded to do a lumbar puncture on me. This was an uncomfortable procedure, but I accepted it, they were only trying to come up with some kind of diagnosis. I was a mystery to them.

Next day I was feeling worse; I felt so sick and ill that I started thinking I was going to die. The nurses were kindness themselves and treated me lovely, but as one nurse came to take my temperature, I decided I had better confess to taking the pills or else I might die. She wasn't very happy when I told her and went stomping off up the ward where she must have notified the doctors.

The attitude of the staff changed immediately and I was more or less ignored then, which hurt a bit I suppose, as I had been enjoying the kindness showered on me up until then.

Mam came in to visit me in the afternoon on her own, as Dad was at work. She wasn't there for long before one of the nurses came and asked her if she would go to the office to see my doctor. When she came back to see me she looked really angry, although she was trying to keep herself under control. I could nearly see the steam coming out of her ears. She started packing my stuff up out of my locker and I thought at first I must be going home, but Mam coldly told me I was being moved somewhere else. I didn't dare ask where I was going. I had shamed her and knew better than to argue. I had told no one what had led up to my taking the pills and never would.

I didn't know it then, but the doctor had asked my mother's permission to move me to Collingwood Clinic, an annexe of St Nicholas' Mental Hospital, and she had calmly signed the papers to allow my transfer. I was transferred there by ambulance. Mam went home and did not accompany me.

It was a shock when I arrived there, where I was duly processed and checked in along with my notes. The nursing staff were different here, not so kind as at the other hospital, and I knew I was in big trouble when they moved me to a room where a man waited in a white coat with a funny sort of machine beside him. They started putting leads onto my head to do an electroencephalogram (EEG). I felt terrified as I remembered Mrs Thompson telling Mam about her electric-shock treatments and thought this was what they were going to do to me. My fears were unfounded, though, and I was eventually moved onto a ward where the doors were locked behind me.

I was taken to a ward and shown to my bed, and when I looked around me at the other patients there, this was when I was truly scared. It was like a scene out of *One Flew Over the Cuckoo's Nest*. Some patients lay in their beds, drugged up by Largactil, while others just walked around in circles up and down the ward. As a young girl in a ward of adult patients, some of who were really demented, some being drug addicts, I felt very vulnerable. Other patients constantly approached me asking me if I had any tabs, cigarettes or even drugs. I was afraid to turn my back and, other than use the toilet, I wouldn't leave my bedside.

After a meal was served in the early evening, drugs were handed out by two nurses. Some of the inmates took their medicines eagerly and continued to follow the nurses on their round, but some had to be force-fed their medicine. I was given nothing, thankfully. After this it was lights out at 10 p.m. and it was bedlam all night long. There was screaming, weeping and wailing, and some patients raided other people's lockers. I had little sleep that night and cried quietly into my pillow. It was too noisy to sleep and I was too afraid. I felt deserted and a long way from home.

Next day brought sunshine back into my life. My dad came to visit me on his own. When he looked around him at my surroundings he looked very sad and sat and held my hand quietly. Other patients approached him while he sat there, trying to scrounge tabs or anything else Dad may have had. He chased them away abruptly, then after about half an hour he said he was going to see someone but would be back soon. He had to be let out of the door, which was locked after him again by a nurse. Not long after, Dad was back, telling me, 'Get your bloody things together, we're leaving this bloody madhouse.'

I was so grateful. Dad had been my saviour; he helped me throw all my bits and pieces into carrier bags and we got out of there as quickly as we could. It was a wonderful feeling to get out into the weak sunshine. I had no coat with me and there was quite a nip in the air but I didn't care about that.

We walked all the way back to Newcastle then caught a bus home to Stanley. Dad had not talked much during our journey, but I could tell he wasn't very happy about the situation, though he had not chastised me about it, which was a ray of light for me. Mam was at home and this time it seemed like Dad was giving her the cold treatment instead of the other way round. Ann had been out playing when we'd got back and, when he spotted her coming up the steps to the house, Dad told me to hide behind the door, which I did. She came bursting into the dining room and I jumped out behind her and gave her a surprise. She threw her little arms around me and laughed and cried at the same time. She was so happy to see me and I was so happy to be back.

I was to learn later that when Dad came home from work to find that Mam had signed the papers to send me to the mental hospital he had gone mad about it, and had been determined to get me out of there straight away. He even lost a shift off work to do so. Mental illness was treated with a sense of shame in those days. To be mentally ill was one thing, but to be put into an institution was much worse and was a great stigma. It was even worse to be placed into an institution if you weren't ill.

It all blew over eventually and everything concerning that incident was swept under the carpet. Mam's pills were moved out of the drawer, but I had learned my lesson and would never try that again. I was left with a lifelong fear of locked doors.

SEVEN

Childhood was not all doom and gloom. Although we didn't go on proper holidays – I don't think we could afford them – I remember with fondness trips to the seaside on warm summer days. These would be day trips, and Mam and Dad would only decide the day before that we'd go.

The coast was not too far away from us. There was Whitley Bay, South and North Shields, Cullercoats and one of our favourites, Tynemouth, which was a tiny little town sat around a lovely bay of perfect beach, not far from the train station. Mam would do her baking the day before we went and make bacon-and-egg pies, apple tarts, cakes and scones. Dad would prepare a mound of sandwiches the night before and get the huge flask out in preparation for the tea to be poured into it early the next morning. He had little bottles that he kept specially for keeping the milk in separately, so he could get as much tea into the flask as he could. These items were all duly wrapped and placed into two large shopping bags, along with our buckets and spades, and we would go to bed and pray for a fine day to come, excited at the prospect of a day at the seaside.

We used to make our way there by getting a bus from Stanley to Newcastle, then a trek to Newcastle Central Station to catch a train to the coast. The train journeys were frequent and only took about half an hour from Newcastle to any of the resorts. We would be woken up very early in the morning by Dad, have a light breakfast, then set off excitedly on our outing.

On arrival at the seaside we would make our way to the beach and, after great deliberation, choose our spot and place a blanket on the sands to mark our territory. If Mam was flush she would let Dad rent out two deckchairs for them to sit on while they watched us playing happily on the sands, building sandcastles or paddling in the sea. We would put on our bathing costumes and brave the cold North Sea. However hot a day it was, the North Sea was always cold. We would be glad to get out and have Mam help us towel ourselves dry, shivering all the while, our teeth chattering – we always stayed in the sea too long. Then we would change back into our clothes while Mam held the big towel around us to protect our modesty. We used to sit on the sands for hours, then we'd have our food spread out nicely on clean tea towels while Mam and Dad supped their cups of tea from the old Thermos flask.

Invariably, by the time we set off back on the homeward journey, the trains used to be packed; sometimes we'd wait for an hour or more as they were so crowded, and we had to stand up on the train all the way back to Newcastle. I remember on one of these journeys feeling so tired out after our day at the seaside I had to lie down on the floor of the train. I felt so tired I just wanted to go to sleep. I was pulled up sharply by Mam and given a clout around the head for showing her up.

Christmas times were exciting as well, though we never got a lot of presents. By far the most exciting part of Christmas was the stockings we hung up every Christmas Eve. It was nearly always the same things we got in them every year: an apple and orange, some nuts which Dad cracked open for us in front of the fire, some small toy and, best of all, a two-shilling piece or even a shiny half-crown. We treasured these.

I suppose we were lucky really. Some of the children where we lived got nothing at all. The poor Wilson girls were sent to ours one Christmas Eve: 'Me mam says, can we borrow a bucket of coal to make a fire?' Dad let them have their bucket of coal. The Christmas spirit must have been on him.

Dad worked hard as a miner but, although he got his coal as an allowance as part of his wage, he still used to chop up wood and burn it to supplement the coal. He liked to see our coal house full, but when he had a load delivered he would sometimes sell off half a load if we could spare it, cheaply to one of the other neighbours.

Dad was always doing jobs for people as well. If any of the neighbours had an electrical problem or something they needed fixing, they would come to him and he never refused them. When he'd completed jobs for people they would ask him how much he wanted paying, but Dad never accepted cash for his toils and would say, 'Ah, just get me some tabs then.' So he would be given ten or even twenty Woodbines for his labours and was quite happy with this arrangement, as he was never allowed to keep money of his own anyway. He was expected to turn every penny over to Mam, so I think the Woodbines he earned for himself were a great help to him.

After the incident with the boys outside Grace's house, the pills and being put in the 'loony bin', I wasn't allowed to play with Grace for a good while, and I missed her. She was my one good friend and I just couldn't mix with any of the other kids any more, being very shy and withdrawn. I had to go back to school, though; the school board man came knocking on our door enough times.

By this time, Betty had met a lad called Eric Platten and they were courting strongly. He lived with his mam and dad at South Moor along with his twin brother, Alan, and their old granddad. Eric worked for the National Coal Board (NCB), but was not a miner, he had a job in the offices. Mam seemed to think Eric was respectable enough to be allowed to court our Betty as he'd been grammar-school educated. Dad wasn't so keen, but went along with it.

As I was meeting Grace at school anyway, or on the way there and back to school, it was decided we could be friends again, but no more stopping over at her house was ever allowed again. Especially as Grace's mam had a new man-friend who took her out and sometimes stayed overnight.

They eventually married but he was not a nice man, Grace's new stepfather. He only had one eye (the other was a false one) and was a very formidable-looking man who beat the kids on a regular basis. Sometimes Grace's mam sported black eyes, but mostly it was the children who were the target. Sometimes when we walked to school we would accidentally touch arms and Grace would flinch, then show me the terrible bruises she had on both her arms from her stepfather's beatings. It was mostly her and her sister, Margaret, who got the worst hidings. This went on for ages and I felt so sorry for Grace and her sisters. She told no one else about it. They were too scared to tell for they knew they'd only get another good belting if they ever did. They didn't get much to eat at home and sometimes I smuggled food out of our house to give to Grace for her breakfast on the way to school.

One particular day I met Grace for school and she could barely walk. In the cloakroom at school she whispered to me and secretly showed me numerous bruises over her arms, legs and back. She couldn't bear to be touched, her bruises were so sore and painful, and I tried to edge the other kids away from her when we stood together during morning prayers in assembly.

That night, when Dad came home from work, I told him about it; he asked me to fetch Grace and demanded to see her arms. I was nervous at spilling the beans now, Grace was crying and Dad was furious, though he treated Grace kindly. He told her she must go home and tell her mother that he wanted to see her, so she too came to our house to speak to him.

Our dad was strict but he did not believe in children being beaten. In those days neighbours more or less kept their family problems inside the four walls of their homes and people tended not to interfere in each other's business, though there was plenty of gossip flying around.

Grace's mam came round and Dad took her in and gave her a good talking to. She was crying but Dad was unsympathetic and warned her, 'If I ever see a mark on any of your kids any more I'll have the cruelty man at your door.' After that, Grace never showed me any more bruises. I don't know for sure if it stopped the beatings completely but I like to think it helped. At least Grace didn't fall out with me and we remained firm friends.

From then onwards whenever Dad used to see Grace's stepfather walking down the street it gave him someone else to vent his spleen on as well as Billy Wilson. He'd look out of our window and be ranting, 'Another idle, lazy string of useless piss, off out to the bloody club.'

I was never such a great scholar at school, I was bored stiff by Geography and History, so much so that I often dozed off to sleep in class. Mathematics I did not find easy. I did try harder in this subject, but confess that when it came time to learn algebra I completely lost the plot. English was the one subject I loved and when we were given essays to write I was in my element. Our English teacher, Mrs Wilson, was so pleased at one essay I had done she gave me glowing praise and told me to take it home to show my parents.

When I took it home Mam read it and told me she did not believe I had written it myself. 'You must have copied it,' she said and, as much as I denied it, she still would not believe it was my own work. I felt very hurt as she would not let me show it to my dad, and told me 'Don't be bothering your dad with that nonsense.'

When we were fourteen, all our class had to sit an English exam and as Grace and I both passed it, we were entitled to go to Shield Row School for shorthand/typing lessons one day a week. We started going there for these lessons but found them so boring that we often bunked off them and spent the bus fare we'd been given to get there in the ice-cream parlour at the bottom of Stanley. We'd buy a hot Oxo drink and listen to the jukebox tunes all afternoon. I regret it now. Even if I had never learned the shorthand, the typing could have proved very useful to me in later life, but I had my chance and I threw it away.

EIGHT

I could not wait to leave school and was desperate to find a job. Both Grace and myself trawled the shops begging for work, but no one would employ us until we were fifteen and had left school.

I finally got my first job after leaving school in a small grocery shop in Catchgate and Grace found work as an assistant in Woolworth's in Stanley. Although our Betty was allowed to pay board, I never was. I started the job at two pounds, seven and sixpence a week and had to tip my wages straight over to Mam every payday. She then allowed me to keep the seven and sixpence for myself as pocket money, which also had to cover my bus fare from Stanley to Catchgate. I could have caught a bus from South Stanley to Stanley, but I always walked up to Stanley and back, saving my bus fare to buy packets of five Woodbines and a box of matches.

I often called in at Stanley to see Aunt Kitty on the way home from work and still stayed with her on some evenings while Uncle Joe was at work on a late shift on the buses. She had always been kind to me and was always pleased to see me. She and Uncle Joe were still poor yet she would always share her last slice of bread or anything. Aunt Kitty would be glad of the company in the evenings when Uncle Joe was at work and I always enjoyed hers. If Uncle Joe had just been paid, she would get me to go to the chip shop for her and then we'd sit and share chips and bread and butter, sitting each side of the fire. She used to sometimes take me up to a little tobacconist's on Stanley Main Street that stayed open late. She would buy Uncle Joe's Woodbines, a packet of twenty Players for herself and, now she knew I smoked, would even buy me a packet of ten Woodbines, which I thought was extremely kind. She sometimes bought a few sweets too, sugared almonds normally, to sit and share in front of her fire. She still shared the same old tales with me as she did in my younger days, but we could have a laugh together now at some of my earlier antics when I'd been younger. We would natter on around her fire with the kettle on the hob, puffing away on our tabs and I remembered how many times I'd shared her bed and my baths in front of her fire. I did love Aunt Kitty so I was overjoyed when Mam put an end to their feud by inviting them to our Betty and Eric's wedding when I was fifteen.

I was bridesmaid for the wedding and Betty and Eric presented me with a lovely gold cross and chain afterwards. It was at the reception afterwards when I got my first taste of Babycham and was quite merry.

I could afford to go to the pictures now, the Essoldo that used to be at the bottom end of Stanley. I would go there with Grace occasionally, and sometimes I was allowed to go to the local dancehall, the Palais, on a weekend, again with Grace, but Dad was very strict about us being home by 10.30 p.m. The dance was never finished by then so we used to have to leave early and would often be running from Stanley, all the way down the hill in my stockinged feet, high heels in my hand, trying to get home for the deadline.

If we were out just roaming the streets, puffing away on our Woodbines 'on monkey parade' as Dad called it, we always knew when it was time to get home. Dad still had the loudest whistle in the whole of Stanley and if we were just five minutes late, he'd be out there, whistling for us to come in. It got to be embarrassing when we were older, but he was a stickler for us being in on time.

We used to enjoy going to the Palais. There was no alcohol served there, though some of the lads smuggled cans of beer in and drank them in the toilets. There was a café there where you could purchase soft drinks during the interval and you were allowed to smoke in the café, though not in the dancehall itself. Often there would be fights breaking out, most times over girls, but the offenders would soon be slung out. On the whole, the girls would mostly dance with themselves, handbags on the floor between partners. They used to have live bands on who played rock'n'roll numbers, and while the boys were busy ogling the girls, the girls would be busy ogling the band. It was the start of the rock'n'roll era, not too long before the age of the Beatles.

I was given my first record player for my sixteenth birthday and started a record collection, which I used to play over and over again in the sitting room – Craig Douglas, Johnny Leighton, Cliff Richard.

I could only afford to buy a new record now and again but I certainly got my wear out of them. It was a quiet little shop I worked in at Catchgate, owned by a nice Scottish couple, Mr and Mrs Fenwick. Though I never saw much of Mr Fenwick himself, Mrs Fenwick ran the shop and I worked alongside her. I learned the ropes very quickly and she was kind towards me, but it was lonely not meeting any people of my own age. One day a lad came into the shop to buy some small item, then he started coming into the shop every day. He used to stutter, but at least made the effort to talk to me. His name was John and he worked for his father out behind our shop, running a local haulage firm of lorries. He asked me out one day and I agreed. Dad said he had to pick me up at the house, as he wanted to 'vet' him.

Well, he turned up looking very smart in his best suit and even brought my mam a bunch of flowers, which went down well with her. He took me to see a film at a cinema in Newcastle, a very posh place and a lot different to the Essoldo in Stanley or the old Pavilion, which was a fleapit really, though I'd gone there lots of times with a sixpenny piece to watch Saturday morning shows of the old Superman re-runs. It had been something to look forward to as a young kid, to be allowed to go to these matinees.

The cinema John took me to was in another class and afterwards we went to a restaurant for a meal. I wore a new lavender suit I was buying on the weekly plan out of a friend's catalogue and felt the bee's knees, yet I hardly knew which knife and fork to hold first and was very shy about eating in the company of someone I hardly knew. I felt very awkward and ill at ease.

John was a perfect gentleman, however, and took me home right to the door that night before going all the way back to Consett where he lived. We had a few dates, sometimes just going for a walk, and his manners were impeccable. Unfortunately, poor John had the most dreadful case of halitosis I had yet encountered and when he tried to kiss me, I would take a deep breath first and keep my lips shut tightly together. He developed a fondness for me but it was a fondness I felt I could not return. I ended the relationship pretty quickly.

Grace seemed happy enough in Woolworth's at Stanley and was on more money than I earned in the grocery shop, so I decided to apply to Woolworth's for a job. I was taken on as an assistant in the grocery department, and now had only to walk up to Stanley to work, so saving on bus fares. My wage had gone up to three pounds and ten shillings and I got to keep the ten shillings for myself, so I was better off all round. Not only that, there were plenty of girls my own age group there as well as my good friend Grace.

By this time Grace was going out with a boy called Jimmy Armstrong; she was smitten by him in his teddy-boy style of dress and winkle-pickers. We wore the bouffant hairstyles of the era, backcombed and sprayed with loads of hairspray and the highest stiletto heels we could manage to totter on.

It was at Woolworth's I was to meet Brian, the warehouseman, who would become my first husband. Brian came from a large family, who had the reputation of being a wild bunch. Brian was older than I was, me being sixteen and him twenty-one. I don't think Mam and Dad were too keen, mainly because of the age difference and his family's wild reputation. His brothers drank a lot and were apt to get into fights, especially at weekends.

Brian, however, did not drink much at all, and didn't smoke either, so this went in his favour. He was my first serious boyfriend and we eventually got engaged. Mam and Dad did not want us to get married – they thought I was too young. I was infatuated with Brian though, and finally my parents gave me permission for us to marry on condition we live with them.

We had a small wedding in August 1963 at St Stephen's Church, when I was seventeen and a half years old. Betty was my matron of honour. Mam laid on a small tea with only our family and Brian's family and that was our reception. I had left Woolworth's by now and worked in a factory in Lanchester where they made make-up bags and toilet bags. Brian now had a job as a bus conductor for the Northern Bus Company, where my Uncle Joe worked. Brian eventually learned to drive, passed his PSV test and became a bus driver.

We lived in with my parents, which soon became intolerable. We paid my mam rent for us both but were also expected to pay half of all the household bills.

We also paid for our own food, so never seemed to get the chance to save up much for our own home.

Mam had always been money-orientated. I was expected to share all the household chores, which I didn't mind – after all, I had been used to doing this from being ten years old or younger – but she didn't enjoy having us there and wouldn't allow a thing to be out of place. Brian had a motorbike and sidecar by now that he used to get to work and back. I worked full-time while always trying to fit in my chores of keeping the house spick-and-span, but it was never good enough for Mam. It all ended up in a big argument one evening between Mam and me when Dad and Brian were both at work. We had a blazing row over a trivial matter and I ended up telling her we were leaving.

'Well bloody well go, then,' Mam fumed. 'You're neither use nor bloody ornament, anyway.'

'I will then, I'll go,' I shouted back, so I marched upstairs, threw our clothes into a big suitcase and stormed out of the house, giving no thought to where we were going to go. I ended up walking all the way over to South Moor to Betty and Eric's house, where they lived with their first son, my nephew Gary. He was only a little boy and was lovely, but Betty was expecting their second child.

Eric was the one to answer the back door when I got there and when he saw me with my suitcase, he said jokingly, 'Bloody hell, you haven't come to stay have you?'

This prompted me into floods of tears and the whole sorry tale poured out of me. Betty and Eric were sympathetic and kindly offered that Brian and I could stay with them while we looked for somewhere else to live. I had to walk up to the Northern Bus Garage, the depot where they kept the buses at night, and wait outside the garage for Brian to finish his last bus run so I could tell him we'd moved.

Dad came over to Betty's next day on his bike (he had had to get rid of his moped by now as Mam decreed the expense of petrol was too much). Dad tried to reason with me for us to return home, but when he went on to say, 'Your mam doesn't know how she's going to manage without your money,' that did it for me and I stuck to my guns and refused to go back.

As Betty and Eric only had a two-bedroomed terraced house, we would have to move out before the new baby came along, so we had to find somewhere to live pretty quickly. Betty and Eric were good to us and told us we did not need to pay them any rent to enable us to try and save up some deposit for a house. To contribute something, we just used to put a bit of money into our Gary's moneybox.

I was working full-time at Randsome and Marles Engineering by now, having been sacked from the factory in Lanchester for being constantly late. The manager there had spied me on so many occasions trying to clock-in with my time card quietly as the whole factory was working away and he would spot me and shout right across the factory floor, 'You're sacked, collect your cards on Friday.' I would just continue on to my line where I worked as a 'turner' and get on with my work. I was late once too often though, and was finally called into the manager's office one Friday when I received my cards. I got a job at Ransome and Marles the following week. It was a ball-bearing factory but had been used during the war to make ammunitions.

While I found the job quite boring, it was a source of income and we saved as hard as we could. I sat on an assembly line fitting rivets into cages that went around the ball bearings. The banter was quite raucous along the line of women whom I worked with. Many of the women were older, married women and I found some of their jokes distasteful. Although I was now married myself, I was still very shy and they enjoyed teasing me as I blushed very easily.

Just before Betty had her baby – Sharon, a beautiful baby girl – we had saved up just enough money to put down on a property on Bircham Street, South Moor. It was a terraced house divided into two flats and an old widowed gentleman lived in the upstairs flat with his two daughters, the Harding family. We managed to obtain a 90 per cent mortgage and as the Hardings paid us seventeen shillings and sixpence a week in rent as sitting tenants, it went a good way towards paying our monthly mortgage.

I had always dreamed of being a nurse but, with only a secondary-school education, felt it was beyond me. One night, I sat and wrote a letter to the local hospital and was elated to get a letter by return inviting me to an interview. I took time off work to attend the interview with the matron of the hospital and was amazed when she informed me I could start on the next batch of nurse training that would commence in the next September. In the meantime, I could start two weeks prior to that as a pupil nurse. I can't describe how excited I was about this and handed my notice in at Randsome and Marles.

So in August 1964, I started work as a pupil nurse at South Moor Hospital, which had once been the miners' welfare hospital. It now consisted of wards, an out-patients' department and an operating theatre for general and orthopaedic surgery. It was to be my 'base' hospital, but we spent a month initially in nursing school, six months at a geriatric hospital in Lanchester, two weeks at Richard Murray Maternity Hospital in Consett and three months at the Ear, Nose and Throat Hospital in Lanchester. The rest of the time was spent at South Moor Hospital on the wards, with six months devoted to training and working in the operating theatre. We had to pass exams at the end of our month in school and I was amazed to find I had not only passed but had come out with top marks. I loved my training, but it was hard work and the shift work I had to do meant Brian and I often just passed like ships in the night at home. We saw very little of each other and when I was not working I was busy studying, so he kind of went his own way and spent a lot of time at his mam's house.

It was during my nursing training I realised I was pregnant. I dreaded having to tell the matron. She was very good about it and told me I could continue with my training and take maternity leave to have my baby. I continued to work at the hospital until I was six months pregnant. I was still only 28 weeks pregnant and not long into my maternity leave when my waters broke one night. I sent Brian up the road to a phone box to ask the maternity hospital staff what I should do and was dismayed when he came back and said I had to go straight in.

Not too long after getting to the hospital, my labour pains began. They kept me in bed and tried to stop the labour for a week, although my baby seemed determined to arrive into the world as early as possible. Exactly one week later, though, on Tuesday 18 January 1966, I gave birth to my first-born, a perfect little baby girl whom I named Helen. She weighed only three pounds ten ounces, but she was a lively little baby, perfect in every way. She was put in an incubator and placed into the special-care baby unit, but other than having to be fed via a nasal gastro tube, she was fit and healthy. They kept her in hospital for six weeks, but I went up to see her every day and spent hours with her.

It was nevertheless a very anxious time. Even when they allowed me to take her home at six weeks old when she had reached five pounds, I was still very anxious as a young mother, especially as they told me she would need two-hourly feeds so as to thrive. She was a sleepy little baby at first and took so long over one feed that by the time I'd finished it was nearly time for the next. I had cried tears of joy when I gave birth to Helen and instantly fell in love with her.

At last, I had a child of my own, a perfect little human being, and I vowed to be a good mother. Helen was born three days before my twentieth birthday. My mam and dad had been to see us; Mam had got over her huff slightly, but she would always remain at a distance from me. Since leaving Mam's home, after we had rowed and I had moved in with Betty and Eric, I gave Mam time to cool down, but had to swallow my pride and eventually started going to their home to see them. I had been desperate to see my dad. Dad was always pleased to see me but Mam stayed cool and aloof, although she tried to stay polite, she never gave me a warm welcome, she would never forgive me for walking out and never showed any warmth in her manner towards me. She liked to play 'the wronged person' and was very unforgiving.

'Don't build your hopes up that this baby will thrive,' she told me coldly. 'It's early days yet, there's still a chance she won't make it,' which did not instil any confidence in me.

Betty and Eric were good to me with Helen, and Betty promised to look after her for me when I had to return to work. I dreaded having to leave her, but I was determined to finish my training. The first day back at work after my maternity leave I left Helen with Betty and was changing into my uniform at work in floods of tears. I remember a friend of mine from the same nursing class, Jean Bewley, putting her arms around me and trying to comfort me.

Every shift after work I always raced back to our Betty's and collected Helen, then took her home. Brian was not much help with her and, even though he seemed to love Helen, he couldn't knuckle down to anything and still spent a lot of his time at his mam's. Even when he was supposed to be at work, I was to find out he'd actually spent the whole day at his mother's house. He was proud of Helen but probably unprepared for being a father at this stage in his life.

Shortly after going back to work I discovered I was pregnant again. My biggest fear was having to tell the matron, but I plucked up the courage to do it one day. She was astounded and very, very angry, shouting at me, telling me it had 'never been known to take maternity leave twice during anyone's training'. Eventually she calmed down and told me to 'just keep working' and perhaps she would think of something. So that's what I did during the year of 1966. I kept working, racing between home, Betty's and the hospital. I had taken my final exams and passed them so I had to continue to work to make up for the time I had lost due to maternity leave.

It was not easy and I had little support from Brian, in fact, I did not seem to see him much at all. When I did see him, in between shifts, I would say to him, 'I can't keep going on like this, Brian, I've about had enough.'

'Well, it's your choice,' he'd reply, 'you're the one who wanted to be a nurse, you were the one who decided that, so don't complain to me about it.' So I just kept on working with a resigned determination.

We had a terrible winter in 1966. It snowed so long and hard and was bitterly cold. I had taken no holiday leave all year, but just kept working as I'd been told to. The other staff at work used to joke with me that they were 'keeping a side ward vacant in case I had the baby at work'. The winds came up hard from the North Sea and as it continued to snow it resulted in snowdrifts up to six-foot high in places. As it was so hilly where we lived, the snowploughs could not keep up and eventually all the main roads were impassable. All of the buses were off. Still, I kept working by getting up extra early, seeing to Helen, then trudging my way through the snow to leave her with Betty, before having to walk all the way to work through deep snowdrifts.

I never missed a shift even though I was heavily pregnant, but I wondered how long I could keep it up. Two weeks before my baby was due to be born, the matron called me into her office and told me I could now finish work. I had completed my allotted time and my training was complete. I was to be placed upon the nursing Register in March 1967 as a State Enrolled Nurse. It was with much relief that I finally finished, but I was proud I had achieved my ambition. I felt I was perhaps not quite as worthless as Mam had always told me I was!

Two weeks later I went into labour. I was having a home birth as I did not want to go into hospital and leave Helen, who was only eleven months old. The midwife was summoned and my mam came over to stay with me for the birth. Labour went on all night, but finally, the next day, I gave birth to my first son, Paul. He weighed five pounds and was long and thin; the midwife said he looked like 'a long skinny rabbit'. He was gorgeous, with fair hair and blue eyes, whereas Helen was dark-haired. They both looked like Brian. I had Paul's cot right next to my bed and even while he slept I could not stop gazing at him in wonder and stroking his little hands. Love swelled up in me for him.

Brian had wanted to call him Wyn after Wyn Davies, the Newcastle United footballer, as Brian was football mad. I would not allow it but compromised by calling him Paul Wyn instead. Brian disappeared soon after Paul's birth to go round to his mam's, only appearing very much later that night, blind drunk, with all his brothers in tow. There was a big row between Brian's brothers and my mam and in the ensuing fracas she was knocked on the face by one of the brothers.

Brian got the cold treatment from both of us that night. I lay in bed feeling helpless.

Next day Dad came over on his bike. Betty had already told him what had happened so when he got to our house he wanted to take Brian out in the street and 'fight like a man'.

'Come on, you bugger,' he shouted. 'You're good at hitting women, let's see what you can do with me, let's see what you're really made of,' taking off his coat, and pushing up his sleeves.

'No,' replied Brian, 'I don't want to fight you, man, it was just a misunderstanding.'

'Misunderstanding, my arse,' said Dad. 'It's 'cause you're not man enough, that's what it is.'

So he ordered Mam to get her things together to go home and I was left to get on with things on my own. I had to get up and look after two babies, and I was totally drained through lack of sleep.

I soon got into a routine, though, and coped pretty well with two children under one year old, considering I got no help from their dad. Our marriage was failing even then and we rowed a lot of the time, yet there were days I hardly saw him at all and he even took to spending some nights at his mother's house, which made our rows worse.

We were slowly drifting a[illegible]

'Why don't you help me more,' I would beg of Brian.

'That's your job, you're the mother,' he told me.

I coped as best as I could, even managing to fit in some part-time shifts at Dunstin Hill Hospital while Betty had the children for me.

It was very good of Betty to do this for me, considering she had two children of her own to look after, Gary and Sharon. Eric helped me out, too. When the snow lay heavy on the ground, he would walk the short distance from his house to mine to help pull the big pram through the snow with a baby at each end of the pram.

'Come on, kidda, let's get these bairns roond to wor hoose, before we all freeze. 'Eeh, man, it's a good job for us we're not monkeys, eh? It's certainly the weather for brass balls, eh kidda?' Eric would laugh. 'Eeh, come on now, hinny, as wor Betty will be wondering where we are.'

My marriage to Brian was doomed to failure, though we decided to give it one last chance by moving away from the Northeast.

Brian had a mate who had found work in Buckinghamshire and offered to help Brian find something down there. He was offered a job in a chicken factory in Bletchley. He had traded in our old motorbike and sidecar by now for a car, an old Vauxhall Victor. He moved away and started his new job, promising to send me money when he got paid. He moved away when our Paul was only seven months old and Helen eighteen months.

I had to pack in my job at the hospital now as it was proving too much for Betty to look after my two young ones as well as her own two children, so I relied on the postal orders Brian would send me on and off, usually for about three pounds. This did not go far as I had to pay the mortgage, utility bills and buy all the tins of milk and baby food out of this. Some weeks there would be no money forthcoming at all but I struggled to manage as best as I could by buying only baby food. I would be starving some nights and after the babies were put to bed at night, I would turn off the gas fire to conserve energy and go to bed myself to keep warm. I was at my wits' end one week after receiving a letter threatening to cut my electricity off if I did not pay the bill.

In desperation I told our Betty and this was how Mam found out about the situation. She came to our house and demanded to know what was going on, then promptly made me get ready, saying she was taking me up to the National Assistance Board in Anfield Plain.

'I can't go there, Mam,' I told her.

'You'll have to,' she insisted. 'You're getting no help from their dad and you need money from somewhere to feed the bairns. We warned you from the start not to get married, but do you ever listen? No, you don't,' she answered her own question. 'You think you know it all, now come on, get your coat on, you're going and that's that. You don't half give me some worry, our Lyn.'

Well, I went with her there as I didn't see what else I could do. When I told them of my plight, they gave me an emergency payment enabling me to go straight out and buy baby food on our way home. I felt ashamed. I was too proud to ask for help but had to feed my babies.

This went on for four months while Brian worked away trying, supposedly, to look for somewhere for us to live. He did on occasions drive back up North late on a Friday night and stay for a weekend, returning on the Sunday.

When he eventually found us a rented house in Wolverton, Buckinghamshire, we sold our house, but had been there so little time we made no profit from it. It was my dad that came over and helped me pack up all my household things. In November 1967 I handed back the keys, then went to stay with Mam and Dad on the Thursday.

The next day, Friday, little Paul went into South Moor Hospital to be circumcised, after our doctor said it was necessary. This was done as a day case and I took him back to Mam's once he was over the anaesthetic. The poor little mite was only eleven months old and was still sore and groggy. Brian came up in his Vauxhall and we set off for the South on the Saturday, after having said our goodbyes to everyone. Our furniture was being moved down separately. Our journey was made via the old A1 and seemed to take forever. Paul was still very sore, bless him, and lay in my lap. The journey was hampered by fog so it was late and dark by the time we reached Wolverton.

I was dismayed when I saw the state of the house. It was the end of a terrace and had been an old police house in previous years. It had three bedrooms, but was a huge rambling old house with a big entrance hall, two main downstairs rooms with old-fashioned fireplaces, a fair-sized kitchen and downstairs toilet. There was a door from the kitchen that led onto a small back garden and another door opposite this one led down to a huge, dark cellar, complete with shackles still left on the walls. We kept this locked and bolted. Upstairs was a landing leading to the bedrooms, then there was another spiral staircase which led up to an attic that contained a big old-fashioned bath and a table. There were bits of furniture left in the house that were extremely old – the owners of the property had left it in so as to charge more rent for it being partly furnished. These owners lived in the next street and ran a local taxi firm. It was quite a spooky old house and certainly not very clean.

Our furniture van had arrived before us and Dad had travelled with them and helped us out tremendously. First job, finding the kettle, next one getting the beds and cots put together. We were all worn out from the long journey. Next morning, by light of day, the house looked more dreary than ever, but we set to work by first giving all the rooms a good brushing-out, scrubbing and cleaning. Then we sorted out the furniture, putting all the old furniture that belonged to the house into the sitting room, which I would never use. After getting the curtains up it was starting to look a bit better.

Dad had to set off back up North early on the Monday and I was sad to see him go. 'Bye, Dad, thanks for all your help,' I whispered in his ear as he gave me a big hug.

'Keep your chin up, lass,' he replied. His voice was choked as he added, 'Look after those bairns, hinny, I will see you as soon as I can.' He turned away from me before I could glimpse the tears in his eyes. He had a last gruff warning for Brian: 'You make sure you look after them all, lad,' before he left. I was so sad to see him go.

Helen and Paul took the move as an adventure, as kids that age would do, but I felt a bit lonely already. Brian had to return to his job in the chicken factory in Bletchley while I continued with my efforts to try and make the old house look homely and finish off our unpacking.

We got into a routine soon enough. Brian worked long hours while I kept the house clean, prepared meals and looked after two lively toddlers. It wasn't long after this that I learned of Brian's infidelity while he'd been living in Bletchley on his own. One of his mates, Pete, told me that he had been having an affair with a woman from the factory where he worked. I confronted him about this and he didn't try to deny it. All my trust was completely shattered and we ended up rowing more than ever. I could not have believed it had I not heard him admit to it with my own ears and it spelled the end of our marriage. Brian ended up moving back up North and moved back in with his mother. I was left after just one month amongst strangers with two tiny children to care for.

Brian and I had parted company as amicably as possible under the circumstances, with me agreeing for him to come down and see the children sometimes and him agreeing to help support them, but we had decided divorce was the only option now.

Although I corresponded regularly with my parents, I found it very difficult to tell them what had happened and then only told them what they needed to know, that Brian had left and was back up North and we were getting divorced. The letter I received back from Mam nearly broke my heart. She complained that I was nothing but a worry to her and always had been.

I wrote back that I was sorry to be such a source of worry to her, that I would keep my troubles to myself in future. As far as I was concerned, I had made my bed and would have to lie in it. I was too proud and independent to ask if I could ever move back up to them in the Northeast.

People down South were not as friendly as people from the North and I found it hard to be accepted. The town of Wolverton was built around the nearby railway works and the printing works, McQuorkidales. It was about two and a half miles from Stony Stratford, about five miles the other way from Newport Pagnell and about a twenty-minute train journey to Bletchley. The people who lived in Wolverton were born and bred into it and outsiders were classed as foreigners, especially me with my Geordie accent. It was before the days of it being turned into a catchment area to be known as the new Milton Keynes area.

I was twenty-one years old with two small children and very far from home. It was a new era in my life.

NINE

My children were my saviours at that time – I had to survive for their sakes. It wasn't easy trying to run the huge old house and keep it clean while looking after two toddlers.

Our main problem was that we never had enough money. Brian started off well after our separation in 1967. He used to send me postal orders for about three pounds and ten shillings a week, but this did not go far after paying the rent. After a while these payments became few and far between and, with the children being so young, I was forced to seek help from the DHSS. Sometimes I would phone them asking for help and they'd tell me I would have to go into the office at Newport Pagnell. I had not got the bus fare to get there and had borrowed the money to make the phone call from a call box, as I told them. They were totally unsympathetic, so I had to put the children in the pram and walk the whole five miles there, then walk all the way home again to await my claim being processed.

I would barely have enough food to give the children, so I went without myself and many a night I went to bed too hungry to sleep and too worried where the next penny was coming from. As the coal fire was our only source of heating and coal was so expensive to buy, I used to walk the surrounding fields and along the banks of the Grand Union Canal, pushing the children in a big twin pushchair, looking for wood to burn in the fireplace. I would spend hours walking the canal banks, picking up old sticks of wood that I would pile on top of the hood of the pushchair to take home. Helen and Paul seemed to enjoy their walks, especially when they spotted the barges on the canal. Then I'd walk home hours later with our precious wood and be able to make a fire in the grate, where I would bath the children in their baby bath in front of the fire. Afterwards, when they were bathed and fed, I would cuddle them into me on my lap until they were sleepy then tuck them up into their separate cots in my bedroom. Then I'd not burn any more wood but would save it for the next morning to light a fire before the children were up. I would put cardigans and a coat on to try and keep warm myself and read library books to while away the hours to forget the hunger I had on me and sip weak tea before going to bed myself.

The days and nights I spent in this way were endless. When I was lucky enough to be sent a giro payment from the DHSS, I was very, very careful as to how I spent the money. My main priorities were food for the children, a bag of coal when I could afford it and sometimes a half-load of wood from a van that delivered it weekly in our back lane. For the most part, I collected our own wood on our walks by the canal.

I remember one particular day when the weather was too bad to go out. I had no wood and no coal left at all. In desperation, I tore up some of the old lino from one of the floors to make a fire and burned that for warmth. We soon had a good fire blazing in the grate while Helen and Paul played happily on the floor, oblivious to our poverty. It wasn't long until someone was knocking on my front door. When I went to answer it some man stood there saying, 'Excuse me, Mrs, do you know you've got black smoke pouring from your chimney?'

I stepped out onto the street and sure enough the black smoke poured forth. 'Oh,' I said, 'I must need the chimney sweeping. Thanks for letting me know.' I had to be a bit more careful after that but still managed to get through all the lino from the sitting room and attic floors.

When I took the children shopping to buy food I was very careful what I bought. It had to be cheap but nutritious food like bread, margarine, potatoes and cheese. Helen and Paul thrived, though I had gone very skinny. We could not afford to buy new clothes so I went to jumble sales to buy the children's clothes. It was at one of these jumble sales where I met Ruby Martin. She lived opposite me in our back lane and had six children of her own. Her husband worked but she loved a jumble sale as much as I did. She befriended me, and I was glad of her company. She would come to my house and share a cup of tea while her children were at school. I think she realised the struggle I was having just to survive, though I never told her all my business.

I met another lady, who worked as a waitress at the Trust House Forte Restaurant at Newport Pagnell Services on the nearby motorway, and she offered to try and get me a job there as a waitress. There was a bus provided to pick up any workers in Wolverton at 6 a.m. and work started at 7 a.m. Ruby offered to look after the children for me and we came to an arrangement where I would share half of all I earned along with half of any tips I made as payment for her looking after the children. I was interviewed and offered the job for two days a week (Fridays and Saturdays) and was extremely grateful to Ruby.

The arrangement worked well, though it was not easy. It meant getting up at 5 a.m. and having a quick cup of tea as I woke up the children, gave them breakfast and got them ready to take them, along with their food, across to

Ruby's. Then I'd run up the road to catch the bus at 6 a.m.

I hated the job; the other waitresses were bitchy and continually trying to steal each other's tips, which we kept under the counter. We had to work hard and at a fast rate, getting the many customers served with their cooked breakfasts. I saw it as providing a bit of money at the end of the week. Helen and Paul seemed happy enough being left with Ruby and seemed to enjoy playing with her youngest children. Nevertheless, I felt terrible at having to leave them there for the few hours I was at work. I tried to console myself with the fact that at least I was helping to provide food and coal for them.

My daily walks with the children collecting wood along the way continued on weekdays and Sundays. The postal orders from their father were sporadic and soon to dry up completely; I was forced to get weekly help from the DHSS, although whatever I earned was taken into consideration. I felt degraded by this, but my children's welfare was my main concern at this time. The rent for the house used to take a big chunk of any incoming money and, though I asked the owners to drop the amount of rent, they were totally unsympathetic to my problems. Ruby had mentioned to me about rent tribunals and I did in fact take the owners to such a tribunal, as a result of which the rent was reduced.

I don't know how I'd dared to do it, being so young, but I did and it was followed by a vendetta against me by the owners of the property to try and get me to leave. I had put my name on the council list for a council property, but the way the council saw it, I already had a three-bedroomed house, more than enough for our needs. The house being so large it was very difficult to manage, but my first concern was food for the children and my second was having enough fuel to keep them warm. It was a perpetual struggle. We had a black-and-white TV I had brought with me from the North, a present from Dad.

In the beginning we used to watch it but, after a visit from two men from the General Post Office who were checking to see if I had a TV licence, I dared not turn the set on again, as I did not have one.

To pass the time in the evenings I would read a library book after the children had gone to bed. I would read everything and anything and sometimes even read horror stories. I used to scare myself silly reading those sort of books and would be nervous to go upstairs to bed. As the spiral staircase to the attic was just opposite my bedroom door, I got quite spooked out about it and had to hang a curtain at the bottom of the staircase.

I had the two cots for Helen and Paul in my bedroom and, though I could have put them in either of the other bedrooms, I preferred to have them in with me. At night when I went to bed, often too hungry to sleep, I would look at Helen and Paul's innocent little faces while they slept; the love I felt for them, the utter joy of having two beautiful little children, was enough to make everything worthwhile. They were blissfully unaware of our difficult situation.

I was not sleeping well and went to see our GP, who prescribed Mogadon sleeping tablets for me. I found these to be brilliant, but having taken one at night often found that rather than make me sleepy, they would perk me right up and so this became the time of day when I found the most energy to enable me to do the washing, peel the potatoes and vegetables for the next day and clean and tidy the house.

I tended to let the children play with their toys and generally run riot within the house and small back garden during the day. These were days when we weren't out walking, trekking the fields and canals in my search for wood. I think the children became so used to our long walks that it made them bored to stay indoors.

Helen was a little terror and definitely the ringleader out of the two. Paul was more placid and easily amused.

When they got into mischief, it was usually Helen being the leader. She was a bit of an escape artist, was Helen. I used to let them play in the garden with the big old back gate locked and bolted for their safety. The back lane had a small amount of traffic on it. Because Helen could not undo the gate, she made a mission out of trying to make holes in the wire fence to wriggle through and escape into the lane, dragging Paul behind her. It got so I dared not turn my back on them. One day, when checking to see they were playing safely, I found Paul to be missing and the dustbin pushed over. A triumphant Helen proudly showed me where he was, in the rolled-over dustbin. I had to pull him out, his lovely fair hair and clothes covered in rubbish and ashes from the grate.

Other times, when I took them to the shops, I would leave them strapped into the twin pushchair with their reins for a moment while I dashed in quickly to get bread or whatever we needed. Sometimes, when I'd left them for just a minute, I would come out of the shop and for a second feel the sheer terror as the pushchair had gone missing. Then I'd spot Helen pushing it all by herself with Paul still in it – usually she'd managed to remove some of her clothes and Paul's as well. The shops were not built for the likes of prams or huge pushchairs in those days and trying to get in and out quickly before Helen escaped became a bit of a battle. As well as their reins, I tied them in with belts and all sorts, yet still Helen would manage to undo them and off she'd be, away down the street, Paul sitting in the pushchair, quite happy.

When I went to the library I had to take the children inside with me while I chose some books. These outings were always a bit of a nightmare as Helen had decided her mission in the library was to clear all the bookshelves of their books.

We had acquired a big ginger tomcat by then and the children made the cat's life a misery by constantly chasing it. Once I could hear the cat howling its head off as if blue murder was being committed. When I ran to its rescue, I found Helen with the cat down the toilet. Not happy enough with the poor animal being in there, she had the toilet brush in her hand franticly trying to push the unfortunate animal round the bend.

It was during this period of my life that I was to receive another blow. I received a telegram from my mother one morning that read: 'Come at once – stop – Uncle Joe died – stop'. I don't think my parents realised how much of a struggle I was having financially and my mother could not have known what hardship trying to find the fare to go back up North for my uncle's funeral was to cost me. I was mostly to blame for this as I was too proud to let my family know of the financial difficulty I was going through. However, I managed to scrape our fares together and I made the journey down to London, through the underground, then caught an overnight train back up to Newcastle. I remember facing an escalator in London that must have been the highest and most congested I had ever seen in all my life. The prospect of getting down it with two small children and a suitcase was very daunting. I achieved this tricky feat by putting the suitcase on first then, with a child on each hip, I managed to get on and tried not to look below me. It was with relief that I reached the bottom where some man had kindly removed my suitcase for me. The journey took me over twelve hours but the children slept most of the way and we finally made it.

Aunt Kitty and Uncle Joe had been moved to a council bungalow in South Stanley by now, as their house in Stanley had been pulled down to make way for new roads. Uncle Joe had had a stroke and died before he reached hospital. It was a very sad time for me and I felt so sorry for Aunt Kitty, who was now left on her own. We stayed at Mam and Dad's house before the funeral, Mam's attitude was still cool towards me and the children but Dad was glad to see us, as always. Mam explained to me that a neighbour had come to her house, letting her know that Uncle Joe was very poorly and Aunt Kitty needed her. She had walked to their bungalow and had found Uncle Joe in a state of near collapse, so had sent for their doctor. 'When the doctor came out, he took one look at him and said he would have to go into hospital,' said Mam, 'I had to go with him in the ambulance, you're aunt wouldn't go, and Uncle Joe died as soon as he was laid onto the stretcher. They still had to take him to the hospital, then I had to get all the way home on the bus, and I'm not well myself you know,' she complained. 'Aye,' Dad agreed, 'your mam was in a state herself, when she came back, I had only just got back in from work, she was so shook up, I had to look after her!'

'She can't come here to stay,' said Mam when I asked 'What's going to happen to Aunt Kitty?' 'She'll be OK, once she has got over the shock,' Mam put in, and she looked to Dad for support. It was clear to me that Dad would back Mam up in whatever decision she chose to make and I just hoped that Mam would give Aunt Kitty the care and support she would need. Her bungalow was not too far from my parents' home so I felt pretty sure Mam would continue to go in to see her on a regular basis.

I returned to the South and 'home' now, and life continued. The winter of 1967 was extremely hard and I found it a constant battle to try and keep a fire in the grate as well as to feed myself and the children. I would make sure they had something to eat, yet often went to bed with pains in my stomach from hunger.

There were to be happier times in the summer of 1968. By then my sister, Ann, was sixteen years old and attending Consett Technical College on a pre-nursing course. It was at the college that she met David Douglas. Ann wrote to me, telling me all about David, and when the spring term was about to end she wrote again and asked me if she and David could come and stay with us for the six-week summer break. Of course, I agreed, and was very excited when I went to meet them at Newport Pagnell coach station.

It was lovely to meet David at long last after hearing so much about him from our Ann in her letters. They were obviously very much in love and their happiness was quite contagious.

It was the swinging 60s, but we were too busy to notice that fact, we were too busy wrapped up in our own battle of survival. A close bond developed between Ann, David and myself during that summer we spent together, with Helen and Paul cocooned between the three of us.

David came from a large family himself. He was one of six children, having two sisters and three brothers. His family had always been close and, though David was only seventeen, he was able to magically weave a sense of family between him and Ann, the children and myself. Even though they were so obviously in love, they settled in so well to include the children and me into their close-knit relationship as if we were indeed one whole big family ourselves. Ann and David accepted our situation at that time – being as hard up as a church mouse – as being the norm and treated everything light-heartedly. They had to support themselves while they stayed with me, so David found a temporary job, sweeping up at a local pet-food factory. If I remember rightly, he earned about fourteen pounds a week, which in those days was a king's ransom. They happily looked after Helen and Paul for me while I did extra shifts at the services, enabling me to start putting some money away to buy extra coal to get stocked up ready for winter.

It was a huge help to me. They were brilliant with the children and made games out of everyday life. We still went on our walks on summer evenings and weekends, and together we'd roam the fields and canal banks. Some weekends we'd all go to a jumble sale and one particular day, David bought himself a waistcoat, which he wore for the rest of the time they were down. I think it cost him about five shillings, but as he wore it in years to come, I'm sure he got his money's worth out of it. We may have been poor but we spent some very happy days together, and a lot of laughter was shared between us.

David's mam and dad, Molly and Jack, came to visit us in Wolverton one weekend. They took us all out to Woburn Abbey, which was great fun. The six weeks were soon to end, though, and I don't know who was more heartbroken when they had to leave to return to college. Ann seemed to be as upset as I felt.

I had to put on a brave face for Helen and Paul's sake, but I missed Ann and David so very much after they had returned to the North – I wept at night I missed them so badly. They had helped me out in so many ways and had lifted my spirits with their laughter and joviality.

After they went home, David and Ann returned to college, then Ann started her nurse training at Shotley Bridge Hospital. She was a brilliant student nurse but soon I was to receive a letter from her telling me she was pregnant and what should she do? As it was over two hundred miles away, I had little advice I could give her other than to tell Mam.

So, of course, Ann's career was to come to an end. She married David and went on to have a beautiful baby girl they named Angela. She had blue eyes just like our Ann and lovely red hair just like her dad's. I managed to buy some new clothes for Helen and Paul and we went up for the wedding. I still have the photo of Helen and Paul, hand in hand, at my parents' front door, looking all smart in their new little outfits.

Ann and David were given a council house at the bottom end of South Stanley and David left college and started work at the Consett Iron and Steel Company, where he was to work until it was closed down in 1980 with the loss of 3,700 jobs.

I had applied to Renny Lodge geriatric hospital for work and was given a job working night shifts. The hospital was about six miles from where we lived. I managed to do this by Ruby having the children sleep over at her house. In the days following these shifts I would be at home looking after the children myself. I would be so tired after working all night, I would let the children play out in the garden while I sat on the step of the kitchen door watching them, nearly nodding off to sleep on the doorstep. I needed matchsticks to keep my eyes open. As I could not go to bed at all during the day, the most night shifts I could manage to do consecutively were two nights, but the money was more than I earned as a waitress. Later on, when Helen and Paul were older and able to attend nursery school, I managed to work extra nights by catching a little sleep while they were there. Once they were old enough to go to primary school all day, I was also able to do more work. Ruby and I remained good friends and she continued to help me out by having the children stay at her house on weekend nights when I went to work.

As Ann and David were married by this time, they also helped me out by offering to have Helen and Paul stay up North with them for a few weeks. This gave me an opportunity to work flat out (and even fit in some sleep!) but the separation from my children proved to be too much for me. Although I was in constant touch with Ann and David and knew the children were quite happy, I missed them too much and decided to go up and bring them home. I had saved as much as I could and had a shed full of coal, along with a load of firewood I had bought. Still, rather than waste money on a bus fare to go up to County Durham, I hitchhiked instead, being careful to only accept lifts from lorry drivers, not cars.

Eventually I was offered a council property. Unfortunately it was a flat in a block of ten storeys and the one I was offered was on the eighth floor. I was full of trepidation about moving into a high-rise flat with two young children, yet at the same time I was desperate to get out of the big old house we occupied, it was such a money pit. The new flat had central heating, something I had never known the luxury of before. I felt between the devil and the deep blue sea but finally accepted the flat, in a block called The Gables.

In May 1969 I moved in. The flat consisted of two bedrooms, kitchen, lounge and bathroom. Once the front door was shut behind us I would soon learn how lonely and isolated a person could feel.

There were four flats on each floor. People tended to keep themselves to themselves but one old lady who had a flat on our landing was quite friendly. Mrs Whiteley was a widow and lived alone. She came from the Northeast herself and this fact cemented a friendship between us. She was a member of a spiritualist church and spent a lot of her time at either her church or spirit meetings in Northampton.

Another good friend I made at the flats was Phyllis, who lived in a flat on the fourth floor with her husband and their six-year-old son, Andrew. Helen would later become good friends with young Andrew, but as he was also very mischievous, they made a right pair of little devils.

While we had good views out of our windows being so high up, it tended to reinforce the feeling of isolation of living in a high-rise flat, watching people going in and out, yet never getting out much ourselves. Our lounge overlooked the railway works, but if you looked beyond you could see fields and countryside for miles on a good day. The bedroom windows faced the town and local church.

After becoming friends with Phyllis and learning she was willing to help out with child-minding to earn some extra money, I packed my nursing job in for a while and started as a petrol-pump attendant back at Newport Pagnell service station. This job was not to last long. I had to stand out in all weathers – there was no canopy for the pumps, then – and on the days when it rained I became soaking wet and had to wring my clothes out once I got home before putting them in the wash. I packed the job in after a few months and returned to working at Renny Lodge Hospital. Helen and Paul were now in school all day, and I could work the day shifts there, which was a lot easier to manage all round.

The feeling of isolation while living in the flats was tremendous sometimes. Though I had Helen and Paul and loved them dearly, I missed my family tremendously and thirsted for adult company.

Some weekends Ann and David would come down to visit and stay with us. We always enjoyed our weekends together, but when they had to return home, I missed them all the more.

I also missed my dad a lot but he visited sometimes, hitchhiking down the whole two-hundred-mile journey. When the loneliness became overwhelming, especially at weekends, I took it into my head to visit my family in this same way. I would take Helen and Paul with me, we would catch a bus to Newport Pagnell Services and thumb lifts up North from there. Again, I would always only accept lifts from lorry drivers, never car drivers. I somehow felt this was safer.

Looking back on these days now, I can see the foolishness in what I did, yet at the time I was driven by a desperation to see my family. I was desperately lonely and missed them so much. I'm sure the fact I was thumbing lifts with two young children in tow often provided me with plenty of lifts out of sympathy.

It would take us hours to get up there via the M1, M18, then the A1, finally getting dropped off near Chester-Le-Street, from where we would catch a bus up to Stanley. We used to eat the sandwiches I had packed for the journey along the way, often at the roadside of a busy motorway, waiting for our next lift. Helen and Paul accepted all this as a big adventure.

Dad was always glad to see us and, oddly enough, never criticised our means of transport. Instead, he readily gave me advice on which lifts I should and shouldn't accept. He also gave advice on pick-up and dropping-off points. He would get his big road atlas out and go through all the roads with me. One weekend I had hitchhiked up North only to find out that I had missed my dad along the way. He had hitched all the way to Wolverton to bring a second-hand pump down for my old twin-tub washing machine. I had written and told him of the problems I was having with it and he had searched the scrap yard to find a suitable pump. His intention had been to come to our flat for the weekend and fix the washing machine at the same time. Poor Dad.

When he'd got to Wolverton, Mrs Whiteley informed him I had gone up to his house. She offered that he stay at her flat for a night's rest but Dad would only accept a cup of tea from her before setting straight back up North again, hitchhiking half the night. He left the pump with Mrs Whiteley and next day, after he had returned home, he drew diagrams for me and told me how to fit the new pump on the washing machine myself.

When I got the children off to school the next Monday I set about trying to fit this new pump to my washing machine. I started the job by tipping the washing machine upside down, then removed the old pump and managed eventually to refit the pump Dad had got for me, working carefully from his diagrams. It was no easy task and took me the whole day to do it but I managed in the end, though I had hardly any fingertips left by the time I had finished. The washing machine worked a treat after that and I felt so proud of myself, another mission accomplished.

TEN

Now we were more settled financially, due to the fact that I could work longer hours at the hospital and the flat was cheaper to run, things became easier.

Paul had longed for a pair of football boots, as he was very much into football at school, and one Christmas I managed to buy him his very first pair. He loved them so much, he went to bed in them on Christmas night and slept the whole night in them.

Helen was more into dolls and prams and was easily pleased with a new doll. A picture I have of the children around this time shows Helen, Paul and Andrew Langley with a doll's pram. They looked so sweet and innocent together with some of their baby front teeth missing, but in reality they were little rascals.

I had made another friend who lived in a house down the road, Margaret. She was also a one-parent family with a little girl. I met her while taking Helen and Paul to school. Margaret persuaded me to go out with her one night for a drink at a pub in Stony Stratford, two miles away from Wolverton.

This one night in November 1973 was to make a big change to my life. It was on this rare night out I met James

Griffin. He was quite good-looking and full of the Irish blarney. He could be very charming and asked me to go out with him on a date. I wasn't very keen; I felt I had enough going on in my life at this time with being a busy working mother with two schoolchildren to look after. I was also happy enough with just the children and myself, even if I was lonely at times.

Jim was persistent, however, and Margaret had given him my address so he continued to call at the door asking me to go out with him. Jim had spent his childhood years in Northern Ireland, but most of the family had moved to England after his father's death. I gave in eventually to Jim's persistence and we started going out on odd nights together while Phyllis or Margaret baby-sat for me. Jim worked on building sites as a general labourer and soon I was infatuated with his Irish charm.

We usually just went to the pub for a quiet drink. I did not drink much at the time, a couple of Babychams or Cherry Bs was usually enough for me, whereas Jim liked his pints of beer and made up for both of us.

I was working on the day-care unit of Renny Lodge Hospital by then and, with Phyllis's help, managed to work fulltime. The hours, eight till five, suited me, as it meant I could give the children their breakfast, get them ready for school then drop them in to Phyllis, who would take them to school for me when she took Andrew. I would run down and catch a bus to Newport Pagnell, then walk to the hospital past the Aston Martin car works. Phyllis collected the children from school and would take them to her home, where they played with Andrew until I got home, usually before 6 p.m., so I had the rest of the evening with the children up until bedtime. They were always glad to see me come home from work and would throw their arms around my neck as I bent to give them both hugs.

Jim had been married before and, strangely enough, his ex-wife Dianne lived in the same block of flats along with their two sons, Matthew and Luke. I had heard rumours about Jim's tempestuous marriage to Dianne but chose to ignore them and soon our whirlwind courtship had begun. We married in July 1974. It was a small civil ceremony, at Bletchley register office, attended by only Jim's two sisters, Anna and Jenny, with Phyllis Langley and her husband as our witnesses and Jim moved into the flat with me.

'You're the best thing I've had,' he told me, 'since sliced bread was invented.'

He continued to work on building sites and I carried on, with the help of Phyllis, working at the hospital. I suppose it was a strange situation, Jim having a wife and an ex-wife in the same block of flats. Matthew even came to stay with us for quite a while.

I was soon to learn that, as well as having a lot of charm and Irish blarney, Jim was also prone to bouts of temper when he could be quite violent. Usually his temper was only directed at me and not the children. Occasionally, he would give them a slap, which made me feel terrible, when I would intervene, he would slap me instead but as time passed, his outbursts became more frequent. He continually pointed out to me that it was all my fault until I felt so downtrodden and brainwashed that I believed it must have been. I felt completely trapped within the marriage, but once again, I felt I had made my bed and must lie in it.

There was a lighter side to our marriage when Jim could be good fun and, while he continued to work, they were not always bad days, but I soon learned to tread very carefully. He was a very jealous-natured person and saw things that were not there. He used to take us all out sometimes, but after a few drinks he would accuse me of looking at someone else and fancying them, which was ridiculous really as I never ever wanted to look at anyone else, never mind fancy them. I became very cowed and tended to hold my head down when I was out with him.

I started feeling very anxious and low. I felt I was walking on eggshells most of the time by now with Jim. We had gone out for a quiet drink one night just down the local pub. Matthew baby-sat for an hour or so, as we weren't going to be long. We sat there having a quiet drink, just the two of us in the little 'snug', which was separated from the main bar by a hatch. All of a sudden I felt a huge pain across my mouth. Jim had given me a back-handed slap across the face for 'looking' at one of his mates in the main bar. From where I sat, I could not even see into there. My front tooth had been loosened and blood poured into my mouth. As tears of shock and injustice trickled down my cheeks, Jim said, 'You can take that looking-for-sympathy look off your face, you little whore,' and went on to tell me I had got what I deserved.

We went home soon afterwards, I was glad to go. I felt such embarrassment when the barman came out to collect our glasses. Next morning my lips were so swollen I looked like I had gone a few rounds in a boxing ring, and had to have treatment at a dental surgery. Of course, as always after one of Jim's violent outbursts, the next day he would apologise profusely and promise never to hit me again, but I never knew when his next violent attack was going to blow up. I became more withdrawn and timid than ever.

The children were beginning to show signs of apprehension around Jim's presence by now, especially when he had a bad mood on him or had been drinking and would start having a shouting match at me.

'You're a little whore,' he would shout at me. 'I know you've been making eyes at someone else.' All I had done was go to the shops to buy groceries with Helen and Paul.

'Hasn't she?' he demanded of the children. 'Come on, tell me who's she been talking to, this slag of a mother you've got?'

'No one, she's not talked to nobody,' they replied, looking worried as they clung to my legs, trying in their own way to protect me. This would infuriate Jim all the more and he would call us all 'fucking little liars'.

It got to the stage where, if I had to go to the shops, I felt under pressure to get there and back as fast as I possibly could, as I feared he would be waiting for me if I had taken too long, ready with his accusations.

I continued to work but was called in to see the nursing officer one day and wondered what I had done wrong. What he had to say surprised me. He told me he had been approached by McQuorkidales, the printing works in Wolverton, who were looking for someone to temporarily work for three months while the nursing sister of their medical centre went on sick leave to have an operation. As the nursing officer pointed out, it would be ideal for me as the printing works was in my home town and would save me travelling to work. The fact I had repeatedly kept my St John First Aid Certificates up to date by doing their courses at regular three-year intervals was another thing in my favour. I went home and talked it over with Jim and he agreed for me to do it. I took over the medical centre, which at that time was responsible for the health and welfare of over a thousand workers, and I had to work in close liaison with the personnel officers.

I seemed to fit in quite well and soon had a good rapport with everyone. There were the various minor ailments and accidents that occurred on a daily basis and one or two more serious incidents that were usually amputations, it being a print works where guillotines were used for cutting through bales of paper.

One day I had a patient whom I suspected had slipped a disc in his back. He lay on the couch in the medical centre while we waited for the local GP who covered the firm to come out to decide what to do about him. Not long after the GP had arrived and was examining the poor patient, the works' alarm siren went off and there were orders to evacuate the whole place. An employee driving a forklift truck had accidentally driven into a gas mains point. It had ruptured and gas was pouring out into the factory. The GP was an old Scotsman who hurriedly called for an ambulance to transfer the patient to Northampton Hospital. He packed up his bag like lightning and shot out of the surgery as fast as his old legs would let him, saying to me on the way, 'I'd get out the bloody building as quick as you can before the whole bloody place blows up.' I had never seen him move so quickly in all the years I had known him.

As the poor patient had overheard all this yet could not move, flat on his back as he was, he said to me, 'You can go now, Sister, if you want to.' I refused to budge and stayed with him until the ambulance arrived and only then would I evacuate the building. It never did blow up, of course, and all the drama was over within a couple of hours.

I loved working at McQuorkidales, but at the end of the three months I duly went back to the hospital to resume my duties on the day-care ward. Not long afterwards, though, my nursing officer called me back into his office to notify me that the sister at McQuorkidales had now left and they wanted me to take on her job on a permanent basis. I refused their offer, telling them that I felt more 'needed' at the hospital where I was working. They begged and pleaded with me to take on the job of being in charge of the medical centre, but I stuck to my guns and stayed where I was.

I met one of Jim's friends one night when we were out. His name was Dave and he was the local funeral director. He wasn't very old, in his thirties I suppose at the time, and had a very dry sense of humour. I was told that if he saw an ambulance go past transporting patients to day-care centres, he would say things like 'that's no good, they're all sitting up'. He approached me this night and asked if we could come to some arrangement whereby if any of my patients at the hospital died, I would take some of his business cards and recommend him to the relatives. I was highly offended by this and refused. We ended up having a row about it and, though neither Dave nor Jim could see any wrong in me doing this, I felt it was totally unprofessional. I got on my high horse and refused to speak to him again. This went on for quite a while until the night of the accident.

I was out with Jim at the working men's club, which was just off the main road between Newport Pagnell and Stony Stratford. Dave had already left the club and we were getting ready to leave when he dashed back in and said there had been an accident on the corner of the main road, would I go out to help, which of course I did. A young lad had been driving his motorbike along the main road when a car came out from a slip road and failed to give way to him. He had been knocked off his bike and lay on the road very badly injured. The police were on the scene and had phoned for an ambulance, but it would take over twenty minutes to get there as it had to come from Northampton.

My first examination of the boy, who was about seventeen years old, proved to be very bad. I started at his head and worked my way down. The poor boy was conscious the whole time, in severe pain and bleeding profusely. He had a broken jaw, his teeth were knocked out and he had a huge hole in his chin. Fortunately he wore a crash helmet, which I'm sure helped save his life. The further down I worked on him the more his injuries were apparent. He'd suffered broken arms, broken legs, broken feet and numerous gaping wounds in his legs where bones were sticking out as well as tissue and huge globules of fat. Dave was behind me while I worked on the young lad, administering first aid. Jim stood on the pavement, watching, along with other bystanders. I shouted orders to Dave to run and fetch me bandages or anything I could use as bandages, clean towels, anything. The police first-aid packs contained nothing more than the odd small dressing and plasters. As the blood pumped out of the young lad I just stayed on my knees beside him, quelling the flow as best I could and reassuring him until the ambulance arrived. When it finally came and they took the boy away, it was only when I managed to stand up that I realised I was soaked in blood, through a new tartan pleated skirt, right through to my underwear.

Although the club was now officially closed, they let me go back in to wash my arms, legs and hands before I went home. The whole time I had worked on the young lad I had stayed calm, but when I got home our baby-sitter got an awful shock when she saw the state of me. I had to strip off and discard all my clothes and have a good shower before having a strong cup of tea, then went to bed, where I hardly slept all night, replaying everything through my mind, hoping I had given the right treatment and not caused any further harm. It was a waste of time going to bed as I worried for the young lad's life the whole night. The adrenaline had worn off by now and I felt totally exhausted.

The next day was a Saturday and I didn't need to go to work. I went out to do my grocery shopping and while in the greengrocer's ordering my usual list of potatoes, fruit and veg, the owner of the shop said to me, 'That was you that performed first aid on the accident victim last night, wasn't it?' He refused to take my money for our vegetables that week, which I felt embarrassed about, but was more embarrassed when I found out the story had made its way into the local newspaper and they were classing me as a heroine. The last thing I wanted was any publicity – I still worried if I had done everything right.

About one week afterwards, the lad's parents arrived at my door. I guessed by the serious looks on their faces who they were and asked them in. We all broke down and cried and the parents thanked me profusely for what I had done for him. They had been told at the hospital of his numerous fractures; in the months to come these would all be pinned and plated, his remaining teeth all removed, his jaw realigned and set. Yet they said staff at the hospital had told them, had it not been for first-aid treatment given at the scene of the accident, he would have been dead on arrival. The parents wanted me to accept some sort of payment as reward, but I refused, telling them it was enough reward to me just to find out he was still alive.

Months afterwards, Jim took us to the working men's club. We were allowed to take in the children at this club and we sometimes went there on a Saturday night where the children could have pop and crisps while we all listened to a live band. Helen and Paul would happily dance to the music on these evenings.

This particular evening I was approached by a young lad on crutches who asked me if I was the lady who had helped out at an accident on the main road near the club. When I admitted yes, it had been me, he told me he had been the victim and went on to thank me profusely. It was a very emotional meeting for both of us. I was so happy to see him alive and well on the road to recovery. 'As long as you are all right now,' I told him, 'that's the main thing.'

There were many changes in the country during the early 1970s. There was decimalisation, then there were the miners' strikes under Ted Heath's Conservative government. The power cuts this led to had a profound effect on the whole country. It certainly affected us badly while living in the flats.

When the power went off it isolated us in our flats completely. The lifts did not work, so to get in and out of our flat we had sixteen flights of stone stairs to negotiate. We sat by candlelight and shared soup from Thermos flasks prepared during times when electricity was on and ate sandwiches. These were bleak times for everyone.

It was while living in Wolverton that I heard from Mam about Aunt Kitty's failing health. Mam wrote and told me she was worried about Aunt Kitty, as she seemed to have gone senile. Eventually, I had a letter saying she had become so bad that Mam had had her GP out to see Aunt Kitty, and demanded she was put into hospital. As there were no beds available in any of the general hospitals at this time, Mam persuaded the GP to have Aunt Kitty put into Saint Nicholas' Mental Hospital. I was dismayed to learn this and went up North to visit her.

I was horrified when I finally got to the hospital to see her. She was only about five stone in weight and was very, very frail, yet her mind seemed clear enough to me. I went to see the sister in charge of her ward and enquired into Aunt Kitty's condition. I learned she had received x-rays at Newcastle General Hospital that showed her to have advanced Crohn's disease. If they had been able to treat her earlier, she could have had an operation to remove part of her bowel, but it was too late for this now. On top of that, when they had finally been able to remove bandages from Aunt Kitty's legs, which she had worn for years, it was discovered she had gangrene in both her legs that must have caused her horrendous pain.

Sadly, the sister informed me that there was little they could do for my aunt other than keep her pain-free. As Aunt Kitty still liked to smoke the odd Players cigarette, the sister said she would allow her to have a smoke while I was with her on condition Aunt Kitty was out of bed, sitting in her chair next to it. Apparently the staff had had to take her Players and matches away from her as she had been trying to light her own tabs while in bed and had set the bed alight.

While I sat holding Aunt Kitty's hand, watching her enjoy her supervised smoke, I felt deep sorrow within me. This frail little person I had always been so fond of was reduced to this. She had always been so kind to me over the years, I could hardly believe she was going to leave me. I sat and chatted to her, trying to be as cheerful as I could for her sake, telling her all about Helen and Paul and the antics they got up to. I'm sure Aunt Kitty knew deep inside of her fate. When it was time to leave I hugged her, stroked her face and said, 'I do love you, Aunt Kitty.'

'I know you do, hinny, I know you do,' she replied. I left her then with a very heavy heart and never saw her alive again. It broke my heart. I grieved the loss of Aunt Kitty for a very, very long time and I will never ever forget her. It pains me still to remember her having to spend her last days in Saint Nicholas' Mental Hospital. I blamed our mam in a way, I'm sure Aunt Kitty had been left to cope on her own after the loss of Uncle Joe and had been sadly neglected.

ELEVEN

When I returned to Buckinghamshire there were more changes in my life.

In March 1975 I started a new job at a new day-care facility that had been built in Wolverton, funded by the British Red Cross. I went there as second-in-charge and helped get the centre up and running. A lot of the patients that came to us were some of the old patients that used to go to Renny Lodge day ward, so they were used to me and treated me like an old friend.

I helped them settle into their new environment. As it was newly established, there was a lot of local publicity. The press came and had a look around and I ended up having my picture taken with some of the old patients. This picture was to make the front page of the local newspaper and I proudly sent it off to my parents. I knew Dad would be pleased for me and felt he would be proud.

I was less proud of my personal life but I kept these facts from my family. Jim's drinking bouts had escalated, and whenever he was the worse for wear with the drink on him, his tempers were always nastier.

We used to go up to Leicester quite often and visit his old mum, who lived in a cottage in Fleckney. Jim's three sisters lived in the surrounding areas, too, and I got on extremely well with them and his mum, and I also liked the town of Leicester. It would have been hard not to like Jim's family and they were always good to Helen, Paul and myself. Jim had hopes of us all moving up to Leicester; he said it would be a new start for us. I have to admit that I found the idea of moving there quite appealing and was eager to leave Wolverton behind me. Of course, we both had to find work up in Leicester first and somewhere to live. Jim's family knew of our plans to move and were keen to help.

One day I received a letter from Jim's sister Jenny, in which she had enclosed a cutting from the situations vacant column of the *Leicester Mercury*, their local newspaper. There was a job advertised for a deputy warden at Stoneygate Hostel, which included family accommodation. It was just off the London Road in Leicester and came under the Leicester Area Health Authority, which included Glenfrith and Stretton Hall Hospitals. I sent off for the application forms, and having returned them I received a letter back inviting me up to Leicester for an interview. Even my travelling expenses were to be paid.

I tried not to build my hopes up too high as I was a general-trained nurse and the patients in the hostel were either subnormal patients or suffered from mental-health problems. I had not done mental or subnormality training during my career at this point so felt I did not have much chance of being offered the job. I was determined, however, to give it my best shot.

Prior to all this happening, Jim's heavy drinking problems had got a bit too much to bear. I refused to go out with him any more at weekends because he had by now even started rowing with me when we were out in company. He still went out on his own and often got into brawls in the pubs. I used to sit in with the children when he was out, dreading the time he was due to roll home, invariably drunk, cursing and swearing at me all the while.

Though he rarely lifted a hand to the children, he was not averse to being violent towards me in front of them, so I made sure to have them in bed before he came home. I felt sure his shouting must have had a bad effect on them and I tried to shelter them as best as I could. 'What time is Dad coming home?' they would ask me, and they needed no persuasion to go to their beds.

On one occasion, he rolled back from the pub drunk and beat me about the head so badly that he ruptured my left eardrum. I had to have an operation to try and repair it. This was done in Northampton General Hospital, where I was told there was only a 50 per cent chance the operation would be a success – if it wasn't I could end up completely deaf in that ear. They grafted a Dacron graft onto my eardrum and fortunately it was a success. Helen and Paul were glad to see me when I came home.

'Don't let Dad hit you again, Mum,' Helen whispered to me, with her arms tightly around my waist. 'I hate it when he hurts you.'

'He won't,' I promised her, hoping this to be true.

Paul was waiting his turn for a hug and said, 'No, we don't want you getting hurt again, Mum, don't let him hit you.'

After this, Jim swore never to hit me again and promised he would cut right down on his drinking.

He encouraged me to go for the interview for this new job in Leicester, swearing that he would be a new man. There was plenty of work available in the building trade at this time so we did not worry about Jim being able to acquire work in Leicester. So I took the day off from the day-care centre and duly set off for the journey up to Leicester on my own for the interview.

Though I had serious misgivings at the state of our marriage, I suppose I was hoping Jim would keep all his promises to change and that this could be a chance for us to improve our lives.

I was interviewed that afternoon, along with several other applicants, by the warden of the hostel, another nursing sister and the head nursing officer from Stretton Hall Hospital. I felt the interview had gone well, but tried not to get too confident as we were all shown into a sitting room opposite the office and given tea and biscuits. In reality, I found it very hard to hide the fact that my knees were literally knocking.

Later, as I was called back into the warden's office and interviewed a second time, it came as a huge surprise when I was offered the job on condition that I do a mental and subnormality nurse training course at Southfields College on an in-service basis. I gladly agreed to this, and after the other applicants had been dismissed I was given a tour of the hostel and shown the accommodation we would be living in.

I could hardly believe my luck. There were further discussions regarding terms of employment, hours I would be expected to work, the type of patients I would be helping to care for and such like. The warden was slightly concerned at the ages of my children and wondered if it would be good for them to live there due to the close proximity of the patients. I assured her they were sensible children and that I felt they would adapt pretty well once I got them settled into a nearby school. She went on to tell me that many applicants had applied with the main purpose of being offered the accommodation that went with the job. They had experienced staff in the past who had worked there, half-heartedly giving a mind to the job, when they had mainly wanted the accommodation. I went on to assure the warden that, as I would be giving up our own home and a good job, I had no intention of using the employment as a stopgap.

I returned home that night on the train and discussed it all with Jim. I had to give a month's notice to the British Red Cross to leave my job and also give notice to the council on giving the flat up.

Jim was enthusiastic about it all and went down the local pub 'for just a couple of pints' to celebrate.

We had five weeks to make all the arrangements, during which time we both resigned our jobs, gave notice to the council and packed up all our furniture and belongings. We moved on a Saturday into Stoneygate and had the weekend to sort out the flat and unpack before I was to start work on the following Monday. I had managed to get Helen and Paul into St John the Baptist School, which was not far away, within easy walking distance of the hostel. Luckily they soon settled in and made new friends.

Jim found a job on a nearby building site in Leicester. An added bonus to the job meant we could take our meals in a staff room on the weekends I worked, alternating with the warden. The whole family could share in these meals, which would be charged for by a minimal deduction from my wages. The flat we were given was also taken out of my monthly wage, but the rent for this was very low. We were responsible for only our phone and electricity bills, as well as our own groceries, of course.

Our flat was on the top of the building and ran the length of it. We had one main front door, complete with Yale lock. The flat had one very long hall leading up to a lounge, our main sitting room. The hall had several windows off it, which overlooked a courtyard. Then there were two bedrooms, a big playroom for the children where we installed a lot of their toys, a kitchen and a huge bathroom. It was very spacious and comfortable. The windows were already curtained with a beautiful fabric, so saving more expense.

The ground floor of the hostel consisted of an office from where we worked, a dispensary where we gave out daily medications, several sitting rooms for patients, a TV room, a large dining room and right at the end of the corridor a huge ballroom. This was used in the day for occupational therapy, the therapists coming out from the nearby Glenfrith Hospital. By night, the ballroom was occasionally used for dances held for the patients of the hostel and other groups of patients from Stretton Hall and Glenfrith – they would come accompanied by their own staff on buses. The staff room, used for coffee breaks or meals, led off from the patients' dining room. The first and second floors of the building both led to the patients' own individual bedrooms. At the end of the first floor was the warden's flat and ours was at the end of the top floor.

The patients, while being able to stay in their own rooms whenever they wanted, were encouraged to share each other's company downstairs as much as possible. We had a chef that came on a daily basis from Stretton Hall and brilliant food was provided for patients and staff alike. It all seemed too good to be true at first.

On the negative side, the long hours I had to work could prove tiring and I was always tied to the job. As the warden and I were the only full-time staff, it meant that after finishing our duties at night, checking everyone was in and accounted for and the main doors were locked, we were still on call. We took it in turns to be on call and if any trouble broke out (which it often did) we would be responsible for sorting it out.

It was an open hostel; most of our patients were what was known as Section 29 patients, who were free to leave the hostel near enough whenever they wanted to. Some of the patients were fit to do little part-time jobs and we encouraged this where possible.

There were a lot of subnormal patients housed in the hostel but we also had a few patients who had been Section 60 or 65 type patients and had been deemed by the psychiatrists to be well enough to be put on Section 29 and moved gently out into society by being at the open hostel. Type 60 and 65 sectioned patients were formal patients who had been detained against their will under the old 1959 Mental Health Act.

A few of the older patients were just subnormal, yet too institutionalised to ever fend for themselves within normal society. They needed a place like the hostel with staff always being to hand.

I cannot say too much at all about our patients, but enough to say that tempers could be volatile sometimes and, as in all institutions, fights could erupt at the drop of a hat.

I soon learned the ropes and got to grips with the various duties that went with the job. I got on very well with the warden, Mrs Henson, who was a lovely Irish lady and had worked there a long time. The part-time staff that came from Stretton Hall Hospital to cover for our days off and off-duty periods were also friendly. Most importantly, I got used to the patients very quickly, earned their trust and respect and soon became aware of all their individual characteristics and illnesses.

I have to say that the children fitted in well to their new environment, especially Helen. Of course, they were a novelty to some of the patients, who for the most part took well to them. On coming home from school at 3.30 p.m. each day, most days the children would share the big TV room with the patients while I continued to work until late at night. They had the freedom to go up and play in our flat, or stay downstairs with me and the patients. I always kept a strict eye on them, however, and if ever a fight broke out between the patients, Helen and Paul always knew when it was time to vacate to our own flat quickly. 'Uh-oh,' they'd say if quarrelling broke out, 'we're going upstairs now, Mum,' and off they would go.

I had the freedom to go up and down to our flat if the children were there and supervise their tea, see they were OK, and attend to their needs for bedtime. 'Wow, that was a good fight started up, Mum,' they would say to me. 'We hid on the stairs and listened a bit before we went into the flat.'

Fights between patients broke out abruptly and often. I used to find myself breaking up these fights, often in the middle of them, and they towered above me. Looking back on it all now, I don't know how I did it, but I didn't have time to think about it or be scared. The fights always had to be stopped quickly.

The patients always got excited when one of our big dances were coming up. These were always closely monitored by staff, but as our family could attend these dances, Helen and Paul used to look forward to them as well and enjoyed them almost as much as the patients. Helen loved it when the younger patients used to dance with her and it made her giggle. Paul was more reserved and would say, 'Look at her, Mum, she's being silly.'

The dances we put on for the patients were a grand affair and took a lot of organisation. We provided lots of food, prepared by the chef, and laid out in the large dining room. We also provided a bar, also in the dining room, where both patients and staff could buy alcohol (the amount consumed by the patients was closely monitored by the staff on account of any medication they were taking). The staff, having come in buses with patients from other hospitals, could also partake in a drink or two. Even nursing officers often attended our dances and usually a great time was had by all.

Jim and the children would attend the dances and, though Jim enjoyed having a free-flowing bar, he did not enjoy my time being taken up by patients or any integration with other staff members. He was still intensely jealous and hated me even talking to other members of staff.

The warden was a gracious hostess at these dances – it was all part and parcel of the job. Jim did not understand this and got so jealous if I talked to anyone that he made me suffer for it afterwards, when he would call me 'a fucking whore' as well as a host of other filthy names he had for me.

When I was on call there was constantly one or another patient knocking on our flat door, mainly with minor problems. I was kept busy but, on the whole, enjoyed my new job a lot. I attended Southfields College on a weekly day-release course and successfully completed the course on mental and subnormality nursing and gained a certificate.

Jim was never very keen at mixing with the patients and soon started to get fed up with how much of my time was taken up by the job. He was working during the day but if he was not out in the evenings, he spent a lot of his time in the flat with a bottle of sherry and a few cans of beer. He did not settle into our new environment as well as me and the children, and resented my being on call so much.

His drinking problems by this time were way out of hand. He constantly embarrassed me but the worst was to come in the privacy of our own flat after these dances. There was almost always a flaming row after these occasions. The warden tried to be neutral about them, but she could not possibly have failed to hear all the shouting Jim did as her flat was directly below ours. Even when he started hitting me again, I did my best to reason with him and plead for him to keep the noise down, all to no avail. I tried to keep my marital problems hidden, but this was hard to do sometimes, especially if I came down to work next morning sporting black eyes and bruises.

Eventually Jim packed in his job, saying there was no work. I knew this was not true, but knew better than to argue with him. He would go out to the pubs at lunchtime then return in the afternoons, where he would sit in the flat drinking cheap bottles of sherry, cans of beer and watching TV. At night, when I had finished work and returned to the flat, he always caused rows and arguments and would become very violent. He would accuse me of flirting and slap me around my head telling me, 'You are a filthy fucking whore who's asking for trouble,' while gripping me by the shoulders, his face red with fury as he shook me violently, like a rag doll, before spitting into my face.

I received a letter from my parents, asking if they could come and stay with us for a visit. I was hoping Jim could control his drinking and his temper while they were there – I had begged him to do so – but remained anxious that he would not.

I arranged some off-duty time with the warden and Mam and Dad spent some time with us together as a family. My hopes for Jim were soon dashed. He continued to spend his days in the pubs while I took Mam and Dad around the town, showing them the market and shopping centres.

At the weekend I took them to Abbey Park with Helen and Paul. It was a blazing-hot day. The children had new fishing nets I had bought them and spent some time fishing for tiddlers in the canal while I sat on a blanket on the grass with my parents. We all enjoyed the day out there. Helen and Paul had jam jars to put their fishes in and while I sat talking to Mam and Dad, they managed to sneak up on me and empty their little fishes down the front of my new sundress. They found it hilarious when I jumped up squealing, whipping the top of my dress down to get rid of the live little fishes. I think it amused some of the other families in the park too. We returned to the flat, tired and hot from our day out. That night Jim went back off to the pub again until closing time.

We all went to bed soon after he came home. Mam and Dad were sleeping in our bed and Jim and I had a mattress on the floor in the toy room. After retiring for the night, Jim tried arguing with me, though in a quiet manner for a change. I refused to take the bait and just wanted to go to sleep, but he would not let it go. He demanded his marital rights – I pleaded I was too tired. He knew Mam and Dad and the children would overhear if we made too much noise so when I would not give in to him, he violently raped me. It seemed to go on forever and the fact I dared not make a noise made it all the worse. My dad would have killed him if only he had known but Jim was very sly, even if he was so drunk. He knew I was helpless. I was his helpless slave and at his mercy. He made me feel like a whore that night as he repeated it over and over again in my ears.

Not satisfied with that, he still would not let me be. While tears of pain and sorrow poured silently down my face, he kicked me off the mattress and violently kicked me in the stomach, back and ribs until I felt I would surely die. He would not leave me alone and his violence went on through a good part of the night. Even when he eventually gave up and went to sleep on the mattress, I could not sleep. My whole body felt battered and bruised, my soul crushed.

Next morning I had to get up early for work. I bathed myself and went down to work before anyone else was up. I left Jim fast asleep in a drunken stupor on the floor of the toy room. He was gradually breaking all my spirit. His words kept echoing through my head: 'You're nothing but a worthless fucking whore.'

Mam and Dad returned home after their break. They had both enjoyed their visit and had been interested to see Leicester and where I worked. I think Dad was proud of me. Little did he know what sorrows I hid from him.

TWELVE

Some of the patients at the hostel could be very amusing at times. They all had their own pocket money and savings accounts and for one week in summer the warden would take a few of them away to a Butlin's holiday camp in Skegness. They used to get very excited at the prospect of their week's holiday. I would take a group of them into town to help them buy new clothes, and those could be eventful days. Controlling six or seven excitable patients around shops, getting them on and off buses yet still trying to keep everyone together could be quite a handful. The rest of the patients who either could not or did not want to go on holiday stayed behind in the hostel. A lot of the patients had either full- or part-time jobs according to their qualifications and the state of their mental health.

One of our patients Shirley had a job cleaning at the local police station. She started work early in the morning and the police thought very highly of her. She looked after them well and always had a nice cup of tea ready for them starting the early shift. Sadly for all concerned, she had to be given the sack when it came out she had been stealing the milk for the policemen's teas from people's doorsteps on her way to work. Shirley just said, 'Well, they enjoyed their cups of tea,' and could not understand why she had been sacked!

We had a shocking event happen while I worked at Stoneygate. I was used to the police turning up at the hostel as if any of our patients went missing we had to notify them. They would then come out, take a description of the missing patient and invariably bring them back to us. This time was different. Someone had been knocked down and killed on the main London Road. It was suspected she was one of our patients but the police needed someone to identify the body. The warden asked if I would go.

They took me to the hospital mortuary, where I was shown the body. At first I had difficulty in identifying her as her poor face and head were so swollen and disfigured. They showed me her clothes, which I recognised, but then I remembered a distinguishing feature the patient had. When I was shown this it helped me to identify her, but the burden of responsibility felt terrible.

It was a traumatic experience, especially as afterwards I had to give evidence in the coroner's court in Leicester. It took me a good while to get over the experience, and the whole hostel mourned her.

My work at the hostel continued. Helen and Paul were happy living there and seemed to be content in their new school, where they were doing well. The only fly in the ointment was Jim's continual drinking and violent tempers. We had been there for well over a year now and he had long ago ceased any attempts to get work. It was as well my job was well paid and at least we had a roof over our heads. I had no support from Jim at all.

I tried hard not to let my marital problems affect my work but this was becoming more difficult, especially when Jim would come rolling in from the pub drunk out of his mind, barely able to manage the stairs. Even the patients noticed this and used to laugh at him. Although

I did not confide in the warden I'm sure she realised the situation. Animosity grew between the warden and Jim.

Matters came to a head in December 1976 when he got so drunk one evening he locked me out of the flat. The children had been staying downstairs with the patients and me. It got late, I had got all the patients off to bed, locked the main doors and still Jim refused to let us into the flat. I had to go and knock on the warden's door eventually and tell her what was happening. She was sympathetic but firm. She rang the on-call nursing officer, who advised calling the police. They came out and talked to Jim but he still refused to let the three of us into the flat. The police told me there was little they could do as Jim was a resident of the flat as well.

The warden notified the nursing officer of the situation again and he agreed to send transport for me and the children to be given temporary accommodation at Stretton Hall Hospital. Poor Helen and Paul were tired out by now and needed their beds, but Jim would not even let us in to collect any clothing or toiletries. We had to leave in the clothing we stood up in. I was still in uniform, Helen and Paul were still in their school uniforms – we didn't even have our coats. We were taken over to Stretton Hall and put into a shared staff cottage. Being wintertime, it was freezing cold, and we had no food. We were given one downstairs room in the cottage and had to share an upstairs toilet and bathroom. There was one bed that the three of us shared, huddled together, feeling ashamed, cold and desolate.

The following day the nursing officer came to the cottage and brought a small portable TV for the children and a small electric heater. He took me over to his office to have a serious talk. I was advised that unless I sought help to get an injunction order to have Jim removed and enable me to get back into the flat so I could continue to work, I would have to be given notice. He let me go back to the cottage to be with Helen and Paul and think the situation through.

While Helen and Paul watched TV, I looked at their young faces and could have wept. I felt totally to blame for our situation – hadn't Jim always told me it was all my own fault. My children did not deserve this. They were innocent victims of the situation. They needed to be home, have their own bedroom and toys and be allowed to go to school and be like normal children. They should not have to live in fear of their stepfather's constant tempers and they certainly did not deserve this, being shut away in the cottage not knowing what was to happen next.

'Don't worry,' I said to them both as I tried to reassure them. 'It will all turn out all right, I promise you that.'

One of the sisters at the hospital knew me, as she was a member of staff who would cover off-duty periods for the warden or myself at the hostel. She came to see us at the cottage and talked to me. She had been very good to us that weekend by bringing over clean clothing that we could wear. They were patients' clothing, but clean and pressed, and beggars could not be choosers. She also brought us some toiletries. Our food had been provided on trays, delivered to the cottage door by a kitchen worker.

I felt sure we must have been the talk of the hospital and felt very ashamed and degraded. However, as I sat and pondered what to do next, I think it was the sight of my poor, bewildered children's faces that helped me make my decision. I realised I could not let them go through the torment and feelings of insecurity any longer.

When the nursing officer returned to the cottage, it was with the news that Jim had already left the flat voluntarily. To ensure this did not happen again, I would have to get a court order against him being admitted to the hostel again. He offered to take us back to the hostel in his car and I accepted.

The health authority could not get the court order, it was up to me, so after seeing Helen and Paul settled back in our flat, I went immediately into town and saw a solicitor. She listened carefully to all I had to say, then offered her advice on how all the legal procedures could be put into action. At the same time as I applied to the court for an emergency injunction order against Jim coming back to the flat or even the hostel, I started divorce proceedings on the grounds of cruelty.

The injunction order against Jim getting back into the hostel was granted by the court within a matter of a few days. The divorce proceedings were put into motion but would take a lot longer. I returned to the flat and when I saw Helen and Paul already looking much better, I knew I had made the right decision.

It would take until the early summer of 1977 before the divorce was finally granted and there were to be a number of court hearings before this. In all, it was a messy divorce and a stressful time for me, but at least I was able to continue working throughout this period and Helen and Paul were back at school. They seemed a lot happier and more relaxed without Jim's presence.

Financially, we were a lot better off without Jim being there. He had made no contribution to our daily living expenses and his heavy drinking habits had been a drain on our expenditure. It was the end of a tempestuous and violent marriage, but it was not to be the end of all contact with him.

THIRTEEN

Though I continued to work at the hostel I had other worries on my mind. My father's health was failing. He had finished in the mines when he was 54 years old, and had the dreaded dust on the lungs, pneumoconiosis, which would get progressively worse.

Though I was happy enough in my work, I still missed my family. Ann and David kept in constant touch with me, and Ann had given birth to another child by now, my nephew Stuart. He was a beautiful baby with his dad's blue eyes and features and fair hair like our Ann. He was doubly precious to Ann and David as they had lost a couple of babies since the birth of Angela. Ann had miscarried twice and Stuart had been an anxious and difficult pregnancy for her. They were well rewarded by his arrival and Angela loved her new baby brother.

David was kept very busy at his work and our Ann had her hands full looking after Angela and Stuart but they always made time for me. I think they worried about me and the children so often phoned me to check we were all OK.

One evening, as I worked late in the office at the hostel, there was a phone call. I picked up the phone to hear heavy breathing, so I hung up. A few minutes later, the phone rang again. I was used to getting weird phone calls, this happened a lot at the hostel. I picked up the phone again and David's voice said, 'What did you do that for, Lyn? You have just cost me ten pence.' He was laughing his head off.

'Well, it serves you right, you silly bugger,' I laughed back at him.

It was good to hear from them, they helped keep my spirits up. It was good to know someone cared about our welfare.

When I was attacked by a patient at work, it was just about the straw that broke the camel's back. I had finished work one Friday evening at 9 p.m. and had handed over to Mrs Henson, who was now on-call. It was to be my weekend off and I was looking forward to spending the time with Helen and Paul. They were in the lounge, watching TV as I had allowed them to stay up later with it being the weekend.

I had run myself a bath and was just in my underwear and an old quilted dressing gown as I walked down the corridor towards the bathroom.

Suddenly, our front door opened and in walked John Baker, one of our patients, with a bottle of beer in his hand. 'Have you got a bottle opener I can borrow?' he asked.

I had forgotten to drop the Yale lock on our front door, a huge mistake on my part!

I was very wary of John, he was an ex-Rampton Mental Hospital patient who had been detained there from the age of seventeen for attacks he had committed against young women and he had been classified as having psychopathic tendencies.

He had been in Rampton for ten years and had come to the hostel at the age of 27, deemed by the psychiatrists to be reformed, rehabilitated and well enough to be classed as an informal patient.

I had read John's notes from cover to cover and they had read like something from a horror story.

Whilst being in Rampton, he had made numerous attempts to escape and had gone on the run from there lots of times during his ten-year stay. During his stay there, he had often attacked female members of staff whilst trying to make a run from there. Some of the staff had been badly injured by his attacks, he had even slashed some of them with knives he had managed to obtain.

I was not the only member of staff at Stoneygate to wonder about the decision of the psychiatrists to have made him an informal patient and have him transferred to our hostel. Other nursing staff members that came from Stretton Hall Hospital, to cover for some of our days off had also read John's notes and they were of the same opinion as myself and were also wary of him.

'You shouldn't be in here, John,' I told him as I quickly went into the kitchen to get him a bottle opener, wanting him out of my flat as quickly as possible.

As I turned to close the cutlery drawer he suddenly grabbed me from behind, swung me round and had me in a vice-like grip, as he tried to kiss and fondle me.

I was terrified and taken completely off guard, John was thin but very tall, being about six feet in height and his strength was enormous.

I did not want to scream, as I feared that would bring Helen and Paul running from the lounge and I did not want them endangered. I fought hard to get out of John's grip but as the struggle continued I sensed that I was in a hopeless position, especially when he suddenly ripped my dressing gown open, buttons popping all over the floor, and he ripped my bra off me, ripping it clean in two which showed the strength he had, it was a nylon bra, not an easy material to tear.

He had me in this tight grip, trying to fondle my breasts and I feared I was doomed. I brought up one of my knees and kneed him in the groin area. It was the first and only time I had ever hit a patient but I felt I was fighting for my life.

I was not proud of the fact afterwards.

Suddenly, John doubled up in pain and this gave me an advantage. He seemed to come more to his senses and started saying 'I'm sorry, I'm sorry, please don't report me.' 'OK John, I won't report you,' I appeased him. 'Just get out now and go back to your own room,' I told him firmly, as I pushed him out of our kitchen and out of the front door, quickly dropping the Yale lock behind him.

Helen and Paul had heard none of the commotion, our lounge was such a long way up the corridor, and of course they had the TV on.

I ran into the bathroom and sank to my knees, trembling in shock. I knew I had to report the attack but was too terrified to leave our flat.

When I finally pulled myself together slightly, I went and phoned Mrs Henson and she came up to my flat and I told her all about it and showed her my bra and dressing gown that John had torn. I had put on a fresh one.

'Stay in the flat, keep your door locked,' she told me, she was going to phone the head nursing officer and consultant psychiatrist.

She did this and John was moved over to Stretton Hall Hospital immediately, in a van which they had sent for him. He was moved in just the clothes he wore, and was placed on a ward at the hospital.

I had to make statements over the weekend and it was all documented in John's notes. I was in a state of shock all weekend and dared not take the children out anywhere, it ruined our weekend.

By the Monday I was still a nervous wreck but had to try and act normal and go back down to work, as if nothing had happened.

Mrs Henson assured me John would not be coming back to the hostel.

When the cleaner, Jane came to work that day, Mrs Henson asked me if I would mind giving her a hand to pack up John's clothes as Jane cleaned his room, so they could be sent on to him at the hospital. It was as we did this that we found several craft knives and numerous spare blades that he had hidden under the paper lining of his drawers. He had obviously stolen them from his work.

Finding all these knives shocked me even more. I realised the attack could have been much worse. I hoped that John would be sectioned again so that he would not be allowed to go out in the community again. I later found out, from staff at the hospital, that this was not the case and John was still allowed to go to work from there and remained an informal patient. The police were never informed, it was all just brushed under the carpet, and I felt I had been let down by the Area Health Authority. I felt it was both wrong and dangerous and I now had serious doubts about my capabilities working with patients in the mental health field. I now also feared for Helen and Paul's safety at continuing to live in this environment.

I talked to Ann and David about it and I mentioned to them I felt I should move on. They kindly offered to share their own home with us should I decide to move back to the Northeast. I decided to take them up on their offer and put in my notice at the hostel.

A nursing officer came over to the hostel and begged me to reconsider. He told me I was an excellent nurse for the job and they did not want to lose me. I myself did not feel up to the job any more, however, and I stubbornly refused to withdraw my notice. After my month's notice was up it was my two brothers-in-law, David and Eric, who came down one weekend and helped me move all our furniture back up North.

We moved in with Ann and David in their three-bedroomed council house in South Stanley. The furniture was put into storage, and I got Helen and Paul into a new school that had recently been built nearby. They seemed to like it there, and I found a part-time job nursing at Shotley Bridge General Hospital on night shifts.

We were very happy staying with Ann and David, though we were way overcrowded, so I put my name down for a council property at Stanley.

We had not been there many weeks when one morning a visitor came to the house. He was from Stanley Council. David was at work at the time, Helen and Paul were in school, Ann was taking Angela to school and I was in the house with Stuart, who was only a few months old.

Incredibly, I was offered the keys to one of the new houses that had been built a few streets further down from Ann and David's home. It was a new estate, built right next to the woods. Having left me the keys to view the property, the council officer left. I was so excited I grabbed little Stuart up in my arms and danced and sang to him like a crazy woman. Stuart was so young he could not understand my excitement, but he was happy because I was so happy, and giggled when I danced him all around the room. After Ann returned, we went and had a look at the house, in Bronte Place. Then we all went back and had another look once David was home from work and Angela, Helen and Paul were home from school. I fell in love with it and next day went up to Stanley to sign the paperwork to accept the property. Even though I had been on night shift, I was too excited to get any sleep during the day.

The furniture came out of storage and we moved into our new home. I felt very lucky. The property was near to Ann and David and I could walk up to Mam and Dad's home via the fields. We were only about two miles away from Betty and Eric and their children at South Moor. Helen and Paul seemed to like the house as much as I did. It was painted throughout the house so I could move in straight away. There were three bedrooms and a bathroom upstairs, and downstairs was a living room, dining room with kitchenette, a downstairs loo and front and back porches, as well as small front and back gardens. It was so close to the woods and fields that I often took the children down the woods for walks, the same woods that I had played in during my childhood. We would laugh and skip about on our walks, enjoying the feeling of being close to nature.

We were very happy there and Helen and Paul soon made their own friends. We had the added bonus of being able to see our family regularly. Ann and David came down a lot with Angela and Stuart, and when Ann started learning to drive they would often drop Angela and Stuart into our house while David took Ann on driving lessons. I would take all the children down to the woods with me, exploring while being followed by Snowy the cat, a new recent addition to our family. Not long after that, Ann and David moved into a house near the library at Stanley that they had bought, but I still saw plenty of them. David would either drive them all down in the car or, if he was at work and Angela in school, Ann would walk all the way to our house with Stuart in his buggy. Our Ann was always in such a rush when the children were young that she became known as the Road Runner.

As Dad was so poorly by now, I eventually packed in my job and went up to visit them every single day. I would get up early, see Helen and Paul off to school, do my housework in rapid time and then walk up the fields to their house, where Dad was always so pleased to see me. It got so that if I was a few minutes late, Mam told me that he would be at the window, watching for me to arrive. Dad started to deteriorate with his illness rapidly now. They wanted to swap council properties with a couple who had a two bedroomed, smaller house in Williams Close. It would be easier on Dad, as that property had central heating.

Dad had got so poorly by now, he could no longer manage the open fire or chop sticks for it, so I took over all of that for him by ensuring I raced up the fields the minute the children had gone to school. Mam and Dad would still be in bed, so I would light the fire for them, chop sticks for the next day and put the kettle on, and take them tea in bed while the house warmed up a bit. Poor Dad got so bad he could only manage the stairs by going up or down them on his bottom. His breathing was dreadful and he lost a lot of weight.

When the swap to Williams Close was turned down, I badgered the council and even wrote to our local MP at the House of Commons. Finally they were given permission to move to the Williams Close house.

I continued going up to see Mam and Dad nearly every day, as did our Ann. When it was time to pick up the children from school, I would race back down the fields, to be at home for when they arrived.

I stayed in touch with Jane, the cleaner from the hostel in Leicester, by post. She updated me on the patients' progress. In one of her letters she enclosed a clipping from the *Leicester Mercury* newspaper. A chill ran through me as I read it. It reported how John Baker had been arrested, charged and taken to court for crimes he had committed against two teenage girls in Leicester. The newspaper reported how John had tried to sexually assault those poor girls at knife-point. One of the girls had tried to protect her throat and face with her hands and he had sliced through her wrist, cutting through tendons and ligaments and she had needed surgery at the Royal Infirmary afterwards.

He was found guilty of those horrendous crimes and more than a hundred other offences were taken into consideration, before he was remanded for psychiatric evaluation and eventually sectioned and sent back to Rampton Mental Hospital indefinitely.

Reading of those horrific attacks made my blood run cold, I felt so sorry that those young girls had had to suffer, it brought back the memory of my own attack by

John when I had worked at the hostel and re-enforced in my mind that I had made the right decision to leave mental health nursing when I did.

I felt I had had a lucky escape, compared to the suffering others had gone through, yet it brought my nightmares back again.

I started having terrible nightmares when I dreamed of maniacs chasing me through corridors or the woods where we lived and I would wake up in cold sweats.

The woods next to Bronte Place did not feel so friendly any more, and I had an irrational fear that John might escape from Rampton and come looking for me. Which was silly, I suppose, but I felt traumatised by it all once more. I felt vunerable once again.

One day I had a surprise visitor. It was Jenny, Jim's sister. She had been visiting an old aunt of theirs who lived in Birtley. I was never quite sure how she had found our new address, but she turned up on my door and it was nice to see her. Jenny had always been good to us and, even though I had divorced her brother, she remained a friend. She shared a pot of tea with me and went on to tell me how Jim was working again and had cut right back on his drinking and was a changed man. She said he would like to visit us.

I was not so sure this was a good idea but finally agreed. Our Ann was far from pleased about it. Jim did come up from Leicester to see us and seemed very subdued, full of regret for his past behaviour, and begged for a reconciliation. He wanted us to move back to Leicester and give it another try. I pointed out that I had a nice house here and was near my family, and the children were happily settled in their new school.

He left me to think things over. When I talked to Dad about it, much to my surprise, he did not seem too averse to the idea. I expected him to be dead against it, but then Dad did not know all that much of Jim's nature, whereas our Ann and David had seen his black side. Helen and

Paul seemed pleased to see him again, but I suppose he was the only father figure they had known, though they both loved their Uncle David dearly. They took Jim down the woods to show him our trails and he truly did seem changed. The whole weekend of his visit he had not had a drink of alcohol. I agreed to think about it and he went back to Leicester.

When he next visited us, he once again begged me to give it another try with him and assured me he would not drink or ever hit me again. He went on to say that his mother was willing for us all to live with her in the flat she now had at Wigston and that we would soon get a council house.

'You know I love you,' he told me. 'You're the best thing since penicillin. I want you and the kids back and swear I'll be good to you if you give me the chance.'

I should have listened to our Ann's advice and my inner reservations, but I'm ashamed to say I chose to ignore them and once again I fell for Jim's Irish charm.

Ann and David were not very happy about my decision at all and I can understand that now – I could never blame them for their misgivings about my future. They had been so good to the three of us and I'm sure it was only our wellbeing they were thinking of and cared about.

Truth be told, I suppose since first moving from the North down to Buckinghamshire, I had always been a bit footloose and found it hard to settle down back in Stanley. Though I did not miss Buckinghamshire, I did love Leicester, so off we went again, back to Leicester, living with Jim's mum in her flat at Wigston. We immediately put our names down on the council list for accommodation and hoped to be given a house quickly. I had, however, not given up our house in Bronte Place just then.

It pains me now to think of the sorrow I must have caused my family, especially Ann and David, who knew so much about my past. I must have been a great worry to them. Yet at the same time, I also felt that my life was mapped out for me by fate.

We had only been with Jim's mum about two weeks when I had a phone call from David. He told me the tragic news that my beloved dad had died suddenly at home. It was August 1978. I was in complete shock and blamed myself for his death. Yet when I had last left him, he had seemed so much better and had been cheerful. He had been sitting out in his little back garden and had caught the sun a bit; he was looking more healthy than I'd seen him in months. Though Dad had lost most of his hair by then, I had spotted new little hairs growing on his bald patch and had joked with him about having rejuvenation in him. He had seemed happy when we bade farewell. Had I known that my father's death was imminent, I would never have left him when I did. I suppose that however ill a beloved parent is, one is never quite prepared for their death.

When Jim came back in that day and I told him the news, he suggested it was better that I left Helen and Paul with him at his mum's and make the journey north for the funeral myself.

I went straight back on a National Express and stayed with Mam until after Dad's funeral. Dad was only 62 when he died. They had taken him to the mortuary at Shotley Bridge Hospital and he'd had to have a postmortem examination; because he had died at home, it was classed as sudden death.

I had hardly cried, was still in a state of shock I suppose. The night before the funeral I slept with Mam in their bed. I awoke around 3 a.m. with tears streaming down my face, looking to the foot of the bed where Dad would be brought home in a few hours before his funeral. I cried scalding-hot tears of utter despair. Mam seemed pleased that at last I was showing some emotion. We eventually got up out of bed and spent the rest of the night drinking cups of tea downstairs, sobbing.

They brought Dad home and placed his coffin at the end of the bed for friends and family to say their last goodbyes. He lay there as if asleep, covered by fancy, frilled, white satin and a little sort of fancy head cover with lace on.

We had all been in to say goodbye to Dad but I felt I could not leave him. I stood by his coffin and stroked his face as he'd stroked mine many times over the years. The little cover on his head fell off and I could see the crude, rough, ropelike stitches that joined his head back together after the postmortem. I was aghast but knew it would be terrible if Mam was to see this. I told Betty and Ann about it and they came up to try and protect our mother from seeing. I had to tell them, as although I did not want to leave Dad's side, my bladder was making me go to the loo every few minutes, either from nerves or all the cups of tea we'd had during the night.

Betty was very upset about it but I whispered that at least one of us should be there the whole time to keep Mam from finding out. She must have spotted something, however, as she wailed that Dad had grown his own dark hair back, as it used to be. I spent the whole morning sitting with Dad, apart from frequent loo breaks and odd fag breaks, but too soon they came to take him away. I placed a packet of cigarettes and a lighter in Dad's coffin for a 'smoke' when he got to the other side. Then I kissed his face and whispered goodbye to him for ever.

The funeral all went by in a bit of a blur for me after that. Afterwards, family and friends gathered at Mam's for a tea that neighbours had prepared. I sat at the table, unable to eat anything at all, I felt I was being choked. Later on, people started drifting away. Last to go were David's mam and dad, Molly and Jack, bless them, they stayed with us until after 10 p.m.

The next few months were very difficult for all of us, really. Dad's death had a profound effect on all of us in different ways.

I lost a lot of weight, as did Mam. I was suffering from bad palpitations; though I had had them for several years, they were worse now. I was sent for a checkup at the hospital and they wanted to admit me immediately. Ann and David had taken Angela and Stuart away camping for a few days, so I had to ask Mam if she would have Helen and Paul for me when I went into hospital. She reluctantly agreed and I left her my family allowance book so she could cash the orders on that. I also left her what money I had on me towards the children's keep.

So I was on a ward again at the hospital, having one test after another. Mam sent Helen and Paul in to visit me on their own as she had gone to her over-sixties night at the local club. I was surprised she had let them come all this way up to Consett on their own by bus, and they didn't look very happy. Even other patients on the ward seemed to pity them and brought them sweets and biscuits to eat as they were there so long. I felt very anxious for them, as they were not allowed to go back to their grandma's until she was home from the club.

It was dark outside and when they left to go back to my mother's on a bus, on their own, I worried for their safety. This went on for a couple of nights, then Mam turned up one afternoon to see me, puffing and panting, saying, 'It's all too much, this visiting. I am not getting any younger, you know, I am not up to this, our Lyn.'

I know Helen and Paul were good children, they were respectful and would not have caused Mam any trouble. They were at school during the day and it was not like she had two babies to look after. They'd told me they'd been helping Grandma and doing washing up for her and such. But Mam complained bitterly, which made me even more anxious, so of course the palpitations then became worse.

The doctors wanted to send me to the Freeman Hospital in Newcastle for further tests and investigations. It was a new hospital at that time. Before this all was to come about, though, I had another visitor come to see me

– a social worker. Mam had been to social services in Stanley complaining she was not well enough to look after Helen and Paul, so they were to be taken into care provisionally by foster parents. I immediately broke down in tears and said I would discharge myself first before I would let that happen. The social worker, on seeing my distress, assured me they would try and keep Helen and Paul together rather than have them in separate families, which made me even more distressed. She looked worried when I demanded to see a doctor to arrange my own discharge, but I was adamant. The worst thing that could have happened to me was to have my children taken away from me. I'm sure any mother, except perhaps my mother, would have felt the same as I did.

Helen and Paul were my life. They were the reason I had striven for my whole life, I could never have been able to bear having them taken from me. I was filled with terror with the very thought of it. When the doctor did come to see me, I insisted on immediate self-discharge and no amount of persuasion from any of the medical staff could make me change my mind. When the paperwork was duly signed and I was busy packing up my things to leave, the hospital social worker came back to my bedside and offered me a lift in her car to take me back to my mother's. I gratefully accepted, as it was pouring with rain.

That evening I walked into Mam's house along with the social worker. Mam was very surprised to see me, and also looked a bit worried. The social worker decided to leave us to it and seemed glad to get out of the way. I wasn't looking for a row so I just told Helen and Paul to get their clothes together, which they quickly did, then I thanked Mam for having them, all very civil, but could not bite my tongue any longer and had to add, 'and thanks for going to social services and trying to have them taken away from me'.

This was like a red rag to a bull. Mam went off into a huge tantrum, screaming and shouting at me, 'It's your fault Dad is in his grave, but you're not going to drive me into mine.' I refused to argue back to her, got the children to put their coats on and quietly we left Mam's house in the pouring rain. As the three of us walked silently home, hand in hand together, I don't know which poured the hardest, the rain or the tears from my eyes.

Once we got home we sat and huddled together – I was inconsolable. I don't think Helen and Paul had ever seen me weeping so much and I'm sure they felt at a loss for what to do, bless them. It was like a dam had broken and I could not quell my flow of tears.

I had to pull myself together for their sakes. They were happy to have me home, but the sting of my mother's words had hurt me very deeply. Mam stayed away for about a week or more, and it was as well she did. I think Helen and Paul had been shocked at the way their grandma had shouted at me so much and been so hysterical. I don't know if they understood the hurtfulness of her words to me, but they did understand how upset I had been afterwards.

I was at a very low ebb. My father's death had affected me deeply but to have Mam blame me for it hurt me to the core. I had tried to be a good daughter, I had given up whole days going up those fields every day to be with Dad, trying to look after him as best as I could, trying to keep his spirits up. I had done this gladly and will never, ever regret it as I know it meant so much to him. Mam had accepted my help at that time, never showing any appreciation (which I wasn't really looking for, anyway) but it was just like years gone by when I had been a young child – the more I tried to do whatever I could to help, it was never enough for Mam.

I did it all out of love for Dad, but now Mam seemed to have forgotten all this. She had even failed to see that Helen and Paul needed me too. To have her blame me for Dad's death was just too much. I tried to forget her angry words, hoping it was only her grief over losing Dad that had got her feeling mixed up. Grief does affect people in different ways, I realised this.

She came back to our house one day, however, knocking on the porch door before walking in. This was something Mam never did; she usually just walked in. I was busy in the kitchen area at the time, and Helen and Paul had gone to school. Mam just said, 'I'm sorry, will you forgive me?' and put her arms around me, something she very rarely did.

I just said, 'Yes, Mam, of course I forgive you,' and I did, but I'm afraid it would be something I could never forget.

Helen and Paul were so precious to me, we had been through so much together. There had been times when they were babies that I had struggled to keep them fed and warm. Yet I had managed it, even if I had sat by an empty fireplace at nights, shivering with cold, then gone to bed too hungry to sleep. I had been too proud to ask my family for help in those days, when the children were so young. To have them taken into care by social services would have demented me. So I would forgive Mam, but I would not forget it.

When Ann and David came back from their few days away, they were shocked when I confided what had happened. Ann told me they would have looked after Helen and Paul if they had been home and I knew this to be a fact. They would have done so gladly, but they were not to find out about it until they got back.

Mam started changing towards all three of us daughters now. Even good friends and close neighbours of hers would stop our Betty on the main street in Stanley and say to her, 'What have we done to your mam, she doesn't want to know us any more?' Poor Betty wondered what we had all done that could turn her against not only us, her daughters, but her own grandchildren too. Neither Betty, Ann or myself could understand why our mother decided to shun all of her family.

Our Ann had been very good to Mam. Now it was like she had no time for any of us. Our Ann worried about Mam so she and David bought her a lovely little terrier dog, a puppy called Brandy. Mam hated it. She kept it for only a short time then gave it back to Ann (she had been threatening to get rid of it she hated it so much). Mam only seemed interested in her over-sixties nights at the club and the new friends she had made there.

Eventually, I was so low and sick of it all I gave in to Jim's persuasions to move back down to Leicester. Ann was not pleased with me and I can't say I blamed her. She worried for Helen and Paul's welfare, as she and David cared so much about them. At the time, I think I just wanted to get away and could not see I would be making another big mistake.

When I married Jim I think I had been looking for a father figure. I had missed my dad so much when I first left the Northeast and moved to Buckinghamshire, where I was left to bring up two young children on my own. I suppose I was easy prey for Jim's Irish charm and his conniving ways.

This time I was to leave the North again, and I suppose it was at a time when I was feeling vulnerable after the loss of my beloved dad and still reeling from yet another rejection from my mam.

I should have been used to her not wanting me by now, but could not come to terms with her trying to have my children put into care. My children meant the world to me, so I would make sure no one would ever take them from me.

FOURTEEN

In early January 1979 we moved back in with Jim's mum, but it was overcrowded. Jim had the idea that if his mum gave us a letter saying we had to get out of her house as she didn't want us there then the council would have no option but to give us somewhere to live.

I just went along with the idea and we took the letter in to the council. We ended up being put into a hostel for the homeless. When we went there I couldn't believe the state of the place. It was run by an Irish couple who had mostly down-and-outs staying there – we were the only family. The rest of the people were mostly men who stayed in the hostel at night and meal times only. They spent what little money they had on drink.

We were put into an extended building in the back yard of the hostel. It was one room with a double bed and two single ones. The mattresses were dirty and the blankets not much better, so Jim's sister let me borrow some of her blankets. We had no hot water or washing facilities and had to share an inside toilet with all the other residents. The room had one small window and was freezing. Helen and Paul were reluctant to go to a strange school but I felt I had to get them into one so I knew at least they'd be warm during the day and get a school dinner.

The DHSS provided vouchers for all the residents, including ourselves, to the couple who ran the hostel. The vouchers they were given were supposed to cover the food and our upkeep, so we had to get in line on a morning with all the other down-and-outs for breakfast, which was a mug of sweet tea each and one bowl of porridge. Lunchtime was another mug of sweetened tea and two jam sandwiches. Thank goodness the children were in school. In the evening we had to queue up once again to receive the main meal. This usually consisted of some dry crusty bread and a bowl of weak broth followed by a cup of, yes, sweet tea. We had been given a small amount of money from the DHSS, which we spent on food for us to eat in our room at night, huddled up in our beds, trying to keep warm.

I was so nervous about the children having to go in to use the toilet where the other residents were, so we would try to wait, then three of us all went in together to share the toilet, then scuttle quickly back to our concrete room in the yard and lock the door. The couple who ran the hostel made an effort on the first Sunday we were there by making a Sunday lunch. We were served with soggy boiled potatoes, soggy cabbage and sheep's heart. We had to leave it; none of us could face eating it.

I noticed the couple running the hostel went out every night to the pub and would return very merry. Jim had given up his job in his effort to try and get us a council house. By the second week we were there, I could see how unhappy Helen and Paul were and they also didn't like their school. I made them go, however, so at least they were warm and had a school lunch.

Jim started getting friendly with the couple who ran the hostel and when he started going out at night to the pub with them, I thought, that's it, we're not taking any more of this. It was not fair to the children and I couldn't tolerate them living like that.

On the Monday, however, the council gave us the keys to a house on Victoria Road East. It was a house just used as temporary accommodation, and we could have it until we could be given a permanent council house. We moved in; it was a bit shabby but I soon cleaned it up and at least we finally had a house to ourselves.

Jim had promised to find himself a job once we got a house, but made no effort to do so and just signed on the dole.

We were not there very long before I realised I was pregnant. As I was feeling so poorly and weak, and still suffering from palpitations, which had been diagnosed as supraventricular tachycardia from earlier tests, I felt unable to work at that time. Helen and Paul had started another new school near Victoria Road and seemed more settled, they had made friends there. Jim got his dole money at weekends and spent most of it on drink. He went to the pub at the end of the road and bought bottles of sherry from the off-licence two doors away from our house. Once again, his drinking was well out of control and I realised I had made a bitter mistake. I felt trapped, however, as I was pregnant, yet I wanted the baby. Jim's tempers and violence escalated once more, as did his drinking. The children and I were walking on eggshells again – what had I done?

When it got to the Easter of 1979, I was three months pregnant and still feeling poorly. On Good Friday I started to haemorrhage and was taken into hospital. They told me I'd probably lost the baby, or if not, that the baby would be dead inside me and they wanted me to go to the theatre for a D&C. I was distressed by this and asked to see a priest. The doctor was not very happy about this but they sent for one anyway. The priest tried to tell me that there was no question about it being an abortion as the young lady doctor had assured him the baby was probably gone and my life may be at risk if I didn't have the operation.

They came and prepared me for theatre, but just before I was to be wheeled down there for the operation, the consultant turned up to see me – they had called him in from the golf course. I think they were a bit worried about me having called in a priest, as well as the fact I was so reluctant to have the operation. The consultant examined me and, as I had nearly stopped bleeding by then, he agreed to let me go home, on condition I returned the following Tuesday after the bank holiday to have a scan; if that showed my baby was lost, then I must agree to the operation.

I willingly went along with this. There had been no scan done by that stage, as there had been no technicians available to do one over the holiday period.

I went home and took things very easy all weekend as I had been advised, my mind in turmoil – had I really lost my baby? But where there's life, there's hope. We had a phone at Victoria Road East and I phoned up Ann and told her what had happened. Amazingly, she said she had guessed something was wrong with me, as she had smelled the perfume I always wore yet had none of it in her house. She had said to David, 'Something's wrong with our Lyn.' She said she would pray for me all weekend and phone me on Tuesday after the scan. There had always been a sort of telepathy between me and our Ann. I prayed to God myself all weekend that my baby would not be dead.

On the Tuesday morning I went to the hospital for the scan. The technician did it carefully and silently but didn't tell me anything. I was told to get dressed and go outside, where the consultant was waiting for me with a junior doctor. He told me with a beaming smile, 'Well, I'm glad to tell you your baby is not lost and the baby's heart is beating strongly.' I broke down in tears of relief and joy. My prayers had been answered.

As my pregnancy progressed, Jim's drinking continued to get heavier. The day he got his dole money he would give me a small amount to buy food. I would go to the nearby shops with Helen and spend all he had given me on groceries before he got the chance to drink the money.

The food wouldn't last the whole week until the next cheque would come so I got what I could.

Tuesday was family allowance day and after going to the Post Office to collect it, I bought more groceries. Jim went mad at me for spending too much on food, but I didn't care what he said as I had already got the food in and hoped it would see us through the week. As Jim was spending so much of the money at the off-licence, they would serve him cheap sherry sold by the pint, he was giving them a good trade. They even agreed to serve him the sherry when we had no money left to pay for it, on condition he settled his bill at the weekend when he got his dole. This created a vicious circle, as he could drink all week long on credit, but when he got his dole money there was nothing left out of it to buy groceries once he had settled his sherry account.

I had to buy what food I could out of the family allowance money. I refused to give Jim any money out of this for drink and he shouted and swore at me, calling me all the names under the sun.

'You stupid, miserable cow,' he would yell at me. 'There was no need to buy so much food. You and your kids are all just fucking, greedy cunts.' Then he would storm into the front room and roll up a cigarette, with the half-ounce of baccy I had bought him to try and appease him. On some occasions, he would give me a slap across the mouth as he stormed out of the front door. 'Greedy fucker!' he would shout at me, sometimes spitting into my face as he left. I knew it would not be too long until he would be back, triumphantly holding up his pint of sherry he had got from the off-licence, on credit. I tried not to cry – I did not want to give him that satisfaction.

I had not been able to buy any baby clothes and even Helen, Paul and myself needed clothes. Jenny bought me a dress from a charity shop that I washed and wore throughout my pregnancy. Jim stopped going out to the pub as it was cheaper to buy the sherry from the off-licence. It meant him drinking it indoors and we watched him go through all the mood swings that the alcohol created. The first few drinks he got happy and talked about the old days in Ireland when he was growing up. He joked and laughed with the children, but I knew this wouldn't last long. Sure enough, after a few more drinks he would become maudlin, which led to more drink, which made him angry and argumentative, ready to start a fight. It was usually just before this last stage that Helen and Paul would go up to their bedrooms. Even at their age, they had started to see the pattern of Jim's mood swings.

His tempers became vicious, even if I refused to join in an argument with him. He found fault with everything I did and everything I said, there was no reasoning with him. He often hit out at me even though I was pregnant. As he sat and watched the TV with his bottle of sherry beside him, he wanted a captive audience who would readily be on hand while he talked of the past. If I tried to get up to do some ironing or something, he would shout at me, 'You just fucking sit down here when I'm talking to you, you ignorant fucking whore.'

He blamed me for everything that had ever gone wrong in his life. He blamed me for the fact our marriage had broke down, blamed me for working and giving too much of myself to the job when we were at Stoneygate. He blamed me for the fact he was not working any more and anything else he could think of. I'd grown used to the horrible, filthy names he called me when he got so drunk, yet still his words could hurt me. He wouldn't let me go to bed while he was sitting drinking. He needed an audience. If I was unable to pacify him, he would swing out with his fists. He told me he would dance on my grave one day.

One night he hit me so hard in the face my nose was pouring with blood. It felt like he had broken it. Then he just looked at me and with no remorse whatsoever told me I had been asking for it. When he went to the toilet I phoned the police and asked for their help. I'd tried to phone them before when he got violent but he usually caught me and replaced the phone before I could get through to anyone. That night I had managed to call them and they came out to our house. 'Please take him away,' I begged the police, 'we can't take any more of this.'

It was obvious to them that he had hit me, the blood still ran from my nose and was all down the front of my dress. Yet Jim still denied hitting me, telling them I was 'nothing but a little liar and devious into the bargain'.

Jim's drunken state was also obvious to the police. While I sat and talked with a WPC, two other police officers took Jim into the front room to talk to him. He had been trying to tell them he was perfectly sober and somehow he managed not to lose his temper with them. I heard no shouting at all from the front room, but when they came out leaving Jim sitting in there, the police officers told me I should not have any more trouble with him that night, but there was little else they could do. It was a domestic affair, they told me.

After they had left I felt sure he would have another go at me, I felt he would be furious at me for calling the police, but strangely enough he did not, he left me alone and I went to bed out of his way.

I blame myself that we ever became reconciled, I should have known better than to believe Jim would ever change or give up drinking. I despaired at what would become of us all. I was heavily pregnant by now and unable to work to enable me to support ourselves financially. I was never allowed out on my own apart from attending antenatal checkups, and I had no one to talk to about our situation.

At one of these checkups I talked to one of our GPs in confidence, hoping I might get a chance to talk to a social worker. Instead, the GP explained that Jim was an alcoholic and unless he sought help for himself, there was little else she could do to help me. I wouldn't have dared to have anyone come to the house to talk to him, Jim would have killed me first. I felt I had nowhere else left to turn.

I went into hospital in October 1979. The placenta was not working very well and I was suffering from hypertension. They decided that labour would be induced at 38 weeks, having ascertained the baby's lungs would be able to function by now.

On a Saturday morning I was taken to a labour room and put on a drip to start my labour. As it progressed, Jim turned up and was given a green surgical cap and gown and paper boots to wear. He smelled slightly of alcohol and had to leave the ward at regular intervals. By the afternoon, I was well into labour, yet still thought about Helen and Paul at home on their own, especially as a particularly bad thunderstorm had begun. Helen was terribly afraid of storms.

It was during this violent storm that I finally gave birth to my third child, a second son. He weighed only four and a half pounds, but he was beautiful. He had all his fingers and toes and was a healthy baby. Jim went home to tell Helen and Paul, and I guessed he would celebrate when he got home. He was in a jovial mood that day.

We called the new baby Wayne James, another little miracle, and I fell completely in love with him instantaneously. We didn't have to stay in hospital very long and were sent home on the Sunday. I had been unable to buy many clothes for him but had the bare necessities. 'Oh, he's lovely, Mum,' Helen exclaimed, as I let her hold her new brother.

Helen and Paul were proud of their new baby brother. Later on that day, Jenny turned up with a pram and a cot she had managed to get for me. She had also bought some baby clothes and I cried when she gave them to me. Bless her, she knew I had not got much and had turned up trumps. I would never forget her kindness. Jim's other sisters turned up to see the new baby, also bearing gifts, which I truly appreciated, but I would always remember Jenny bringing the pram and cot. At least I now had somewhere to lay the baby.

Helen was like a second mother to the new baby, she was so proud. She helped me a lot with him and we got to go out for walks to the shops with Wayne in his pram. Helen was thirteen when Wayne was born and Paul, at twelve, became more protective towards me, though he was still nervous around Jim.

For a short while after Wayne was born, Jim had tried to moderate his drinking – it was not to last very long.

FIFTEEN

When Wayne was nearly six months old, we were given the keys to a council house in New Parks. I had no idea where that was as it was the other side of town to us.

We went by bus to see it and found a three-bedroomed semi-detached house on the very end of a street. There was a cherry blossom tree in the front garden, as well as fir trees and an apple tree in the back garden. The house itself needed decorating throughout. In the kitchen was an old iron stove for heating the water. It had open coal fires and no central heating, yet we decided to take it, as we did not know how long we might have to wait for another property.

We moved into the house in April 1980, Easter time. There were a few shops down the road from us and further shops on the main road, less than a mile's walking distance.

After the Easter break, I managed to get Helen and Paul into the nearby school. They settled in there well again – it would be the last time they ever had to change schools. As Jim was still out of work, it was a struggle to buy them the uniforms they needed, but somehow we managed it.

Jim continually badgered me into remarrying him once we had Wayne, but I refused. As we both went by the same surname, I didn't see the point, but that was not the only reason.

Jim was still drinking and his moods were still volatile. As one of the local shops contained an off-licence, it was too easy for him to walk down there and purchase drink, which he began to do on a frequent basis. His violence towards me continued and I knew for sure it was affecting Helen and Paul. He shouted at them a lot of the time and I could sense their fear of him. He started drinking so much again that he hardly knew what day it was; it went on well into the night and often ended in him being violent to me. One night, on the landing, just outside the children's bedrooms, he smashed my head into the light switch so hard that blood poured out from my scalp. It was so painful, all I wanted to do was be allowed to go to bed and sleep, but while Jim wasn't sleeping neither could I.

'You'll fucking stop down here where I can keep an eye on you,' he shouted.

It had got to the stage where Jim hardly seemed to need much sleep – he hardly knew the difference between night and day by now. The rest of the family still needed our sleep but we weren't getting it.

Jim now ordered me out to buy his bottles of sherry. I had to do it or there would be terrible rows. He even tried to get Helen and Paul to go down and buy it, even when I insisted they wouldn't be served as they were underage. He still insisted they go for his sherry or else we'd be out, so they set off down the road with fear on their faces. I knew they would return empty-handed, which they did, and then he stormed off down the road to buy it himself. We were all very anxious when he was gone and dreaded what he'd be like when he got back.

He constantly belittled us and told us we were scum and that no one else would have us. My self-confidence was virtually nil by now, my spirits at an all-time low. Jim had humiliated me and treated me as worthless for so long that I was now beginning to believe it. One morning I got up about 5.30 a.m., after he had finally fallen into a drunken stupor. I had had virtually no sleep all night, in fact none of the family had. I opened the front door and was looking out into the garden wondering what on earth I was going to do. I could see no light at the end of the tunnel and no way out of our situation. Wayne cried all the time as he was scared of the shouting; he was tired and needed sleep. Helen and Paul were too scared to answer him back, and we were all so weary.

One night, when Jim had gone to the toilet during one of his drinking bouts, I quickly crushed up a few phenobarbitone tablets that I had in the cupboard. I had had them for a long time, from when our Paul had been ill once. I should have thrown them out a long time ago. I wasn't thinking straight, I felt so desperate that I tried to crush about three of the pills and get them into Jim's sherry before he came back down from the toilet. It was meant only so as he would go to sleep and enable all of us to get some sleep. My hands shook so violently, however, that I could not get all the powder from the pills into his drink before I heard the chain flush. He seemed to look at his bottle of sherry suspiciously before pouring himself another glassful. I was in terror the whole time he drank it. Being a nurse, I should have known better than to mix drugs with alcohol, but I only wanted us to be able to get some sleep.

I needn't have worried – I waited and waited and yet nothing happened. Jim continued to drink and talk well into the night again.

His abusive behaviour continued. He was drinking mostly all of the days and evenings and kept telling me to 'get out and take your three bloody children with you'. I really did not know where or whom to turn to and felt that we could not continue to live in this way. My confidence was all gone, I felt as worthless as Jim said I was. I was continually anxious over my children's welfare and our future. Deprived of sleep, I was completely browbeaten and full of despair. If we went out, I had to keep my head bent down and my eyes averted from looking at anyone else so he could not accuse me of being a whore.

Then Jim had an accident.

He had been drinking continually for about two days and nights with very little sleep for any of us. He got up from the settee and fell over, catching his ribs on the wooden arms as he fell. He howled in pain and needed help to get up from the floor. He demanded I get him some help so I went down to the phone box and called for an ambulance. When I got back he was yelling at me for being 'fucking useless' and shouting about how much pain he was in.

When the ambulance arrived Jim refused to go with them to hospital. He said the pain was now much better. The ambulance men were amused by his inebriated state but could not force him to go with them. Instead they got him to sign a form discharging them of any responsibility. 'That's got rid of those bastards,' he laughed when they had gone.

Then he spent the rest of the night shouting and yelling how much pain he was in and how useless I was. 'You can't do nothing right can you, call yourself a nurse, you're no fucking good at anything, never mind being a fucking nurse.'

The next morning, Helen and Paul were glad to go to school. I tried to care for Wayne while Jim screamed at me all the while and ordered me to get him some help. I took Wayne down in his buggy to the phone box and phoned our doctor to ask him to come out and see Jim. The doctor insisted that either Jim was to go up to the surgery or, if he was unable to do this, I was to call the ambulance out again. I returned home and told Jim what the doctor had said. He screamed at me that we were all useless and that I had to walk up and see the doctor myself and order him to come out.

I was so worn out with it all I just did as he ordered and walked up to the doctor's surgery with Wayne in the buggy. I sat and waited my turn and duly went in and begged Dr Humphries to come out and visit him. When he refused again, I just put my head down on his desk and wept. I cried and cried and, in between sobs, the whole sorry tale poured out of me. It was like someone had released a safety valve in my head and our months of anguish all came pouring out. The doctor looked startled; he had not realised at the time we had been suffering in silence and I'm sure he felt sorry for me. He treated me with kindness, gave me a prescription of analgesics for Jim but, more importantly, advised me to try and get some help for our situation, though he failed to say where to turn for it.

I went miserably home, glad in a way I had unburdened myself, but knowing we could not continue to live like this. Jim complained that I had taken long enough but took the tablets anyway. He still drank his sherry and that night none of us got much sleep again with his cursing, ranting and raving. The next morning, after Helen and Paul had gone to school, Jim threw me out with Wayne, telling me to 'get out and take your bloody kids with you' once again. I walked into the town centre and sat in the square with Wayne on my lap, watching the fountain and pondering in my head where we should go.

I just had no idea who to turn to. Then something seemed to click inside my brain and on impulse I walked to the solicitors' office that had handled my divorce. They got me in to see a solicitor urgently and I poured my heart out to her, asking if I ought to go to the council for help. 'No, no, no,' she insisted. 'It's not you that has to leave or the children.' She told me I must apply for an injunction order to get Jim removed from the property.

I said how scared I was of him and the repercussions that could follow, but she told me I had to be brave, that it would not take long. So, for the children's sake, I agreed to do it. The solicitor explained what would happen next and advised that if he got too violent, I was to call the police.

I went home that afternoon before Helen and Paul returned from school in mortal fear of Jim. I had to tell him what I had done and felt sure he would kill me.

I was wrong. When I explained where I had been and whom I had seen, he seemed to accept it, as if he knew it would come to this. It took about one week for the injunction order to be granted and Jim was given two weeks to leave the property. It slowed down his drinking slightly and he left within a week of receiving the court injunction order, going to his mother's to live once more.

'I'll be glad to get away from you bastards, you've been nothing but a rope around my neck for years. Don't ever try to claim any money from me, I would kill you first' was his parting shot.

The Saturday morning he left, I sat on the bottom of the stairs and cried, but they were tears of relief. I knew I had done the right thing, yet was amazed at how long it had taken me to finally see the light.

It is very easy to criticise someone for continuing to live within an abusive relationship, but unless you have actually been in that situation, it is very hard to imagine how difficult it becomes to remove oneself from it. If a person is beaten and browbeaten into believing themselves unworthy for long enough, it becomes impossible for that person to have faith in themselves or have the confidence to try and change the situation they have become trapped in. Looking back on it all now, I realise I should never have gone back to Jim after our divorce.

I do not feel sorry for myself for having suffered through Jim's alcoholism. What does cause me pain is the sorrow I feel for having let Helen and Paul suffer during the time we were with him. I only hope they have forgiven me for putting them in that position. I have suffered for years from nightmares over Jim. I hope with all my heart that my children have been able to put it behind them and not dwell on the past. They remain close to me and have never shown any blame towards me. I thank them for this, as I always loved my children with my whole heart.

Wayne was too young to remember his dad's violence, but I know Helen and Paul have their memories of him. I just hope these have become faded with time. It certainly did not stop them from growing up into lovely individuals, with their own lovely natures. They are now settled and have their own children and are both wonderful parents. I am now, and always will be, proud of them. My children will always hold a special place in my heart and I know for certain that when it's my time to go, I will live on in my children's hearts, as my dad will forever live on through mine. I feel truly blessed at having such wonderful children.

Never again will anyone be able to put me back into that cowed, frightened person that I had been with Jim.

Never again will I have to hold my head down, eyes averted, too scared to look someone in the face. I can hold my head up high now without fear of accusation.

Never again will I feel worthless, as I was led to believe I was, first by my mother's rejection, then by Jim as he continually strived to beat all my spirit out of me. He may have damaged my self-esteem and robbed me of all self-confidence but he never stole my soul.

Now I would try to put my bad life behind me and put the fragmented pieces of my shattered soul back together.

SIXTEEN

As Wayne was still a baby, it was not practical for me to find a job. Helen and Paul were young teenagers in school. They had made friends of their own by now and our lifestyle was poor, as I had to rely on DHSS benefits. At least we could spend more money on food now, though, and we didn't have Jim there with his drinking and tempers and tantrums. Peace reigned once more in our household. Jim was granted 'reasonable access' by the courts to see Wayne. He used this to his advantage to 'keep an eye on me'. He did not want me himself but neither did he want anyone else to have me.

At that stage, I was happy enough to be on my own with the children. Wayne grew into a mischievous little toddler and I swore to myself I would never let his spirit be broken. As he got older, he was into everything and loved to climb up the apple tree in the back garden. He climbed up the tree then onto the roof of the shed, where he chanted, 'You can't catch me.' He did it so many times we eventually had to chop down the tree to stop his climbing.

Our first Christmas without Jim was a tranquil one. About two weeks before Christmas there was a knock on our front door one evening. I'll always remember, I had Wayne sitting on the potty at the time. Paul answered the door and in walked Dr Humphries. I was surprised to say the least; we were all well and had not sent for him. He told me he was a member of the Freemasons' Society and had brought us a hamper of food they had been given to distribute to poorer families. I was extremely grateful to him. Although he could be brusque, his kindness at that time touched me greatly.

We did not have much money to spare during Wayne's early years but we got by. The peace that we had more than made up for any lack of cash. The bags of coke I had to buy for the kitchen stove and open fire in the sitting room were expensive at £5 per bag. That ate into our meagre budget, but I had to buy it to provide warmth and hot water.

During the following summer, we went out together as a family some days, during the children's summer breaks from school. As we did not have much money, we could not go far. Seaside breaks and things like that were impossible. Instead, I would make up picnics and we would go to Western Park or Abbey Park, where the four of us would spend whole days there. Although Helen and Paul were getting older, I think they enjoyed their days out with me and Wayne when he was so little. We all shared a sense of liberation that summer.

When Helen and Paul returned to school after the holidays, I took Wayne into town in his buggy during the day. We sat in the square where he loved to watch the fountain. I used to take him out of his buggy for a better view of the water and throw him gently up in the air. He would giggle with delight as I continued to sit there and play with him. These were joyous little moments with my youngest son and passers-by would remark on my happy baby. I spent numerous days with Wayne sitting by that fountain.

At weekends, we would all go to the park again with our picnic. We could once more enjoy the simple things in life. Paul had made a lot more mates and was very much into sports at school. Helen was still very shy at that time. She had a good friend, Sally, just down the road from us who she went to school with. Evenings they would spend either at Sally's house, or the two of them would be up in Helen's bedroom. They were into listening to records together, Meat Loaf and UB40. I used to worry a bit about Helen being so shy, while Paul was more outgoing in nature; they had both developed a good sense of humour, though. Their individual characters were already developing, and they kept me going and helped me retain my sanity.

Ann and David came to visit us on several occasions with Angela and Stuart. We always looked forward to their visits, as they always seemed to be able to make us all laugh.

They realised how hard up I was at this time and always brought enough food with them when they came down to feed the lot of us. They would even bring all the vegetables and a big joint of meat so we could all enjoy a big Sunday lunch together.

Ann and David used to take us all out, to Abbey Park or Bradgate Park. Helen and Paul adored their aunt and uncle.

We went to Twycross Zoo one day, which was great fun. While looking at the pigs I asked David, 'Is that a boar?'

'Well, it's certainly no conversationalist,' David replied, deadpan, and we cracked up laughing.

On one of their visits to Leicester to see us, Ann and David told me of their intention to try and emigrate. They wanted to go to Australia.

Consett Iron and Steel Company had by now closed down. As most of the pits in the Northeast, as well as some of the shipyards, had also closed, it had caused many jobs to be lost and there was a severe recession in the area. When David had lost his job at the steel works, rather than be on the dole he had attended Newcastle University, eventually earning his BSc Honours degree in Metallurgy. The whole family were very proud of him.

I was devastated by the fact that they might leave the country, yet I could see they would have a better future in store and could not blame them. They put their house up for sale and went ahead with their preparations. David secured himself a good job in Australia with another steel company and obtained their visas. I had to accept they were definitely going.

As they could not take their little dog Brandy with them, they asked me to have him, which I did. Sadly, several months later we lost him as he ran away.

Mam had still turned her back on us all. She had made new friends at her over-sixties club, including a close relationship with Dick, the organist who played at their club. David's mam and dad, Molly and Jack, went to the same club as Mam and had told her of Ann and David's plans to emigrate. She still failed to have any contact with them whatsoever.

The weekend they were finally due to leave the country to start their new life, I went up North and stayed with Betty and her family for the weekend with my own children. Betty had hired a minibus to take us all to Newcastle Airport to see them off. They were due to fly from Newcastle to Heathrow before catching their flight to Australia. So we all piled into the minibus and off we went to the airport. I clung on to our Ann's arm, not wanting to part from her, but eventually they were called for their flight.

I had always been so close to Ann and David, I could barely believe they were going. I felt like I was cracking up but I knew I had to put on a brave front for their sakes. It must have been much harder for them to leave all their family and friends behind. I whispered to our Ann to 'be a brave soldier', something I had told her when she had been a little girl. We all hugged and kissed each other and once they had been called through to departure, we all went upstairs to watch them board their plane through the glass windows of the airport. I strained my face to the glass, hands cupped around my eyes, and eventually saw them walking across the tarmac to their plane. David was carrying their hand luggage, and Angela and Stuart were both holding onto Ann's hands. Their little figures looked so small. They boarded the plane and we stood there waiting for it to take off – no one could have dragged me away from that window. When the plane finally took to the sky, I almost collapsed. I was utterly brokenhearted.

I thought I would never, ever see them again and I sobbed bitterly. I cried all the way back to Betty's house in the minibus and could not stop. I was inconsolable and had to go upstairs where I cried for hours. When I finally was able to pull myself together, I joined the rest of the family downstairs and asked Betty if I could use her phone and asked her for my mother's phone number.

I phoned Mam and said Ann and David and the children had got off safely. At first she was surprised to hear from me then calmly said, 'Yes, well, thanks for letting me know.'

Then I went on to tell her that while we were all surprised by her behaviour at turning her back on us all, that one thing I would never, ever forgive her for was the fact she could let her youngest daughter and her family leave the country without even saying goodbye to them. When Mam tried to make excuses, I pointed out that she might never get to see Angela and Stuart, her grandchildren, again and that I failed to see how she could have let them go without even a farewell.

Then I hung up the phone. I had phoned my mother on the spur of the moment, in anger, I suppose, but felt glad to have gotten things off my chest. Mam had told me on the phone she had nothing or no one to answer to and that her conscience was clear. I realised then that we would never be able to penetrate Mam's shell.

We returned home to Leicester the next day. Life had to go on. I would stay in touch with Ann and David regularly by letter over the following years. Ann always wrote back to me and kept me up to date with their new life 12,000 miles away in Australia. She was also to send me many photos of the family, and also of the many, many children they fostered while they lived out there.

SEVENTEEN

When Wayne was three years old, I got him into full-time nursery school and applied for a part-time job as a nurse at Glenfield Hospital. I was successful, so I was able to stop relying on DHSS benefits. Money was still tight for us but at least now I could work and try to earn our own living. Having to live on benefits was demeaning to me and I wanted to be able to support us to regain my dignity and sense of pride.

I worked the days while Wayne was in nursery, taking him there then making a mad dash up the road to the hospital to work. Then after work it would be a mad dash back down to the nursery school to pick him up again. Nine times out of ten, I would be the last parent to arrive and Wayne would be the last child to be collected. However fast I tried to run, I always seemed to be late.

Some days I got the chance to work overtime, which I managed to achieve by relying on Helen and Paul – they were old enough by then to look after Wayne for short periods. I used to come home from work exhausted, as I was doing geriatric nursing, which was very hard work.

I had some friends at the hospital, one of whom was Barbara. On our days off from work, Barbara would come to our house and stay for a few hours. She was having problems with her husband at the time, who was seeing someone else. She was very distressed about this and would confide in me or anyone else who would listen to her problems. I gave her a shoulder to cry on as I had an idea what it must have been like for her.

When she came to our house, she always brought sweets for Wayne and would laugh at his little antics. Helen and Paul were less enthusiastic over Barbara's visits as she would stay for ages and they would be wanting their tea.

'Bloody hell,' Barbara would squeal at them, 'aren't you all growing big, then, what's your mum feeding you on, eh?' as she shoved sweets at them.

Helen left school when she was sixteen. She had obtained a place on a pre-nursing course at a local college. She had the six-week break from school to prepare for it, but when the day finally arrived to start college, she set off only to return later in floods of tears. She had been unable to face going into college, she was so painfully shy. I tried hard to persuade her to do it, but to no avail. She had a dream of becoming a nurse, yet felt unable to go on the course and mix with students she didn't know. Short of physically dragging her there by the hand, which would have been impossible at her age, I felt there was little else I could do. At Helen's last school, she had gained quite a bit of weight which had made her self-conscious.

She decided to get a job instead and started work at a shop in town. It was a decision she would regret, although her dream of becoming a nurse would later be fulfilled.

Paul left school a year later and gained a place on a course at Charles Keene College studying Physical Education. He wanted to be a PE teacher or do something in sport. He had grown up into a tall, fine-looking young man by now and had a keen interest in all sports.

He joined the basketball team at college. I would take Helen and Wayne to the Granby Halls some nights to watch him play. Paul was good at basketball and had dreams of playing the game as a professional, perhaps even going to America. I always enjoyed watching him play and was very proud of him.

Helen was paying me some board money now, which helped out on the financial side of things. I had also started doing some private work for the British Nursing Association, an agency that dealt with private patients in the community, moonlighting from my job with the health authority to supplement my part-time wage. I managed to fit in some night-shift work, nursing for the BNA. I had to juggle the hours around my work at the hospital and the time Helen would be at home to look after Wayne.

My friend Barbara's birthday was coming up. She was very depressed at this time as her husband was talking of leaving her completely and she didn't want him to go. 'What will I do if he goes, Lyn?' she kept asking me. I tried to reassure her but still she worried.

On a whim, we decided to go out one Sunday night. It was the night of Barbara's birthday and I was hoping it might cheer her up. Our Helen had turned seventeen by then and I persuaded her to come with us, while Paul looked after Wayne for me.

Neither of us were used to going out far but we got the bus and set out for town. Barbara and I had both worked at the hospital all day, so it had been an effort to summon up the enthusiasm to get ready to go out, but I made the effort for my friend's sake. Helen still felt reluctant at tagging along with us, but I wanted her there, I thought it might be good for her to socialise too with her being so shy.

We went to a pub in town and had a couple of drinks and a giggle together then we ended up gate-crashing a dance being held at the St James Hotel. We did not realise it was a singles night – we were only out for a drink and a laugh together.

This one night would change my whole life.

It was a hot July night and the hotel dance room was splendid with a lot of people there. The three of us chose a table and sat there shyly watching the dancers and listening to the music.

I finally plucked up the courage to go to the bar and buy us all a drink. Helen and Barbara sat waiting at our table and as I got our drinks, I also ordered a small whisky for myself and knocked it back as I stood waiting for my change. It was for a bit of Dutch courage really. The next moment a man at the bar was saying to me, 'You must be thirsty.'

I just told him, 'Yes, I have been at work all day and I am thirsty.'

'What sort of a job do you do to be working on a Sunday?' he asked.

I looked up and saw this tall, handsome man with big dark eyes talking to me. As our conversation progressed, I explained I was with friends and I had better rejoin them with our drinks. 'OK,' he said, 'see you later, then.'

He came to our table towards the end of the night and asked me to dance. I did dance with him, though he was certainly no Fred Astaire. We ended up out on the balcony where the curtains blew gently in the summer night's breeze. As it was a high floor of the hotel, we had a good view of all the lights twinkling over the city.

I was enthralled by the view; it was wonderful to look out for miles on this warm July night. I was captivated by it all and drank in the freshness of the night air as the music drifted over us on the balcony. My new friend put his arm around my shoulder and pulled me to him and our lips met as he gently kissed me. It was so romantic, I felt like Cinderella at the ball. The alcohol had relaxed my mood and I felt at peace with myself as he drew me closer into his arms. The close proximity of his body next to mine felt so right somehow. As he gently kissed me again, I could feel a magic atmosphere blow gently round us.

His name, I learned, was Richard, he was a plumber and recently divorced. I told him I was also divorced and lived with my three children at home. I was certainly not looking for any romantic attachment with anyone. We had set out only for a drink and to cheer up Barbara. Little did I know that Richard was my Prince Charming in disguise. He was to be my knight in shining armour.

Richard offered me a lift home. When I explained we all had to get home, including Barbara to her house, he said this was no problem, he had room for all of us, so I accepted. By the time I got back to our table and told Helen and Barbara we had a lift home, Barbara was quite merry. She was not used to drinking much and was extremely jolly by the end of the night. As we went to the car park with Richard we had a surprise when we saw his transport – it was a big white van he had borrowed from work. Helen and I managed to get in the front seats with him, while Barbara sat in the back of the van.

We took Barbara home first. She was in fits of giggles by now as she rolled around in the back of the van squealing 'Bloody hell!' at every corner. After dropping her off, Richard took Helen and myself home and I asked him in for a cup of tea. It was the least I could do after all his trouble.

Wayne was in bed when we got home and as soon as we got in, Paul went promptly up to bed. He was surprised we had a visitor. After having her cup of tea, Helen soon went up to her bed, too. Richard and I sat and chatted over our tea and he told me he had three daughters who lived with his ex-wife. He lived in a rented house in Blaby. When he asked me to go out with him for a drink one night, I agreed without even thinking.

When the night arrived for our date, Richard turned up on our doorstep, all dressed up and ready to go, but unfortunately I had been asked to work some overtime. I did not have a phone number to ring him and let him know about this and felt dreadful when I opened the door in my uniform and had to explain I was going to work. I saw the disappointment on his face and felt truly sorry.

We made a date for another night, however, and I am so glad he asked me again and doubly glad that I went.

Richard was a lovely man. He was a real gentleman, like no one I had ever met before. He was only 32 years old, whereas I was 37. The difference in age bothered me yet Richard did not worry about it.

He had regular access to his daughters, took them out every weekend and it was obvious he loved them very much. He had been through a painful divorce and still felt very much let down, though he was not a man to talk much of his problems. Though he only told me the bare bones of his past life, I could still sense the rawness of it all for him.

Gradually, as we continued to go out together on a regular basis, our trust in each other would develop, and we fell in love with each other. I soon absolutely adored him, yet Richard was slower to show me his true feelings.

In the beginning, once I realised how much I loved him, I was never quite sure how he felt about me. I now realise that I had to earn his trust a bit more yet. He had been married for thirteen years, his divorce had hit him harder than he would admit and I think he did not want to be let down again. The longer we went out together, the more my love for him grew, yet I felt unable to let him know how much I really did care for him in case it scared him off.

On one night out together, I felt things had gone far enough with us that I must tell him the truth about myself. We went out for a quiet drink together and I braced myself. I was terrified it would mean the end of us being together, yet felt sure it was time that Richard knew all about my past.

I confessed I had something to tell him, swallowed my nervousness and admitted to Richard that rather than having been married once before, that I had indeed been married twice and went on to tell him quickly of my past. When I was finished I told him he could take me home then and dump me there if he wanted to.

To my great relief he just said, 'I'm not dumping you anywhere.'

That night we shared a lot of confidences with each other and talked of our past lives. We each talked of our past problems and failures, then set them aside.

Our trust in each other was beginning to grow. Richard had only recently got back from a holiday in Spain the night we first met – he had a lovely tan – and he continued to talk of foreign holidays he had enjoyed. I told him I had never been abroad before.

After we had been courting for several months, Richard told Helen and I that if we both saved up hard, he would take Helen, Wayne and myself to Spain.

It gave us something to look forward to and we both worked and saved like mad for that holiday. Paul was still in college at this time. Richard had managed to win Helen's confidence and gain her trust, yet Paul still held himself back. I think Paul's memories of Jim were still raw in his young mind, or perhaps Paul had been the man of the house for a while now and felt reluctant to have another man in our home. In later years, Richard and Paul would become closer together, but they did not bond straight away.

I never quite believed we would ever get to Spain, yet I took on extra work and continued working at the hospital by day and doing private night shifts. I often worked day and night shifts back to back, getting little sleep but earning extra money.

The following summer, 1984, we went off to Spain on a two-week holiday.

We were all excited, though Wayne was too young to appreciate where we were going. He certainly enjoyed himself once he got there. I found it all thrilling and could not believe how hot it was. We were in Benidorm at the

Hotel Torredarada. Wayne loved the pools and Richard played with him in the water. It was waiter-service for drinks at the poolside bar, where we sipped iced Cokes. Some of the waiters were cheeky, trying to chat up some of the younger women guests. One of them asked Richard, 'Which one of them is your woman?'

Richard told him sternly, 'Both of them.' They left Helen and me alone after that. We had a wonderful holiday and came back refreshed and sporting good suntans.

We were not back from holiday very long when Richard asked if he could move in with us, and I readily agreed. After a while, Helen decided she wanted to move out and get her own flat. She told me she was happy at home but wanted to try her independence. She found somewhere not too far away from us, but I missed her dreadfully.

Some nights, if Richard had gone out down the club to his bingo, I went down to her flat with Wayne. The fact that she was living on her own was driving me crazy and I felt she would be lonely. I told her how I felt, but Helen reassured me that while she loved us all very much, she just wanted to 'enjoy her independence' and come home after working all day to a place of her own. She assured me she was enjoying herself, so I had to stop worrying so much about her and give her some space.

Richard's eldest daughter, Mandy, then moved into our home. She was fourteen years old and had been having some teenage tangles with her mum. Paul had been visiting Helen a lot at her flat, they remained very close, and it was not long before Paul moved into a flat directly above Helen. He, too, wanted to find his independence.

I missed both of them, though we saw them regularly. The first Christmas Helen was in her flat, she decorated it up with so many Christmas lights and decorations it looked like Santa's grotto. Wayne loved it when he saw it. Helen loved her Christmas decorations so much that she left them up until the following March!

Paul finished at college and took up work with someone he knew on a window cleaning round. Everything started happening so fast, it was difficult to keep track of it all.

In the midst of all these comings and goings, Richard and I decided to get married. Mandy was elated. We booked the register office for 24 May 1986.

A week before the wedding I had a heart attack. It came on me like a bolt out of the blue, when I was at home, I had been doing some cleaning when I developed a sudden chest pain which would not go away. Helen phoned an ambulance for me.

I was taken to the coronary care unit (CCU) at the Royal Infirmary, where they told me I wouldn't be able to make the wedding. I got so distressed about this that they tried to contact Richard, who was at work and unavailable by phone. When he finally arrived at the hospital, the doctor was waiting for him. He took Richard into a room to talk to him and it was agreed they would allow me to go ahead with the wedding if only he could calm me down.

When they let Richard in to see me, I did calm down when he told me we'd still be able to get married, as long as I settled down and concentrated on getting better. Fortunately it was only a mild heart attack, and it did not take me long to get better and get out of hospital, just in time for our wedding.

In light of what had happened, we had a very small private ceremony, attended only by Wayne and Mandy and our witnesses, Ann and George, who were good friends of ours. We had not planned a bigger wedding, fortunately, which was just as well in light of the heart attack. Helen and Paul were unable to attend the ceremony as they both had to work on that Saturday, they had been unable to get the time off work.

I was still feeling a bit fragile on the day so we got married, went to Brucciani's Café for a cup of tea afterwards and then straight home, where we unwrapped our wedding gifts. After having done this, Richard made me go upstairs to bed for a rest while he went off to have a game of snooker!

That was our honeymoon. Still, the day I married Richard was one of the happiest days of my life.

We loved each other so much and that love would continue to grow with every passing day. Whatever trials and tribulations we were to go through together, nothing would ever shake the love we shared.

Besides being a good husband, he also became a father figure to Wayne. Wayne had started to call Richard 'Dad' and Richard treated Wayne as if he were his own child. He would prove to be a better dad to Wayne than Jim could ever have been. I was so lucky to have met him.

EIGHTEEN

Helen had been going out with a young man from Coalville called David, and she fell pregnant. They came and sat and told us together. I think David was more shocked at the news than we were. Richard reassured them that they were not the first couple this had happened to and they would not be the last. It was not the end of the world.

They started making hasty plans for a wedding. Helen asked if she could give up her flat and move back in with us while they saved up to get married. This proved no hardship to us and we were glad to have her back home. The wedding was arranged and Helen asked Richard to give her away, which he was proud to do. David asked Paul to be best man. After their wedding, Helen and David moved into their own home, a house they were buying, at Coalville, about 12 miles from Leicester.

I had given up my job at the hospital in 1986 and was working instead at a factory, Corah's, in the city. I worked in the medical centre there and loved the work. I took an Occupational Health course at Wigston College, which came in very useful.

Corah's was a huge clothing firm with a number of smaller branch factories, each of which had their own small first-aid rooms and employees that had attended first-aid courses. I was to be responsible not only for our medical centre in Leicester but to be in overall charge of all the other factories' first-aid treatments and supplies. I seemed to have found my niche in occupational health and was in my element working there. A good friend of mine was later given a position there as a nurse, so there were the two of us there full-time. Maria and I got on extremely well together and worked well as a team alongside the health and safety officer. As the factory employed in excess of two thousand employees, it was a responsible position to hold, but I loved it.

We had a medical officer who came in on a weekly basis to do company medicals and was on hand to give us advice. We also had to arrange courses for a certain number of employees to ensure enough first-aiders would be on hand in the event of a large-scale accident. Other employees had to be given basic first-aid practices and knowledge of resuscitation, people like the electricians, maintenance employees and security men. Maria and myself instructed them in first aid with the help of Annie, the plastic model we gave them to practise on.

Maria and I split the different areas of the factory between us. One of my areas was the dye house, where the fabric was coloured. It was a hazardous area and messy as well, but I loved it and guarded my area of it zealously.

If we were called out to an emergency in any part of the factory, we had to run quickly, but it could be very hazardous running through the dye house in a pair of wellies. We had to learn all the different processes in the factory and all about the machinery that was used there, as part of our job was to try and prevent any accidents as well as treat them.

There were many aspects to the job of running the medical centre, and it kept us constantly busy and alert. We both carried bleepers and could be called out to an emergency at a moment's notice. It was inevitable in such a huge factory, with so many employees working there and all the different types of machines that were used, that accidents would happen more or less on a daily basis. Most were minor and a few more serious, but Maria and I thrived on the adrenaline of it all. It was never boring working there, and I loved it.

Helen was married now, they'd had a lovely wedding and we were eagerly awaiting the birth of our first grandchild. Helen had found work at Corah's, as did our Mandy, coming to train as a machinist when she left school at sixteen, so it became quite a family affair.

As Wayne was still young in junior school, a friend of mine, Corrine, who lived on our street helped me out by having Wayne at her house from about 7.45 a.m. until it was time to go to school, which was just around the corner from us. He also went to Corrine's house after school and played with her children until we finished work.

Wayne loved his school and was a good boy but quite a little character by now. He came home one day with a letter from his teacher. He looked very sheepish as he handed it to me, saying, 'I couldn't help it, Mum, it wasn't my fault.'

As I read the letter, I found it difficult to try and look stern. It explained that Wayne had been suspended from school at lunchtimes for a whole week. This was because he had been trying to look up the girls' skirts during playtimes. I sent him to his room until his dad got in from work.

When Richard came home I called Wayne downstairs while he read the letter. Poor lad, he looked so contrite, while we dared not look at each other in case smiles of amusement passed between us. As Wayne got older, we would often recall that time, much to his embarrassment.

As well as Richard and I getting married in 1986, we obtained a mortgage and bought our own home from the council. We had central heating installed so were able to get rid of the open fire and old coke stove in the kitchen, and over the years we would gradually make lots of changes to the house.

1988 was an eventful year for us. In May, Helen's husband David phoned me late one night – Helen had gone into labour. As David did not want to be at the birth, she had asked me to be with her and I was glad to do so. This was my first grandchild, after all. David called to pick me up at our house on his way to taking Helen to the maternity hospital.

Helen was in labour all through the night and part of the next morning, until just after eleven o'clock on 19 May she finally gave birth to a beautiful baby girl. I was so excited and full of love for my new granddaughter. She had blonde hair and beautiful blue eyes. She looked very much like her daddy. Later on during the morning, after I had phoned David and given him the good news, he came to the hospital to see them both and was very proud.

David finally gave me a lift home and I tried to get some sleep after being up all night. Sleep would not come, however; I was on too much of a high.

Richard was very happy when he came in from work to learn the news, and could hardly wait to go and see mother and baby himself. I phoned our Ann in Australia, who answered the phone in a very sleepy voice and, when she realised it was me, said, 'Lyn, do you know what time it is?' I said the time it was in the UK and Ann replied, 'It's bloody three o'clock in the morning.' When I went on to tell her about the birth of Helen's child, though, she too was excited and said it was wonderful news.

Helen and David named their daughter Gemma. She was a beautiful child and is stunning now she is eighteen years old. It had been a great privilege to be at her birth.

Paul had given up his flat by now and was living back home with us, but still had dreams of moving to America. A good friend of Paul's, Ricky, had an aunt who lived there and, after a visit from her, Ricky had decided to go to America to stay with her. Paul was very keen to go too and saved up as much money as he could.

At the end of May, not long after Gemma had been born, Paul decided to give it a go. So off Paul and Ricky went, supposedly to have a holiday with Ricky's aunt and uncle. Paul soon found a job over there and stayed there working for nearly two years. I missed him dreadfully and worried for his safety in a strange country. He wrote to me and phoned occasionally to let me know he was all right, yet still I missed him.

Although Paul was doing well for himself, I suspected that he missed us, too. One time I had a surprise package from Paul with a letter in it. When I opened it, it was a little witch on a broomstick that he had seen and bought for me. I hung it up in my kitchen and treasured it for years, until it finally got broken by one of the grandchildren years afterwards.

Eventually, Mandy left home and moved into a place of her own.

This left just Richard, Wayne and myself at home now. There had been a lot of comings and goings. I was always sorting out pots and pans and household things for one or another of them and our attic had become full of stuff left in storage by the children.

There began to be rumours at Corah's about more redundancies – a lot of employees had lost their jobs recently and it was an anxious time at work, waiting to see who might be next to go. Maria and I were quite worried about it, but the company doctor assured us we would be the last to go should the company go bust.

It was around this time when I started having some pains in my chest and neck. I had suffered from indigestion for quite a while but these pains were more severe and seemed to come on worse with exertion. I tried my best to ignore them, hoping they would just go away.

It was a foolish attitude to have, I suppose. If one of my patients had come to me for advice on the very same symptoms, I would have referred them to a doctor immediately. I, however, chose to plod on. That was until they got so bad that even walking across the huge courtyard of the factory brought on the pain.

As the pains grew worse, I knew something was badly wrong, but I still tried to ignore it. After finishing work one day I had to return to the factory that night for a meeting. Richard gave me a lift back there before going out himself for a game of bingo (Wayne was staying at Helen's house for a few days at the time). As I walked across the courtyard to the personnel department where the meeting was to be held, I had to stop to catch my breath several times as the pain worsened. After the meeting finished, I went home to an empty house, as Richard was not yet back. Going upstairs brought on the pain again, but much worse, and I could hardly breathe. I knew this time I had to seek help, so calmly phoned myself an ambulance and, before I knew it, I was admitted onto the intensive CCU ward.

Richard had arrived home in time to see the ambulance, which he followed, and he showed up as soon as I was put into bed. The next day I was moved onto a medical ward but I just wanted to go home. Richard came in to visit me and I was insisting on going home. The doctors were exasperated with me but I discharged myself and went home anyway. I had promised them I would attend as an outpatient for further tests, which I did during the following two weeks. I did a stress test on the treadmill that was stopped after only minutes. I had not felt any pain by then and had been determined to go as far as I could with the test so they could obtain a good result. The test was abandoned quickly, though, and there was much consulting between technicians and doctor in hushed whispers. Then I had to see a consultant who told me I had to go home and rest – I was being referred to Groby Road Hospital for further tests. He also warned me it could be so serious I might even need heart surgery. I was to go home carefully, he said, not to run or even try to hurry a few steps, it was so serious. I still buried my head in the sand and refused to believe this was happening to me – I even returned to work.

Not long after that I was taken into Groby Road Hospital where an angiogram was performed. When the cardiologist came to see us afterwards – Richard was with me – he patiently explained the results. My right coronary artery was severely obstructed by 90 per cent. I needed an operation.

I was stunned. They sent me home to wait for bypass surgery and I had to go on sick leave from work while waiting for a date. It was while I was waiting for this that the company doctor from Corah's phoned me at home. I guessed what he had to tell me before he said it. The firm was closing down completely and both Maria and I were to be made redundant. Mandy had already left Corah's and was working in another factory.

Poor Maria was left to sort things out in the medical centre on her own and I felt very bad about this, as it all happened so quickly and all the employees were despondent. There wasn't much I could do about it at the time though. I was worrying about my health situation too much.

Richard tried to keep my spirits up and keep me cheerful before the operation, but I worried for my children, our young Wayne especially. I set to work tidying all my cupboards and drawers out at home, just in case. Richard came in one day as I was having a few tears.

'What's wrong, ducky?' he asked. I explained I was scared. 'Here, this will cheer you up,' he said, as he put some music on the stereo and out blasted Gene Pitney's 'I'm Gonna Be Strong'. In fact, it made me feel even worse, as the first line, to which Richard sang along, is 'I can see, you're slipping away from me'!

I finally went in for the bypass surgery, having the operation on 8 August 1988.

Wayne was only nine years old at the time and, as it was during the summer break from school, Helen and David had agreed he could stay with them for two weeks while I had the surgery and recovered a bit. Richard was self-employed at the time and needed to go to work or he would not get paid. We still had to pay our mortgage and other household bills. I was really grateful to Helen, as it meant Richard could visit me after work while I was in hospital and I knew Wayne was being looked after well.

I did not want Wayne visiting me at such a young age, I felt it would be too upsetting for him. That's when he sent the letter to me, which Helen brought in, telling me he was having a good time and hoped I was too. Bless him, he did not understand. He has told me years later that he thought I had gone off on a sort of holiday.

Wayne's letter cheered me up immensely when I read it in hospital. I quickly wrote him a short reply to send back with Helen, reassuring him I was well, and that I was looking forward to seeing him soon. Wayne was to tell me later he had kept the letter in the pocket of his jeans and treasured it. One night, after he had gone to bed at Helen's, he suddenly remembered he had put his jeans to the wash. He panicked, in case Helen had started the wash, got up and ran downstairs, where he managed to rescue the letter. From then on for the duration of his stay at Helen's, he had kept it safely tucked up inside his sock, and would not be parted from it. When Wayne told me that tale, it made me realise the importance of staying in contact with your children during periods of separation, however short that period may be!

The surgery went well and I was discharged after only one week. Richard was fitting a new bathroom for us at the time and, though he'd managed to refit a new bathroom suite, he had not finished the tiling before they sent me home. He had been trying to surprise me and looked crestfallen when I told him I was being discharged.

'What's wrong, ducky, don't you want me to come home?'

'Well, yeah,' he replied, 'but I've not finished the bathroom yet.'

NINETEEN

It took me about three months to recover properly. We had been booked to go to Spain on holiday that year, with Wayne and good friends of ours, George and Ann, but had to cancel the holiday at the last minute as I was not allowed to fly.

We did, however, manage to get the all clear from the surgeon on my six-weekly post-operation checkup. As soon as the surgeon informed Richard and I that I could fly, Richard was in the car and straight to the travel agent. He very soon arranged another holiday for us. We set off for Spain in the September and, though I was still a bit frail, we still managed to have a lovely holiday.

Our Paul, of course, was still in America. He had been worried about me but I assured him I was fine on the occasions he phoned. I always loved hearing his voice when he called. On one occasion he phoned me to tell me he had bought a new car. 'It's a Toyota Tercell, Mum,' he told me proudly.

I replied, 'Well what do you want to sell it for, Paul, if you've only just bought it?'

'No, Mum, that's the make of the car,' he informed me, giving a hearty laugh.

We had lost Richard's father in April 1988. Richard's dad, Albert, was a lovely man, a retired shoe clicker. This was an occupation that meant that Albert had to cut out heels and uppers in leather for shoes, by hand, in the days before machinery took over this task. They had been married since 1946. Richard's mum Dorothy, known as Dot, had lost her first husband during the war. She married Albert, and they had two sons, Robert and Richard. Albert had two sons from a previous marriage and Dot had a son and daughter. They had brought all six children up together as one family. Richard's family was not a close-knit one, but I had got close to Albert and Dot from when Richard and I first met. Albert, an athletic man in his youth – he was Midlands high-jump champion in 1933 – had been frail for a number of years and Dot looked after him herself at their flat.

As his health deteriorated, it became increasingly difficult for Dot to cope. Albert suffered a number of falls around the flat and she needed a break, so we arranged for Albert to go to a nursing home for two weeks, while Dot came to our house. It was while Dot was with us that we received the phone call late one night to say that Albert had died. His heart had failed him, at the age of 82.

Richard arranged the death certificate, the funeral and everything for his mum, while she remained with us until after the funeral.

We offered her a home at our house, but she wanted to go back to the flat and keep her own home. We understood this and visited her as often as we could and had her to our house every Sunday. Wayne was very close to Dot, his adopted grandma. He used to put the TV on for her as I prepared lunch and get her to watch *Lost in Space* and other kids' programmes with him. I've got to say, Dot seemed to enjoy watching these programmes as much as our Wayne did.

This set the pattern for years to come; Dot was part of the family. She was in her seventies, but still managed to go down into town some days with her friend to the bingo hall. Dot had always liked her bingo, and I guess this is where Richard got his liking for it. So Sundays became a regular family day at our house, as Richard's three daughters and Helen and Paul and their families often came round too.

As our family continued to grow, Christmas days could be very hectic. It was not unusual for us to have up to eighteen or more of the family as more of our children grew up and brought their respective partners and our grandchildren to our house on Christmas Day. We still have Christmas family videos of when our home would be packed full of kids. I suppose it was a bit like that TV series, *The Royle Family*, only there were more of us.

In November 1988 I applied for a job at Groby Road Hospital. It was a bit early to be thinking of returning to work following the bypass surgery, but we still had a mortgage to pay as well as all the other household bills. Richard continued working as a plumber, in fact, he would never miss a day's work. He had been brought up that way and he was always a good provider. I had worked for a good part of my life, though, and felt I wanted to be able to contribute to our earnings.

I was offered a post on the outpatients department at the hospital and started there in early December. It was a very busy department as it not only covered Leicestershire and surrounding areas, but also had a huge catchment area as far as Lincoln. The work there was not only busy but could also be very stressful but, on the whole, I enjoyed the work and found it a challenge.

In 1989 I was to learn of my own mother's death. My sister Betty contacted me and told me that Mam had cancer. She had been taken into South Moor Hospital where both Betty and I had completed our nurse training. As Mam had severed all contact with us all, Betty had only found out about her because a sister at the hospital phoned her to notify her of Mam's deteriorating condition.

Betty went to visit her in hospital where she was indeed very poorly. I chose not to go up North to see her in her last days – I felt it would have been hypocritical. Even when Mam died on 21 September 1989 I did not go up for the funeral. I believe our Ann was upset at the news, but she was unable to attend the funeral as they were in Australia. I felt very sad at losing my mother but more saddened by the fact that there had been no reconciliation with her. She had made it so plain to all of us daughters that she wanted nothing more to do with any of us. The night I had phoned her, after Ann, David, Angela and Stuart left for Australia, was really the night it finally drove it home to me that she wanted to sever all contact with her family. There were still feelings of guilt left in me, for our failed relationship and there always would be.

In December 1989, Helen was due to give birth to her second child. It was planned for her to have the baby in hospital but it did not work out that way. We received a frantic phone call from David, who told us she had already had the baby at home. He was a bit incoherent on the phone. Richard and I got in the car straight away and drove to their home.

It turned out that when Helen had gone into labour, everything happened very quickly. She'd got David to phone for an ambulance, but this had to come all the way from Loughborough and David had been warned it could take some time to get there. As the birth became more imminent, Helen had told David to fetch Judy, the next-door neighbour.

She had to shout to David, 'Don't you dare faint on me!' as he had gone very white and slumped against the wall.

By the time David managed to get their neighbour to come around, Helen was upstairs in their bedroom, giving birth to the baby while she stood up. Helen told her neighbour to hold on to the baby, as she was terrified he would fall to the floor.

A midwife eventually arrived and between the neighbour and the midwife, they managed to get Helen onto the bed, where the midwife quickly cut the umbilical cord and sorted everything out. The ambulance finally got there to find mother and baby fine, though David nearly needed it himself.

In the end, the midwife decided all was well and Helen and the new baby could stay at home. It had literally been 'stand and deliver'. We got over there to find Helen tucked up in bed with her baby son, our grandson, whom they named James Andrew. I held him in my arms and felt my heart swell with love and pride. He was gorgeous, with blonde hair and blue eyes like his daddy.

James was grandchild number two. Richard and I now had six children and two grandchildren between us. We were very proud.

It certainly gave me something to tell my friends and fellow nurses at work, and caused some amusement. And when I phoned up my sisters to give them the good news, I made sure I was careful of the time I chose to phone our Ann in Australia.

TWENTY

I continued working at Groby Road Hospital and would have my checkups with my cardiologist while I was at work. I just got on with my work in one of the surgeon's clinics until it was my turn to be seen, then I got another nurse to cover my clinic while I nipped across the corridor to have my checkup.

One day in May 1990, after finishing one of our clinics, I was sorting out the patients' notes when I started getting in a big tangle with the Sellotape and seemed disorientated. I looked at the clock in the room but I could not see the time. The sight in my left eye had gone. It was like a curtain had come down over it, obscuring my sight. I told another staff nurse that I worked with and she soon had me in a wheelchair, as by then I had lost the use of my left hand, arm and leg. She took me to our staff room and called one of the surgeons, who was on his way out of the department back to the wards.

He quickly came up with his diagnosis; I had suffered a stroke. I was immediately admitted to one of the wards. Another good friend of mine from the department, Doreen, sat with me as I was put into bed. She sat beside me and stroked my hand and arm so kindly while they tried to contact Richard. He was told to get to the hospital at once, but it was not until he got there that the doctors told him the diagnosis. The following morning I had an angiogram of my brain to confirm the diagnosis.

When Richard was allowed to visit me the next day, the cardiologist also came to see me. I expressed a wish to go home and my doctor agreed, as he said not much more would be done for me right away as it was a weekend. So Richard brought me home and cared for me himself. We had not told the rest of the family yet as we did not want to worry them. Richard coped extremely well and even went up and collected his mum on the Sunday and brought her down. He made the Sunday lunch for us all, but in the afternoon Helen and David turned up with Gemma and James.

Richard had to jump up quickly so he could take Helen into the kitchen and explain as gently as possible what had happened to me. I sat helplessly in an armchair. Naturally, Helen was shocked and tearful but pulled herself together for my sake. I found it difficult myself to accept what had happened and probably would have gone into a state of depression had it not been for Richard. 'Don't worry, ducky, you'll soon get better, we'll manage, just you wait and see,' he assured me.

So he ran the household, looked after Wayne and me, as well as himself, did all the meals, washing and shopping and still found time to go to work. Wayne was a good little helper himself and Richard used to leave Wayne in charge and give him instructions about keeping an eye on me and reporting back to him if I tried to do anything I shouldn't.

'You tell me, Wayne, if your mother tries to do anything,' he'd say.

'I will, Dad, I'll watch her,' Wayne would reply, feeling important at being in charge.

Richard would nip home from work in the day to take me up to physiotherapy two or three times a week. Even days when I did not feel like going, he insisted.

I rebelled. The physiotherapist made me work so hard and even smacked me lightly on the bottom if she thought I wasn't trying hard enough at my walking exercises. I wanted to stop going, but Richard would not give in to me and made sure I attended all my physiotherapy appointments and continued my exercises at home.

'I'm not going back,' I would tell him after one of the sessions.

'Oh yes you are,' he'd say to me. 'You'll go back and you'll do those exercises and you'll keep doing them until you get right again.'

I could easily have given in to my stroke had it not been for Richard. He pushed me and pushed me to try harder, and he kept my spirits up when I was low. 'You *will* get better,' he insisted. 'Just do as you are told and keep going.'

Eventually, after months of hard work and sheer determination, I recovered from the stroke and went back to work in the outpatients department, having been on sick leave for six months.

Paul arrived home from America in the winter of 1990. I was so glad to see him again. He looked tanned and fit and was now an extremely handsome young man. It was so good to have my eldest son home again, he was as good as a tonic to me, as he made me laugh with all his tales of America.

Though he was happy to be back home, he soon noticed the difference of being back in the UK. He said the whole place looked littered compared to the state of the streets of New Hampshire in America. He also missed the sunshine and was still filled with a sense of travel and adventure. He was happy to see Helen and Wayne and, of course, Gemma, who had been a tiny baby when he had left. He was also able to make acquaintance with James, his new baby nephew.

While Paul was back from America he met Becky, and they started dating. Becky was younger than Paul, a lovely girl with very dark brown eyes and hair so dark it was almost black. She lived at home with her mum and dad, Bev and Jim.

It was not very long before Paul wanted to return to America, but he and Becky were very much in love by now and he wanted her to go with him. He spoke to Bev and Jim about it, as Becky was still young. Her parents finally agreed to her going, so once again Paul set off for America, this time with Becky.

He found a job working on a huge golf course, attending the grounds. They also had a house to live in together, but it was so remote that poor Becky got homesick. She was left on her own while Paul had to work long hours, and the loneliness proved too much for her; she eventually returned to her parents' house in the UK.

Though Paul enjoyed working in America so much, he felt desolate once Becky had left. He realised how much he loved her, so it was a very short time afterwards that Paul followed Becky back home. This time, he moved in to Bev and Jim's house to be with Becky, while they saved up for a home of their own. I was so glad to have them back in England.

While all this was going on I had suffered another mild stroke at work. This time I was off sick for about four months and, although I eventually went back to work, I was not as good as I should have been. I had lost a lot of peripheral vision in both eyes by now. My blood pressure was sky high and I had some partial blockages in my femoral and both carotid arteries.

My cardiologist sat me down and talked to me during one of my checkups. 'Don't you think enough is enough?' he asked. He also warned me my health was in danger if I continued to work on the busy outpatients department, and it was his opinion that I be retired out of the NHS on health grounds.

I was completely devastated. Richard came to pick me up from work that night and could see I had been crying.

When he asked me what was wrong, I was unable to tell him for fear of breaking down in tears again.

He waited until we were home and managed to get the whole tale out of me. When I had told him, Richard said, 'That's it, then, get your coat on, I'm taking you to the doctor's.' So he took me down to see our GP, Dr Goodchild, who gave me a medical certificate so I could stay on sick leave until my retirement date was set.

'What will I do with myself now?' I asked Richard. I knew I would miss my job, and I would miss the patients as well as my fellow nurses.

Richard assured me, 'I'm sure you'll find something to fill your time in, you still have me and Wayne here.'

Though I was so devastated at that time, it was for the best, I realise that now. I continued to suffer from TIAs – trans-ischaemic attacks – for which I was put onto aspirin and warfarin for anticoagulation, as tiny blood clots were breaking off from my carotid arteries and going to the brain.

TWENTY-ONE

Jim had still been having access to Wayne while he was young. He would pick Wayne up from our house on a Saturday morning, then bring him back to us by about 6 p.m. The court had ordered reasonable access, but his visits were sporadic and often Jim would be obviously drunk when he returned Wayne to us.

Wayne also used to tell us about his time spent with Jim and it was obvious to both Richard and me that these visits were doing him more harm than good.

Jim had remarried by then and had another baby daughter. Wayne often told us of the rows between Jim and his new wife, and of the violence that often occurred between Jim and her on these occasions. I decided to take the matter of access back to court again.

After numerous meetings between social workers, they agreed that it was not in Wayne's best interest for Jim to have any more access. Jim even turned up drunk on a few occasions at meetings with the social workers. It was eventually heard in court and the judge spoke to us all in turn. At one stage in the proceedings, Jim was nearly thrown out of court as he continually interrupted the judge. He was warned by his own solicitor to keep quiet or he would be in contempt of court.

The judge even took young Wayne – he was eleven at the time – into his own chambers, took off his wig and gown and spoke to him on his own. After this, the judge returned to his bench and ordered that all access to Wayne from Jim was to be stopped until such time as Wayne was old enough to decide for himself if he wanted to see his biological father again.

It was a good decision as far as I was concerned. Jim had done enough emotional harm to myself, Helen and Paul, and I did not want Wayne to suffer any more trauma from him.

Richard continued to bring Wayne up as if he was his own son and a close father/son relationship is still there today. Yet Wayne is always very close to me too.

He was my baby, I suppose. As far as Wayne is concerned, I think it's fair to say the cord has never been cut. He made lots of friends as he went through school, bringing lots of them home. A great mate of Wayne's, Steven, stayed at our house so much I think he was with us more than his own home.

Richard and I became so used to having Steven stay over we would think it odd if we got up in the mornings and he wasn't there for his breakfast. They became soul mates and still are to this day, even though they're both married and have their own families.

After all contact with Jim was stopped in March 1991, Wayne was able to enjoy a proper family life and childhood.

Ann and David had been over to the UK a few times. David frequently had to travel to the UK and other countries as part of his job. He had worked his way up in his company in Australia and was now a manager.

We were all very proud at how well he had done since moving to Australia. While we still missed them all, I realised they had a much better lifestyle there than they ever would have had in this country.

It was February 1982 when they had emigrated. Angela was eight and Stuart five years old at the time. Ann and I exchanged letters regularly and Ann sent me photos of the family on a regular basis so I could see how they were growing up.

She also sent me photos of all the different children that she and David were short-term foster parents for. They fostered mentally and physically handicapped children for seven years, including once a pair of Siamese twins. All of the children would be welcomed into their home and received loving attention from not only Ann and David but Angela and Stuart as well. The fact that a lot of the children they looked after were handicapped never fazed Angela and Stuart. They always shared their own toys with them and sometimes their beds.

I could not believe it sometimes when I received photos of the children – when Stuart was only twelve years old, he was already five feet nine inches tall. Angela was also growing up tall and was a beautiful-looking girl.

Ann and David were so good to all of their children, and I felt very proud of them.

Ann had suffered a lot of health problems herself since moving to Australia, and it was fortunate that David had private health care in place. She had to have a hysterectomy because of a cancer scare. I bought a tape recorder, did a pep talk for her and sent it off for David to take into the hospital for her.

She also suffered terrible arthritic joints before it was discovered she had a disease similar to lupus that was causing acids to eat into her joints. She had many, many operations to try and relieve or repair her poor joints and, after several operations on her hands, eventually she had to have a finger amputated. She went through all of this and soldiered bravely on, even after two operations for bowel obstructions. I worried about her a lot.

Then we got a shock one year when we found out that David had been very ill with legionnaire's disease and had been in intensive care in hospital. David has always been one to plod on – he doesn't like hospitals. He had no choice that time, though, as he could have died. At first, when they tried to trace where he had caught the disease, it was thought he might have caught it from his work. Inspectors had been all over New South Wales until they finally discovered the cause – bags of compost that David had been using on his garden!

Towards the end of 1991, David had to travel to the USA and Canada for his work and managed to make it a family trip and pull in some holiday time to include a stay in the UK. We were all very excited at the prospect and could hardly wait to see them all again, though this was not the first time they had been back on a visit to us. After they finished their stay in the USA and Canada, they finally made it over to Britain, where they all stayed with David's parents, Molly and Jack.

It was arranged with Betty that we would go up to their house for Christmas and would all have Christmas lunch out at a local restaurant and would make it one big, happy family gathering. When we finally met up we were all over each other. Our Angela was by then eighteen years old and Stuart was fifteen. Even though Ann had sent me photos, we still found it hard to believe how much they had grown, they were so tall, and Angela was a beautiful young lady with her hair permed, all glorious red curls. Stuart was very tall too and looked a proper young man. It did not seem possible to me that this was the same boy that I had changed nappies for when he was a baby. It was hard to believe that here was my niece and nephew I had looked after so many times while we lived up in the North. I had taken them on so many walks into the woods and here they were now, all grown up.

'I've seen your bare bum a time or two,' I joked with Stuart, much to his embarrassment, as he blushed bright red and gave me his lovely, shy smile.

'You won't be seeing it again, Aunty Lyn,' he quipped back to me.

We all spent a wonderful Christmas together but too soon had to return back down to Leicester. It had been arranged that they would all come down and stay with us later before making the final journey down to London to fly back home. At least we had that visit to look forward to.

Plans changed with our Angela though. I think she got bored being in the UK, but whatever the reason, she got her dad to fix her up with an earlier flight and returned to Australia on her own.

When Ann, David and Stuart finally came down after Christmas, they stayed with us and we spent some quality time together, though it was freezing weather at the time. Wayne took Stuart round to one of his mate's who lived nearby. Stuart left a good impression on the whole family, especially Emily, one of the sisters. I think he had a secret fancy for Emily as I caught him peeping out our dining room window early one morning trying to catch a glimpse of her.

'What are you doing up so early, Stuart?' I asked him.

'Just looking out of your window, Aunty Lyn, to see what the weather is like,' he replied with his special, wonderful smile.

I had startled him slightly, but he would not admit to this. 'As long as that's all you're doing,' I said, giving him a hug.

It was good having that time with them all and they regaled us with their tales of the different countries they had visited. We all got on extremely well together, and it was a very happy time.

As it all too soon became time for them to return to Australia, Richard and David sat with their maps out planning the route for London. Richard suggested we should say our goodbyes at home, but that we would still get in our car and drive ahead of David in his rental car as far as the motorway, to ensure they joined at the right junction, number 21. Richard warned me that we had to get all the goodbyes out of the way at home, as they would have to get on with their journey to make sure they made it to Heathrow on time. 'I know you, ducky, you'll be wanting to give them tuck bags for the journey and all that, but they won't have time to waste,' he warned me.

It was very early in the morning that they had to leave, and still dark. We had breakfast, said our goodbyes and off we went, Richard and myself in our car leading the way for David in theirs.

When we came to the slip road for junction 21, I insisted Richard stop the car and flag David over. I had forgotten in our haste to give Stuart some spending money for him to use at the airport. In reality, I just did not want to part with them. 'Hurry up, then,' said Richard. 'I warned you last night they haven't got much time, so be quick.'

We pulled over, I hurried to their car, gave our Stuart some money and just had to give them all a last kiss and cuddle. After that, we watched their car disappear onto the motorway on their way to London, then turned our car around on the island to drive home again. A rabbit ran out in front of our car. Fortunately for the rabbit, we missed it, but when 'Bright Eyes' came onto the radio, I felt it was an omen and I cried all the way home.

'Don't cry, ducky,' Richard comforted me. 'We'll see them all again, I'll see to that.'

Later that same year, 1992, we learned that Becky was pregnant with her and Paul's first child. They were still living with Bev and Jim but were hoping to get a home of their own in time. As it rolled around to Christmas, we were all anxiously awaiting the birth of Paul and Becky's baby.

We were having Richard's mum round for Christmas lunch, then Helen, David and their family were due over for tea. We were also expecting Richard's daughters, Mandy, Wendy and Joanne, all with their respective partners, and Paul and Becky were invited too, so it looked like being a full house once again.

On Christmas Eve, though, Becky was taken into hospital. Paul stayed with her throughout her labour and in the early hours of Christmas morning she gave birth to a beautiful baby girl, Brogan. Paul phoned us to let us know and it was the best Christmas gift we could have wished for. Paul said 'it had been the best and also the worst' day of his life. He had spent all night with Becky up until the birth of their daughter, but then had to go and get some sleep as he had a terrible migraine. Richard and I went later in the morning to see Becky and our new baby granddaughter. She was beautiful with very dark hair like Becky, but lovely blue eyes. I sat with her in my arms and felt so lucky. Richard was busy capturing it all on video.

When we got back home and all the rest of the family arrived, we could proudly show them the video of Becky and Brogan on the TV. That was a happy Christmas.

The following February Paul and Becky were married. Betty and Eric were invited to the wedding and came and stayed with us for a week. We all attended the register office where the ceremony was held and later went back to Bev and Jim's, where a small reception was held with close family and some of their friends.

I felt extremely proud of all my family that day. Betty was in her element to be able to hold little Brogan, in fact, we all had to take it in turns to hold her. Paul and Becky made a lovely couple and Paul gave a lovely speech.

The only blot on their wedding day was when my grandson, James, got overexcited and was sick all over poor Bev's floor. But, all in all, it was a marvellous day and I gained a wonderful daughter-in-law.

TWENTY-TWO

It was not all good news in 1993, however. Later on that year we were to get a terrible shock, when a tragedy happened that would shake all of our family to its very core.

This is a part of my life I am going to find very painful to narrate. I have to include it in my story, yet I know it's going to cause me great pain and sorrow as I write of it.

It was in June 1993 that we received the phone call from David in Australia. His voice heavy with pain, he told us that Stuart had been in a car accident and, tragically, had been killed. At first I could not believe it. Surely it could not be true. My beloved nephew, Stuart, only seventeen years old, had died. We had seen him last as a lovely young man when they left us in early 1992.

We had all enjoyed their visit so much. When I had made Richard stop the car so I could run and give Stuart some spending money for the airport and have my last kiss and cuddle of them all, little did I know then that it would be the last time I would ever hug Stuart. The baby I had looked after when he had been so young. I had changed his nappies, and had teased him over this on their last visit to us. He had grown up to be a fine young man, such a pride and joy to Ann and David, such a wonderful brother to Angela.

Stuart had always loved children. As Ann and David had fostered handicapped children over a period of seven years, Stuart and Angela had always been so good with them, sharing their toys, their rooms, Stuart had even shared his bed with those children. He would always treat them as if they were his own brothers and sisters. He had been so much like his dad, always ready to see good in other people. He had loved his friends and took gifts back for all of them on that last visit abroad.

At one time, Stuart had thought of becoming a priest. He had a Bible that his Aunty Jean had given him and our Ann often found him in his room, reading his Bible. He had also been learning to play the guitar. His favourite song was 'Knocking on Heaven's Door'. I found it so hard to accept he had gone – I did not want to believe it.

David had phoned us on the Saturday in the UK, and as they were twelve hours ahead of us, it meant Stuart had died in the early hours of their Sunday morning, 13 June 1993.

Richard pointed out that we had to inform our family and took it upon himself to phone Helen's husband. He told him to sit Helen down gently, to explain to her what had happened. He then phoned up our Paul and notified him of the sad news of his cousin's death. I was too distraught to be able to do this. Wayne and his mate Steven were just coming in now, so he had to be told; he and Steven went upstairs to Wayne's bedroom. I think they found it too painful to listen to my howling.

Next thing, our Betty was on the phone to me, she too was distraught and was asking me to go with her to Australia for Stuart's funeral. I could not talk to her much and said I would discuss it later. I had been having angina for a while, and was waiting for results of an earlier test, so Richard was worried about me going all the way over there.

I asked Richard to take me to see our Paul. We got in the car and went to talk to Paul, who was himself in tears and very distressed. Paul, who had always been so close to his Aunty Ann, Uncle David and his cousins, was feeling the shock of it all. When Richard discussed the possibility of me going to Australia with Betty, Paul was worried about me going as well. Between Richard and Paul, they made me promise to think twice about it before deciding. Paul had tears streaming down his cheeks as he told me, 'I don't think you're up to it, Mum, Richard is right. We would all worry about you if you try to go. Aunty Ann and Uncle David would not expect you to go.'

We came home and I cried all evening. I imagined the pain that Ann, David and Angela were suffering and found that so hard to bear. I managed very little sleep that night, even though I had taken a sleeping tablet.

Next morning, on the Sunday, I was up at the crack of dawn. I was thinking of Molly and Jack, Stuart's grandma and granddad and how they must be feeling. When Richard came downstairs I told him I had to go and see them, and he agreed immediately. We told Wayne we were going and would be home that night, and off we set for the trip up North, where we went straight to Molly and Jack's. Molly was coping; she had to, as Jack was devastated. He was crying and looked like a broken man.

We sat with them awhile then went and saw Betty and her family. They too were devastated and we all cried together.

We had to set off back home to Wayne, I had cried all the way there and I cried all the way back again. Richard was so distressed at my pain and could only keep patting my arm and leg all the way home as he was driving. I could see how concerned he was for me, though he, too, was very shocked. I was inconsolable.

I went to church on the Monday. There was no service on but I wanted to sit in the empty church and pray for

Stuart and his sister and mum and dad. I felt I was in shock – it was like a nightmare I could not wake up from.

I sat there for ages and ages in the deserted church, saying my prayers, awash with scalding tears streaming down my face. Eventually, the cleaner of the church, an Irish lady, came out and told me to 'Stop all that crying and get your prayers said.' I think she was impatient to get all the aisles swept up so she could go.

Later that day, I phoned up and spoke to my cardiologist's secretary about the possibility of me flying out to Australia. She told me it would be unwise to travel at this time as I was waiting for another angiogram to be done on my heart. I had to let Betty know I could not go with her. We'd spoken to Ann and David and they agreed that it would be better if I did not go. Instead, Molly and Jack flew out to Australia, as did Betty and Eric.

I bitterly regretted not being there for the funeral and not being able to say my last goodbye to Stuart. He was given a wonderful service, where the church was packed with family and many, many friends. Stuart's guitar tutor sang 'Knocking on Heaven's Door' at the funeral and they played the music 'Tears in Heaven'. David later sent me a tape of the funeral service. My beloved nephew Stuart was cremated and they had a further service for him privately on a ledge off Sugar Loaf Mountain, where his ashes were scattered to the winds. It was a mountain he had always loved as a child.

My pain at losing Stuart was immense, so I could not imagine the pain that Ann, David and Angela would be going through. My heart ached for them all.

I felt a bitter regret that twelve thousand miles separated us at a time as drastic as this. I wanted to be there with them to try and offer them some comfort, yet my heart told me that no one could ever console them enough to ease the pain of losing a son and a brother.

I prayed hard for them all.

TWENTY-THREE

Joanne, Richard's youngest daughter, got married and went on to have two children: Thomas, who is now twelve, and Ashleigh, ten.

Mandy met and married a nice lad, Tim, and that was another happy wedding day. They had their reception in Tim's parents' garden on a hot summer's day. Richard, as father of the bride, made a lovely, laid-back speech. They later went on to have a son, George, on 31 January 1996, another lovely grandson for us.

Sadly, neither of their marriages lasted, but they are both now happy and settled once more. Mandy brings George to see us nearly every single weekend, although she lives well over an hour's drive away from us.

What happened to their marriages are their stories to tell, not mine. We worried a lot at the time, that's natural for parents however old our children are, but they sorted themselves out and we are glad they are once more settled.

George is growing up so fast now, he's a lovely lad and I often find chores for him to do now he's older. I'm sure he's going to be an enterprising young man in a few years' time.

'Sweep the yard for me, please,' I'll ask him.

'OK,' says George, 'what rates do you pay?'

Mandy has become very close to me in recent years. She is very much like her dad and has a lot of Richard's characteristics: she is easy-going and a hard worker. She is dependable and has been there for me a lot in these last few years, when I needed help. She's her dad's girl, but is still close to me, and has been a good daughter.

Wendy, Richard's middle daughter, has not yet married. She is engaged and, who knows, perhaps we'll have more grandchildren.

Unfortunately, Helen's marriage also broke down, but once again, that is her story to tell. She later moved to a house nearer to us. We were always very close to Helen. As she matured, she grew out of her shell more and is certainly not as shy as she used to be. She is a lot more outgoing now and has a wonderful, caring nature. She became very close to Richard from the first onset of our relationship together in the early years and looks on Richard as her father figure. Indeed, Helen would often heed Richard's advice much more than she would ever heed mine.

When Helen had to look after the children on her own they would be at our house most weekends. We took them out to parks and the seaside whenever we could, right from when Gemma and James were little children, and we gained a lot of enjoyment in doing so. We have had so much pleasure in watching them grow up.

Now Gemma and James are growing older, they are more independent. Gemma has always been a close and loving granddaughter and I don't think that will ever change. She is eighteen years old now, has done her A levels and has a boyfriend of her own. Yet it seems no time at all since she was about two years old and Richard and I had taken her with us one day, when we went to Plumb-centre in town. Whilst we discussed the price of something we were going to buy, I had looked around suddenly for Gemma who had escaped my hand, and she sat there innocently using a toilet that was in the middle of the showroom, and was not even properly installed! It caused much amusement to other customers and staff. 'Don't worry about it, they all do that,' one of the staff assured me! James has a lovely nature. He is a very loving boy, who is sixteen years old and has turned into a handsome young man starting to show an interest in girls. He comes to cut our hedge and lawns now – he's a good little worker. He is building up a thriving little business, gardening for people. Yet it does not seem long since he was very young, and at the age of about two would eat worms or anything else that crawled.

They have shared so much love with us over the years, yet I can close my eyes and still see them as babies. Where has the time gone?

Helen always regretted not having followed her dream to become a nurse. After she moved over to Leicester, as Gemma and James became older, she got a job in the x-ray department at Leicester Royal Infirmary as a helper. As she was doing this work, she also studied very hard and finally got A levels in many subjects, including psychology. She then went on to do a degree course at Leicester University and completed her nurse's training. We were very proud of her the day we attended De Montfort Halls to watch the degree-presentation ceremony. It was all done with pomp and ceremony and I almost cried with joy as I saw Helen receive her degree in her gown and mortarboard. It had been her dream for so long, I was glad to be able to witness her achieving it.

As soon as she qualified, she got a job as a district nurse, and enjoys her work. Helen seems to have found her niche in her chosen field of work. She has also met someone else now, Steve, and they are engaged. They have bought a house of their own together where they have set up home with Gemma and James, and new baby Jamie.

After Paul and Becky's marriage in 1993, they eventually bought their own home. Paul had to do this house up from top to bottom and it took him some time to do it, as he works long hours as manager of a well-known shop Pilot in town, where he has worked for a good number of years.

It's now a lovely house with French doors that open onto a huge back garden with trees and lawn. It's lucky they have such a beautiful garden, where they have slides and swings and loads of room for children to play. Paul and Becky went on to have three more children. Millie, who is six years old, looks like a little angel, she is in fact called Millie Angel. She is a lively, free-spirited child who is adorable. Then they had Finn, born in July 2002, their first son. He is such a happy, lovable child. In July 2005 they had their fourth child, a second son they named Tate. He is beautiful and such a happy, placid baby. Tate looks so much like Paul did when he was a baby of that age, that when I hold him in my arms, it's like stepping back in time 38 years ago. All of Paul and Becky's children look just like their daddy, but Brogan has lovely dark hair like her mum. Though Brogan is now thirteen, it seems like yesterday that I held her in my arms and she sweetly sang most of the words to 'I Will Always Love You' a song by Dolly Parton that we had on the stereo at the time, as she snuggled onto my shoulder. Millie, Finn and baby Tate are all blonde-haired and blue-eyed, and they look so much like Paul.

Becky is a wonderful mum and Richard and I often wonder how she copes so well. Paul is an excellent father and provider for his family.

Wayne was the baby of the family. He enriched not only my life but Richard's life too. As Richard and I met before Wayne was four years old, he accepted the role of being a dad to Wayne with no qualms at all. Richard has been an excellent dad to Wayne and Wayne knows this. Their relationship has always been a two-way one. Wayne has always showed Richard his love and respect.

Wayne has brought a lot of joy into our lives. He has always been like the Pied Piper as far as other children are concerned and remains the same now at 26 years old. He has always been like a magnet to all the grandchildren as they have come along in later years. He has a way with children.

Wayne used to love it when our house was full of family, he would be in his element. With being so young when Richard and I got together, he was the luckiest child out of my three children, inasmuch as we had got over the poorer times and were able to take him on holiday every year with us. Christmas times were not so much of a struggle as when Helen and Paul were young, when I was on my own with the children. Yet Wayne remained unspoiled and never in his life took anything for granted.

We were able to take him away so much more than our other children, but that was a sign of the times. We encouraged Wayne to take up a paper round, which he did for many years. He would save up his wages from the paper round until he wanted to buy something for himself. Wayne always wanted to be busy doing something and helped me a great deal. We used to work well together, either in the house or on the garden. He was always a good little worker.

We took him to Spain, Tenerife, Cyprus and Florida. To be honest, I think it was Richard who wanted to go to the States the most. That had been a childhood dream of his, to go to Disneyland. We were to go there four times over the years.

We even witnessed a twister on one of our holidays in Florida. It had been a bright, sunny day as we frolicked in the pool of the Ted Williams Motel. The three of us had the pool to ourselves that day. We were relaxing in between busy days spent visiting theme parks. A black American gentleman walked by us saying, 'It's gonna rain, I can smell it,' in a Southern drawl. There was hardly a cloud in sight. Less than half an hour later, dark clouds had started to form and we decided to go back to our room. When afternoon rain showers come in Florida, we had learned by now that they tended to come quickly.

'Come on, Mum,' laughed Wayne as he sprinted off, 'I'll race you.' He knew full well my racing days were over. 'You took your time,' he observed as I puffed and panted up the stairs.

We put on the TV to watch the news, as there was a hurricane warning at the time. Just as the weather forecaster was updating on the forthcoming path of the hurricane out in the Atlantic Ocean, everything went black. The TV went off, as did all power in the motel and surrounding areas. The heavens opened up with rain and an almighty wind got up. Within a few minutes, the twister was all around us. Thunder and lightning crashed and flashed as the roof of the walkway where we had been minutes earlier flew past our window, along with light fittings from the pool and other objects. It was quite terrifying and Wayne and I huddled together on the bed as Richard watched the storm, with me screaming at him to get away from the windows. It was over in less than an hour, but everywhere was left without electricity as bare power cables floated in the pool. The car park outside was half-covered in water. We were amazed and our mood was slightly more sombre by now, though Richard took it all in his stride.

Richard used to tease Wayne so much when he was a young boy and Wayne would fall for it over and over again. We would be out in the car somewhere and Richard would say to me with a wink, 'Do you know, Lyn, I think Wayne is sprouting a moustache like me.' I would carry the joke on by gently having a stroke over Wayne's top lip.

'Yes,' I would agree, 'I can feel the whiskers starting to grow,' and for the rest of the journey we would watch him on the sly as he kept feeling his top lip, for the hairs he could imagine he was growing. We would compound the joke then by saying, 'I reckon he's soon going to grow a beard, like his uncle Eric,' and Wayne would be convinced by the end of the trip that he was indeed growing whiskers on his chin! It gave us great amusement and passed the time of the journey for him. Nowadays, it's Jake, Wayne's son, that we tease instead. He's four now and spends a lot of time with us. Our time spent with Jake is precious, he keeps us young at heart and looks so much like his daddy, when he was of the same age, it's amazing. He thinks that our home is his second home and is a very loving child. He tells me he loves me but adds 'he is Grandad's boy'. He has told us recently 'that he's eating up all his dinners, so he can be big and strong, like Granddad and have a big belly just like him'! When Richard had a recent haircut, Jake told us 'he wants a haircut just like Granddad's, with a hole in the middle'. As Richard's hair is receding now, on top, we think Jake may change his mind about this as he gets older! Jake feels the back of my head for 'the invisible eyes' that I tell him I have there, he also believes I can see around corners and that his granddad can tell what he wants, by reading his forehead. Oh the innocence of children!

Although Richard and I have remained closely in love during our years together, Richard always sensed the special bond that Wayne and I had. He never minded that fact and Wayne would always be my close little companion.

The nights Richard chose to go out to his bingo, Wayne and I shared many happy evenings together watching videos or films on TV, with our bags of sweets or chocolate.

When Richard is at home, he is like Jim out of *The Royle Family* on TV. He is possessive over the remote control, as all the family know.

'Let's watch *Mary Poppins*,' he'll say, 'or how about *The Sound of Music*?'

'Oh no, not those again,' I groan. He loves the kids films nearly as much as the kids themselves.

He likes his own armchair by the fireside with the remote control by his hand. Occasionally, I've had little spats about this with him, then he'll be all contrite, but Richard likes his TV, while I can quite happily be engrossed in books. We never fall out and have rarely rowed in our lifetime together.

The odd occasion I've had moods on me when we have slightly disagreed, it's nearly always been my fault. At times like when I was going through the menopause and suffered a bad bout of depression and took it out on him, bless him, he's always avoided arguments and he loves a peaceful life. Fortunately my depression was not to last long, following my hysterectomy in 1999.

'God bless the HRT patches!' says Richard.

TWENTY-FOUR

In October 1996, my niece in Australia, Angela, was due to be married to Joshua.

We were invited to the wedding but I doubted I would be up to such a long-haul flight. Richard desperately wanted us to go, so we saved up long and hard and finally decided to give it a try.

Wayne, at sixteen years old, had decided he was too old to be going on holiday with us any more. Once we had made the decision to fly out to Australia, however, he decided it would be too much of an opportunity to miss and agreed he would come with us one last time. So our flights were all booked and we were ready to go.

Richard and Wayne were very excited at finally making it to Australia, whereas I was both excited, yet full of trepidation at our reunion. It would be the first time we were to be reunited following Stuart's death.

Richard nearly had to drag me through to the lounge where Ann and David waited. I was so nervous. At last we were through and I caught sight of their smiling faces. Our Ann and I fell into each other's arms where we hugged, laughed and cried together, all at the same time. Then David had his arms around me and I was glad we were together at long last.

Richard and David shook hands warmly, then Ann hugged both Richard and Wayne. They were surprised to see how much Wayne had grown, he was a young man himself by then. I had been afraid the sight of seeing Wayne might upset them as he was around the same age as Stuart had been when they had lost him, but I need not have worried. Both Ann and David were delighted at seeing him.

We were welcomed into their home, where Angela and Joshua waited to meet us all, along with Betty and Eric and David's parents Molly and Jack. They had all travelled to Australia a little earlier than us. Joshua was a very handsome, dashing young man. He was quite shy, yet extremely sociable. Everyone was excited over their forthcoming wedding. Joshua had formed a good relationship with Ann and David and it was so obvious that Angela and Joshua were such a well-matched couple.

It was lucky for us that we could all stay at Ann and David's home during our stay in Australia. It was a gorgeous bungalow with an extensive back garden that David had recently completed. It had a wonderful view of Sugar Loaf Mountain, where the sun set each evening. I spent many an evening out in their garden, watching the sun go down over the mountain. I knew it was the mountain where Stuart's ashes had been scattered and I prayed for him a lot as I sat out there alone.

He would stay forever in my heart.

The wedding of Angela and Joshua took place at Terragon, a coastal area of New South Wales. It was a beautiful service and was followed by a splendid reception at a hotel where we had all booked rooms for the night. Angela made a beautiful bride and Joshua was handsome in a formal suit. The following day was our Wayne's seventeenth birthday. As a surprise to Wayne, Richard let him drive our rental car around the car park. It was also a surprise to me too, and my hands shook as I caught it on videotape. Angela and Joshua came to Ann and

David's home the day following the wedding, where they had another small celebration tea and opened their wedding gifts. I later got to walk around the garden with Angela and we talked together before they left to go on their honeymoon.

After the wedding, we were all able to have many days out. We shared days at zoos and the different coastal areas of New South Wales as well as the famous Lake Macquarie. They were happy family outings.

The holiday was nearly at an end when I finally managed to get to talk to David properly and I expressed a wish to go up to Sugar Loaf Mountain to pay my respects to Stuart and take flowers to the ledge where they had scattered his ashes. I wanted to say my goodbyes.

David understood this and privately approached Ann about it. It was two days before we were to leave Australia that we all got ready to drive up the mountain. Betty and Eric also wanted to go, but Wayne stayed with Molly and Jack that day. Betty and Eric came in our car while David led the way in his car with Ann.

Ann had been out in her garden early that morning, had picked flowers and prepared our own individual posies to take with us. I had wanted to buy flowers, but Ann insisted that Stuart would prefer flowers picked from his mum's garden.

We finally arrived at the ledge where they had had the service and scattered Stuart's ashes. We each laid our flowers and said our own individual prayers and goodbyes. It was such a sad day, with lots of tears from all of us, but at least I felt I had been able to say goodbye. I would never, ever forget our Stuart.

I always think of him, and the songs 'Knocking on Heaven's Door' or 'Tears in Heaven' still provoke tears in me when I hear them.

Stuart will forever be in my memory. He was such a lovely boy; as a young child, he never ceased talking. His constant questions always amused me, his lovely nature and his love of other people always shone through. His humour and his love will stay, curled around my heart-strings, always.

Our two weeks in Australia had flown by. We all said our sad farewells and Ann and David drove us to Sydney, from where we returned home to the UK.

Wayne started taking driving lessons and managed to pass his test and went on to purchase his first car. He had gained his NVQ in motor mechanics but decided this was not to be his vocation. He got a job working in a shop in town where he worked hard, long hours.

At seventeen, he met Nicola, and they fell in love. Nicola was so young that Richard was very dubious about their courtship. Wayne told us Nicola was only fourteen – we were to find out later that she had only been thirteen years old at the time. Richard thought of his own daughters at that age and felt Nicola was too young to be getting seriously involved with anyone. I was more open-minded.

They were to let no one get in their way, however, and over the next few years, Wayne and Nicola were constantly together. They would let nothing or no one come between them. Wayne even neglected his best mates so as to spend most of his time with Nicola. She was a lovely girl but was so young when they were first together that she was still painfully shy and had little self-confidence. As time went by, Richard and I could both see that no one could part them and we had to leave them alone.

Wayne decided to leave home, get a flat of his own and stand on his own two feet. I was devastated at the time. He was still my baby and I did not feel ready for him to leave home. He was determined to try it on his own, though, so we had to let him go. I was so upset about it that when he had found his flat and was due to move out, I got Richard to take me away so I would not be at home to see him leave. When we came back home and Wayne's bedroom was all bare, it finally hit me that all my children had flown the nest now. The house seemed so empty. There was only Richard and myself at home, and I had to come to terms with that.

When we went to visit Wayne in his new flat, we could see how nicely he had settled in and that gave me some comfort. The fact that his flat was only a five-minute drive from our house also helped. I was soon to find out that I wasn't losing him, as he and Nicola were frequent visitors; Nicola was also close to me by now.

Their courtship continued and as soon as Nicola reached the age of sixteen, she moved into the flat to be with Wayne. She had left school by then and had found a job, where she worked hard, as did Wayne. They later on found the flat to be too expensive to run and managed to obtain a small, one-bedroomed council flat only a little further away.

They continued working hard and had soon turned their little flat into a beautiful little home. We stayed close on hand for them and visited whenever we could. The main thing was they loved each other and were very happy together.

When we went to see them at their flat, Nicola would proudly show me the household purchases they had bought and would beam with pride when I admired them. 'You've got the place looking lovely,' I would tell her in all honesty.

They did not go out much, as money was tight for them, yet they were quite content to stay in and watch the soaps on TV together after work, like an old married couple. It was obvious they were happy together. I told Richard, 'They are going to be all right together, those pair.'

'I told you they would be, I don't know why you worried in the first place,' he replied.

'I never worry,' I lied.

'Well, somebody does,' he laughed.

TWENTY-FIVE

Angela and Joshua had already been blessed with the birth of Jake and now had a new baby son, Kye. We had been asked to attend Kye's christening.

This time we decided we would have a stopover on each leg of the journey. So in February 2000, after much planning, we set off. On the way out we stopped in Singapore, where we spent three nights.

The night we got there, we slept straight through for twelve hours. We spent a wonderful few days in Singapore, visiting the beautiful island of Sentosa and enjoying a cable-car ride back from there. We also got to visit Chinatown where Richard was measured up for a tailor-made suit and some lovely silk shirts and ties, which were all hand-made and delivered to our hotel room before we left.

In Australia we were once again met by Ann and David in Sydney. Angela and Joshua lived in a lovely house that Joshua had built himself. It was in an amazing spot, set back in woods with a beautiful view and only a ten-minute drive from the beach. They lived in Avoca Beach on the central coast, New South Wales. The house really felt like a home. It was lovely to be reunited once more with them and meet their two beautiful sons. Jake, who was only going on three years old at the time, had Angela's red hair and Joshua's dark-brown eyes. He looked so much like our Stuart, however, it was quite amazing. New baby Kye sported a mop of dark curly hair.

We attended Kye's christening then stayed overnight at Angela and Joshua's home after a lovely celebration tea with family and friends. We spent a happy evening outside, on the veranda of Angela and Joshua's home with them, along with Ann, David and Joshua's parents.

We were woken very early next morning by the screeching of cockatoos outside our bedroom window. There was a balcony outside the house from where the view was splendid and colourful parrots and cockatoos came to the veranda looking for food.

After the stay at Angela's, Ann and David took Richard and myself to Sydney for a couple of days. We stayed in a hotel and got to visit the opera house, Sydney harbour and many places of interest. The weather was sunny and warm and the four of us managed to get our faces sunburned. 'Our Angela will go mad at us,' moaned Ann, 'we look like a couple of Pommie tourists.'

We left Sydney and drove up to the Blue Mountains, where we spent another couple of happy care-free days. The views up in the Blue Mountains were amazing and David took us to see the Three Sisters rock formation – he joked that it was me, Betty and Ann, cut out of the mountain. There were several lookout points where a lot of coach parties stopped, and the views certainly were spectacular. Way up high, we looked out at miles of dense, thick forests of trees. It was uninhabited land, as far as the eye could see.

There were people of all nationalities there, all of them poised with their cameras or camcorders, all of them trying to capture the beautiful views. It was there that we saw a huge, aboriginal man. He was a giant of a man, looking to be nearly seven feet tall. He stood in native costume as he played his didgeridoo, with a hat on the ground, for coins to be dropped in from tourists as he played his tunes. Ann and I approached him and asked if he would mind if we took a photograph of him. He happily agreed to this and we even managed to get photographs of him as he stood poised with Ann and me by his side. When our films were developed, the photographs would show just how tall he was. We looked like dwarfs beside him!

We stayed overnight up in the Blue Mountains, and I was surprised to see how many blankets and quilts the hotel had provided for our beds. The reason soon became apparent – temperatures plummeted quickly in the mountains and it got cold at night. Ann and David took us to a club there where they served good meals. This club also had numerous slot machines, which they call pokey machines in Australia. As Ann and Richard are both partial to the pokey machines and played them enthusiastically, David and I were content to watch them. Neither David nor I are into gambling, but were happy to see them enjoying themselves as they put their dollars in. They had a few drinks and Ann got quite merry as the evening wore on. Richard has a favourite saying, 'Give it some welly', which means to give it your best shot. Ann got the saying mixed up and the more merry she got, the louder she cried, 'Go on, Richard, give it some willy!' as she watched him play one of the machines. We watched them squander a few dollars with a lot of amusement and it gave both David and myself great pleasure that evening to hear our Ann's laughter; it was music to our ears.

After we had driven back to their house, Angela visited again. She had missed us all. Together we visited beaches and spent many happy hours together. Angela and I even managed to get out shopping, just the two of us, while Ann looked after Jake and Kye. I bought some presents to bring home for the children.

David and Ann took us to see some of their friends who we had met on our first visit to Australia. Betty and Rowan Evans had us all over for a meal at their home, which was in Meadowie, in the outback. We all went out walking nearby where the kangaroos ran wild.

Following our walk in the outback, we returned and sat outside their lovely home, enjoying a drink while Rowan grilled steaks and sausages, which we ate with salads and fresh bread and butter. Then we retired indoors, before dusk descended, when the mosquitoes would come out in full force. We were then served the most delicious desserts that Betty had prepared herself. She is a wonderful cook and a gracious hostess.

After such a wonderful meal we sat in their lounge and shared more drinks, though both Richard and David had to be careful with their drinks, they had to drive at the end of the evening. Betty and Rowan had spent a recent weekend in Sydney and were regaling us with their memories. They had gone out and got tipsy and had ended up visiting a sex shop there. We were all laughing about this when suddenly Rowan left the room. When he next put his head around the door, he said he would have to put the light out for a moment as he had something to show us! He told Ann and me that we had to keep our eyes tightly closed until he said we could open them. What happened next came as a huge surprise! When Rowan told us we could open our eyes, he stood there poised with a huge vibrator that was lit up like a beacon. Everyone howled with laughter, but when Rowan tried to put our Ann's hand on it, she squealed and we laughed all the more.

Rowan is such a character and had us in stitches all evening, especially when it was time to leave and we had said our farewells. As we went to our cars to drive away, he proceeded to guide us down the driveway in the darkness, while he guided us like a traffic policeman with the huge illuminated vibrator in his hand. We were still laughing as we drove away, Rowan still waving to us with his unusual torch! We keep in touch with them to this day and Betty writes to me every Christmas and gives me a rundown on the year's events.

A couple of days before we were due to leave Australia, David and Ann took us out in their boat on Lake Macquarie. I have always had a fear of deep water, but once we set sail, all my fears disappeared. We spent the whole day out on that vast lake, and even stopped so they could all try their hands at fishing. Richard managed to catch a small fish about six inches long that, upon reeling it in, he promptly let go onto the deck. It was a very small fish, but whatever it was it had a set of vicious, snapping little teeth. I screamed my head off while Richard and David tried to catch hold of it by its tail to throw back into the water, though not before we had taken a photograph of the 'huge whopper', as Richard was later to call it in his retelling.

At the end of a wonderful day, Ann drove me home while Richard helped David sort out the boat. They got back to the house just as dusk was setting in and poor Richard was bitten from head to foot by mosquitoes.

Next day, he was covered in enormous bumps – he had had an allergic reaction to the bites. As it was the day before we were due to fly off to Dubai on the next leg of our holiday, we visited a pharmacy in Newcastle, New South Wales, where the pharmacist sold him strong antihistamines and a foul-smelling body lotion to apply. I felt so sorry for him, covered in all those bumps, which were extremely itchy and irritable. We said our goodbyes once again and left for Dubai.

During this visit to Australia I had been able to spend more time with Angela and the bond between us was strengthened. We had managed to share some intimate conversations together and had even talked of the loss of Stuart. I was made to realise during our talks how profoundly Angela had been affected by the loss of her brother and I felt so sad that I had been unable to have been more use to her at the time she needed someone most. Twelve thousand miles is a long distance to be from family, it is half a world away. It's during times of crisis within the family that we feel it most.

Leaving Angela and her boys had been so hard to do and I worried for her safety as she left her mum's house in floods of tears to take her boys home on the fifty-mile trip to their house. It was also hard to leave Ann and David when they took us to Sydney Airport, yet these were more settled times for them now and I had been able to see them as the proud grandparents they were now.

I looked forward to our stopover in Dubai, where we had arranged to stay for four days. Dubai was so different to other countries we had visited before, but their beaches are the most beautiful beaches of anywhere in the world. The ocean was so clear, and little fishes swam right up to the edge of the beach.

Dubai was to be like a proper honeymoon for Richard and me. We were so happy and so much in love. We had been advised to visit the souks (markets) and Richard had promised to buy me an eternity ring when we visited the gold souks. The first couple of days we rested up either on the beach or by the hotel pool to recover from our flight from Sydney. Then, the second night we were there, we got a taxi to the markets. The smells of all the different spices assailed our nostrils on reaching them. We browsed all the different kinds of exotic spices, then set off for the gold souks, the sights of which neither of us had seen before. There was street upon street of gold shops. All the streets and lampposts were decked in pretty lights and there was such a sense of festivity all around us.

We slowly trailed the many gold shops and looked at trays upon trays of gold rings, some set with the most brilliant jewels I had ever seen in my life. We finally chose the first shop window we had looked at on arriving at the market. Richard would say that it was typical of me.

Richard bought me a beautiful gold eternity ring with seven sparkling diamonds. He also bought Helen an Italian gold bracelet.

We went back to where we were staying to have a meal and Richard fancied a beer or two to celebrate. We could certainly enjoy a meal but all Richard's hopes of enjoying a celebratory drink were quashed – it was the Eid festival in Dubai and no alcohol could be bought anywhere in all of the country. So he slipped the ring onto my finger in the Indian restaurant we had chosen for our meal and we toasted our love together with water that night.

For the next couple of years, Richard and I chose to have our holidays in Tenerife. It was not so far to travel as I was starting to feel my health problems could be a hazard. I was getting too scared to travel too far by now, as I felt my body was letting me down, though in my mind I still felt young.

TWENTY-SIX

In 2001 Wayne took a short break from work and came to see me. He had something to tell me, he said. I guessed what it might be but was delighted when he told me that Nicola was pregnant. She was only seventeen years old but they had been together for four years. They had remained childhood sweethearts and were devoted to each other. When I told Richard, he was as delighted as I was for them.

As Wayne and Nicola had only a one-bedroomed flat at that time, they decided to look for somewhere larger before the birth of the baby. They ended up buying a property on the same road we live on, within walking distance of our house.

They were due to move into their new home on 23 February 2002. Nicola had been kept busy packing up all their belongings ready for the move, and then went into labour the night before. Wayne phoned us from hospital to let us know Nicola was in and that he was staying with her for the birth. During the early hours of 23 February, Nicola gave birth to Jake, a healthy, bouncing boy, and both mother and baby were well. This was the second Jake in our family, so became known to us as baby Jake, while Jake in Australia is big Jake.

Wayne had been up all night long, yet still had to move all their furniture into the new house that day. We planned on going to the hospital to visit Nicola and our new grandson later on in the day. Nicola's mum and her husband were helping Wayne move their furniture.

In the afternoon we had a surprise phone call from Nicola asking if she could come to our house. I told her, 'Yes, of course, but where are you?' She had been let out of hospital and Wayne had brought her to the new house, but all the hassle of the moving was too much for her. It had only been hours since giving birth to Jake.

Richard said he would go and fetch her, so they came back to our house, Nicola and baby Jake, complete with the new sterilising unit she had, to make up Jake's bottles. Unfortunately she had no baby milk. Richard dashed off to the chemist to buy the tin of baby milk and then, as Nicola rested, we tried to work out between us how to work the sterilising unit and prepare some feeds. I suppose we made a comical pair, both of us with our reading glasses on, trying to fix those first feeds for Jake.

We both fell in love with baby Jake instantly and were so proud of Nicola and Wayne. Jake looked so much like Wayne, it was unbelievable.

We had been booked for some time to go on holiday to Tenerife again that February. I was glad Nicola had given birth before we left as I had not wanted to miss this happy event. They soon got settled into their new house and Jake was only six days old when we left for our week's holiday.

It was the only time I ever felt reluctant to go on holiday. I did not want to leave them but, as it was only for a week, I consoled myself that we would soon be back and able to enjoy seeing Jake in his early days.

How wrong I was. He would be a month old when I next got to see him. If I had known what lay ahead of me, I would never have gone to Tenerife.

We were staying, not for the first time, at the Santa Maria Hotel in Torviscas. We spent a week in the lovely sunshine and enjoyed our holiday, but were already looking forward to coming home and seeing our family and new baby grandson again. On the very last day of our holiday, we had packed and checked out of our room. Our flight home was not until much later that night so we had the whole day to ourselves to spend beside the pool, then we would use the courtesy room to shower and change, ready to be picked up from the hotel about 9 p.m. that night. As the day progressed, however, I started to feel unwell. My stomach started to swell up and I was feeling sick. At first I thought it was just a bad bout of trapped wind. We had a light lunch at the poolside bar but this only made me more nauseous. Richard helped me walk about, hoping I would be able to pass wind, as my stomach continued growing bigger.

This did not work so we tried cups of hot tea to try and relieve it. This only made things worse and I started suffering from vomiting and diarrhoea. I thought by now I had caught the 'Spanish tummy' and felt that as long as we caught the plane I could cope with all of that at home. As the time approached for us to get ready for our journey, I was starting to feel really ill. My stomach had grown so large by this time that I looked pregnant myself and was suffering terrible stomach pains. When we eventually got use of the courtesy room, I could hardly stand up. Richard helped me shower and dress as best as I could, then we had to wait in the hotel lounge ready for the bus to come and take us to the airport.

I had been determined to make our flight as I just wanted to get home now, but it was not to be. Richard was very concerned for me and he sought the help of our holiday rep, who came to see me. She suggested that I was too ill to travel and should go to the hospital. I was upset about this but on the verge of collapse by then, so she called a taxi for us, which she said would be quicker than an ambulance, and off we went to Hospiten Sur in Las Americas.

Once we had been seen by an interpreter and our insurance details had been ascertained, I was quite quickly examined and x-rayed. The results showed I had a bowel obstruction and needed to be kept in hospital. A surgeon came to see me and assured me it was only for observation and to be able to get me rehydrated.

I was taken up to a ward and put into a room shared by another patient. Poor Richard was then told he had to leave me. I was aghast and could see the concern on his face. We had checked out of our hotel and he had nowhere to sleep at this point. Richard had to leave and I worried about him, but felt helpless.

A couple of hours later, the nurses got me up out of bed and moved me to another private room, which had two free beds in it. I was put into one of the beds and shortly afterwards there was a knock on the door and there was Richard, accompanied by a security guard and a nurse. I was so relieved to see him, dragging our suitcases with him. He looked a lot happier now and explained that he had phoned a helpline and spoken to someone, who had made arrangements for Richard to be able to stay with me at the hospital. He had been given a choice of either staying with me or being put in a nearby hotel. He chose to stay with me and was given the bed next to me. The language barrier while in hospital was to be a constant battle. We did not speak Spanish and the hospital staff's English was very limited. Richard was constantly up and down between floors trying to sort out our problems between our insurance company and the hospital. We were terrified the insurance company would refuse to pay out and had visions of having to sell our house to be able to cover all the costs. Eventually it was sorted out and the insurance company agreed to pay, as I had never suffered any bowel problems before.

I had been admitted to Hospiten Sur on the Friday evening. All weekend Richard had been kept busy sorting out insurance details and phoning Wayne and Helen back home to let them know where we were – they had expected us back by the Saturday morning.

On the Monday morning, I was visited by the surgeon, Dr Cherubino. He was a handsome young Spanish doctor and after a quick examination of my tummy, he took pains in his best English to explain my problem.

'The bowel was obstructed completely,' he told us, and as it had not managed to clear itself in the couple of days I had been in hospital, he said I would need an operation where he would either attempt to cut free the obstruction or he might have to remove part of the bowel itself. I was aghast and expressed a wish to be flown home and have the operation in England. Dr Cherubino advised against this as he said the bowel could rupture and I could die. He was hoping to be able to do the operation that day but found out I had been taking my warfarin tablets as prescribed by my GP. They were also giving me heparin injections, prescribed by Dr Cherubino. There had been a mix-up with my medication due to the language difficulties. He stopped the warfarin and I went on yet another drip of vitamin K to try and get my blood to a level where it would be safe to operate. Richard now had the task of phoning the family at home and updating them on my progress on a daily basis. I'm sure that the whole time we were in there, Richard was still hoping the obstruction would clear itself and I would not need an operation. I was scared but felt everything was out of my control.

Richard kept cheerful and lifted my spirits but he was also confined to that hospital room for most of the time. Fortunately the room had its own *en suite* shower room and toilet, so we had some amount of privacy. It also had a small TV set in there but most of the programmes were in Spanish naturally, so we passed a lot of the time doing crosswords. We had taken enough clothes for one week's holiday so Richard took on the task of washing out our underwear in the bathroom and hanging it up to dry.

He used to walk down the road every day to purchase a newspaper, but always rushed back so as to be with me. He could also go down the road in the evenings and buy himself a meal and a couple of quick pints, as the hospital food was atrocious. He had to make sure he was back at the hospital by 10 p.m., though, or he would find himself locked out.

He was absolutely devoted to me and we managed to keep each other's spirits up during this time. He phoned our family every night and I would be waiting for him to get back, eager to find out how they all were.

By the Tuesday evening, I realised my problem was not going to sort itself out and that I would indeed need an operation. Richard, however, was still hoping for the best, bless him, and I was worried for him. On the Wednesday morning, Dr Cherubino visited me on his daily morning rounds, examined me, checked my blood levels and said, 'Marilyn, I need to operate.'

'All right, Doctor, when?' I asked.

'Now,' he replied. I asked him for ten minutes with my husband first and he agreed. Richard looked panic-stricken and helpless now and I knew I had to be strong for his sake. We held hands and I told him how much I loved him and that he was to take care of himself while they took me away, but we never did get the ten minutes together. They were pushing a trolley into our room to take me and we had little time to have our last kiss and reassure each other before they whisked me off down the corridor to the operating theatres. I prayed quietly all the way down there, not for myself, but for my husband and all of my family, as I felt sure I would never see them again. It was all of them that I worried for, not myself. I felt I was in God's hands now.

They brought the consent form for me to sign but I felt reluctant to sign it as it was all in Spanish. The nurse got cross with me and managed to point out the word laparoscopy, which I was able to understand, so I just signed it then. I was pushed into the operating theatre and left on the trolley as all the staff went busily ahead with their chores of setting up their apparatus and instruments as I watched. I was afraid they were not going to give me an anaesthetic. Then they spoke in Spanish to me, making signs that I was to climb onto the operating table. I found this a bit of a manoeuvre due to some weakness in my left side and the fact that I had drips going into my arms. I was trying to hitch over when suddenly one of the male staff said in stilted English, 'You, er, like music?'

That did it for me – I felt sure they were going to operate with me still awake and I now refused to budge off my trolley. There was much ado now, but I did not understand as all the bickering was in Spanish. Finally, I felt I had no other choice and managed to clamber slowly onto the operating table. The staff then placed boards on the table onto which they strapped my arms, then cuffs were put on both of my legs and I felt truly helpless by now in a position similar to a crucifixion. Then Dr Cherubino looked through the door and proceeded to rap out angry-sounding instructions to the staff in Spanish, after which I was given the anaesthetic.

Next thing I knew I was being transferred back into my bed in our room. I was in considerable pain and Richard begged the nurses for some pain relief for me. He was told I was already receiving paracetamol via my drip. After getting me back into bed, Richard's face showed such relief at having me back. He lovingly stroked my face and told me how brave I had been. I had not been brave at all, it had all been taken out of my hands really, but I was so glad to be back there with him again. My mouth was very dry as I had been given no fluids for days, but I still managed to tell Richard about the events in the operating theatre and tell him how very much I loved him. He did not leave my side that day or night and in my waking moments I could see him constantly beside me, tears on his face as he watched over me.

Richard was able to tell me that the operation had been a success. Dr Cherubino had been in to see him and told him he had managed to free not one but two obstructions, and had not needed to remove any of my bowel. I was thankful for that.

I spent one day in bed then they got me up and I was encouraged to keep walking. I was in a lot of pain but I still obeyed their instructions and managed to walk up and down the corridor with my drip stand with me. Richard and I spent hours walking up and down that corridor, which I called my green mile as it was covered in green tiles, walls and floors alike. I had been allowed no food or drink for ten days, so was extremely weak.

I was kept in Hospiten Sur for ten days with Richard by my side the whole time. He lovingly helped me shower and even washed and conditioned my long hair. I could not have managed it without him. He was so caring and devoted to me, he deserved a medal for the loving care he gave me.

After ten days in hospital, I was discharged and we were put into a hotel down the road, Noelia Sur. I still had all the clips in my wound then and we had to attend the hospital on a daily basis to check my blood. I had to give myself heparin injections daily but grew tired of this and got Richard to give me the injections instead. I told him how to do this and he managed it as confidently as any good nurse.

Seven days after the operation, the clips were removed and Dr Cherubino gave me a certificate of flight so we could make arrangements to fly home. We were given various options of flights, but our car was still parked at Birmingham Airport, so it was decided that we would be put on a flight from Tenerife to London, where a car would be waiting to pick us up with a chauffeur and we would be driven from London to Birmingham to pick up our own car to travel back to Leicester. The insurance company were very good about all the arrangements, I could have had a nurse flown out from England to accompany us on our flight, but I turned down this offer as I felt I could manage as long as I had Richard by my side. As I had recently had an operation, they insisted that we fly back business class so I could have plenty of room. Richard was delighted by this. He had always wanted to fly business class but we had been unable to ever afford it.

I was euphoric to be going home. I was still in a fair bit of pain and had developed a lump in my left groin, but I kept quiet about this as I only wanted to get back home. I would have sailed back by boat if we had to.

We arrived in London on Saturday afternoon and were then taken to a huge limousine and driven up to Birmingham, where we collected our own car and drove home. As I was in so much pain after the two-hour drive from London, we had to stop at motorway services between Birmingham and Leicester for a rest, and it was late on the Saturday night when we finally made it home. We were glad to get into bed, it had been a long, tiring day.

Next day Richard had to go shopping to buy us some provisions. I had managed to get up but found it difficult to walk around. I had a phone call from a friend of our Helen's and as I was talking to her I felt something wet dripping onto my feet. I looked down and realised my nightgown was soaking wet with blood. It looked as if I had been shot. I quickly ended the phone call and tried calling Richard on his mobile, not realising his battery had run down and he had left it on the kitchen worktop charging.

In a panic, I phoned our Wayne and said I needed his help. He walked into our house in less than a minute and promptly flew into a bigger panic than I was. He wanted to call an ambulance but I refused, so we had just started arguing when his dad walked in with the shopping. Richard had a look at me and we could see part of the wound had burst open – no wonder I was in pain.

Wayne had been saying to me, 'Where's your dressing gown, you're going to hospital.'

'No, I'm not,' I argued back to him.

'Yes, you bloody well are,' he insisted, 'I'll take you there myself.'

Richard calmed both Wayne and me down and phoned our doctor, Jeremy Goodchild, who agreed to come straight out. Jeremy and his wife Hazel soon arrived, and Jeremy wanted to send me into hospital again, fearing I could have an infection, but I begged and pleaded not to go. Hazel was most understanding about this and eventually they gave me strong antibiotics and some pain relief with instructions on daily salt baths and such. The wound would heal itself in time.

So I stayed at home and followed the instructions I had been given. Jeremy and Hazel called in again that night to see me and Jeremy took some wound swabs to send off to the laboratory. They made me comfortable before they left. They were very good to me, bless them both.

As the days passed, I followed my instructions, rested and had daily salt baths, and all our family visited me. It was lovely to see them all again and be reunited with them all, especially baby Jake.

Wayne and Nicola came to see us and Wayne proudly told me I had to get better quickly and put on some weight as they were going to marry on 2 August that year. I had lost loads of weight during my three weeks in Tenerife and was a bag of bones. Their happy news gave me the will to want to get better quickly. I needed to be well for the forthcoming wedding and promised them I would sort out all the catering for their evening reception on the big day.

I had to see another surgeon at the Leicester Royal Infirmary. He told me I had an inguinal hernia and needed another operation. I did not want it, but he insisted that if it wasn't done as an arranged operation I could end up having it done as an emergency and that if the hernia was to strangulate, it could cause serious complications.

I felt then that I had no choice and had to agree to the

operation, but managed to get it postponed until just after Wayne and Nicola's wedding.

Betty, Eric and Sharon, plus Sharon's children, Ross and Tamsyn, were all coming down to stay at our house for the week of Wayne's wedding. It was lovely having them all but I still felt very weak and frail. Betty had agreed to help me with the catering for the wedding reception, which she did, and Richard was also a great help to me at this time.

I still found it difficult to even walk but I was determined I would not give in. I could not seem to put on any weight, however, and found it hard to buy a nice outfit for the wedding. My weight had by now fallen to only seven stone six pounds. I really did look a bag of bones.

Wayne came home to sleep the night before his wedding. It was a bit of a tight squeeze in our home as we had six adults and two children sleeping over at that time, but we managed.

On the morning of Wayne's wedding, as usual I was last to get ready. Richard had taken everyone down to the register office and Wayne and I were left alone. He was busy pacing the lounge, practising his speech as I got ready. We had a quiet little time together before Richard came dashing back to collect us. As I was late he had to put his foot down a bit to try and get us there in time.

'How is it that you always manage to be late, Lyn?' Richard asked me, slightly cross.

'It's not easy, it's something that you learn over time,' I calmly replied.

Wayne was very smart and Nicola made a beautiful bride in a long satin-and-chiffon cream dress. The wedding went very well and afterwards we all went for a meal together, which Nicola's mum had arranged. Paul was Wayne's best man, but Wayne had forgotten to ask him so Paul only got to know of this fact the night before the wedding, so he had not had long to prepare his speech. I knew Richard planned on giving a speech at the wedding but he had not written one out and intended to give it from off the top of his head.

After the meal, Paul and Richard made their speeches, which were lovely. Richard started off his by saying, 'I suppose most of you here realise I am not Wayne's real dad,' when Wayne interrupted to shout, 'Who is then?' This caused great hilarity. Then Richard continued his speech and ended up by saying 'but Wayne is my son' and his voice was choked with emotion.

After the meal Wayne and Nicola went home with Jake and we all came back to our house where we were kept busy by the final preparations for the catering for the evening do. It was all a bit of a mad rush but eventually we managed it. Betty came up trumps that afternoon and evening and we had the room that was to be used for their reception all nicely decorated by 7 p.m., for when it was supposed to start. Helen had baked a beautiful wedding cake as a gift to Nicola and Wayne.

That Sunday, Mandy brought George to our house for a while and along with Betty and her family we watched the video recording we had made of the wedding. I became quite emotional while watching it. I was so proud of them all but I also had the worry in the back of my mind knowing that in a couple of day's time I was to have another operation. It had only been five months since my last one in Tenerife and I did not relish the thought of another. I went into hospital on the Wednesday and they operated on the Thursday, repairing the hernia and putting a huge graft in to help retain my abdominal muscles. The operation went well and they sent me home the following Monday.

I took things easy when I got home; I did not have much choice. Poor Richard had to see to everything once again. He managed so well, as he usually does. I still seemed to be in a lot of pain and, all in all, did not feel right at all.

Two weeks exactly after the hernia repair operation, Richard was busy watering the flowers in our garden when a friend of mine, Pat, came to see me. I confided in her that I did not seem to be recovering as quickly as I thought I would. Pat reassured me that I would soon be well again and that it was early days yet. We enjoyed a cup of tea together then Pat went off home. Richard had gone upstairs to have a bath, and as he came downstairs, I suddenly felt a pop inside my tummy and immediately felt severe pain on my left side where I had had the operation. I just knew something bad had happened and hardly dared to take my hand away to show Richard. He could not see anything drastically wrong, but the pain kept getting more and more severe. I needed to pass urine but was in such agony that, even as Richard helped me to our outside loo, I howled with pain. It was worse than even the pains of childbirth.

Richard got me onto a sofa and dialled 999, but as the paramedics arrived I begged them not to move me, the pain was so horrific and my tummy was once more starting to swell up very quickly. They had to bring in gas and air to try and relieve the pain as they moved me into the ambulance. I felt every bump of the short journey to the hospital and sucked away on the gas and air until I slipped into unconsciousness, yet the pain always brought me round again. Richard had followed the ambulance in our car and I screamed for him while they transferred me to the A&E department. It was so busy that evening that we were parked up on a trolley in the waiting area, but no one could part me from that gas and air.

I was x-rayed and sent upstairs to a ward on the trolley, still with my faithful gas and air cylinder beside me. They had a problem with me again as I had already been restarted on my aspirin and warfarin tablets and my blood was thin. The doctor treating me felt a scan was needed to help him in his diagnosis, but they were so short-staffed there were no porters to take me down. It was apparent something was dreadfully wrong, as my stomach had swelled up so much the sutures were giving way on my recent operation scar. It looked like I had a football inside me. It was like something you only see in horror movies and I was very scared. The doctor eventually helped a male nurse move me, still on my bed, into the lift to take me for a scan. Richard had to run beside them opening doors for them. They had given me morphine for the pain but it barely did anything. They increased the dose, but still the pain was terrible.

The poor young doctor had been about to finish his long shift and still carried his backpack on his shoulder as he studied the scan alongside two consultants who had been called in. Richard was still by my side as the doctors shared differences of opinions. They saw a mass, but one consultant thought it was blood and the other thought it was bowel. They needed to operate as quickly as possible, but first had to try and get my blood level just right.

I was taken back to the ward again and given more morphine and hourly blood tests. During the early hours of the morning they advised Richard to go home and get some rest, as it would be much later in the day when they would be able to operate safely. He had not long been home and had just got into bed when the hospital called him back. I was refusing to sign the consent form for the operation as the word 'colostomy' was on the form as a possibility and I did not want to have that done. I begged the doctor just to put me to sleep to get rid of all the pain. I think he took it in the literal sense and thought I wanted to be put down like an animal at the vet's as he told me, 'We can't do that yet, it's illegal.'

Richard returned to the hospital and made me sign the consent form. He would not leave my side after that. They took me off at about 11 a.m. that Friday morning and, after putting a central line into my heart via a vein in my neck, they finally put me under anaesthetic.

I woke up in intensive care, where I spent the next few hours before being moved back to the ward, where Richard waited patiently for me in an armchair.

Blessedly, the intense pain had been relieved. The following day, I was told a huge blood clot had been removed, but the worst news was that an artery had burst in my abdomen and this had caused all the swelling and pain. As fast as they had transfused me with blood, it had kept pumping out. I was lucky to be alive. I was also fortunate that I did not need that colostomy – I would have hated that.

I must have looked a sorry sight when Wayne and Nicola brought baby Jake in to see me that Friday night of the operation. I had wires and tubes all over the place, but Wayne came to my bed and let little Jake touch my face. They all looked so worried about me, bless them, and I regretted them having to see me like that. Nevertheless, I was glad at the same time to be able to still see them at all.

Next evening, Paul came to see me as soon as he finished work. He and Richard joked together yet I could still tell they were concerned. Richard had had no sleep now for two nights and he left then to get some rest himself while Paul stayed with me. He sat beside my bed and stroked my face gently. I told him how much I loved him and how proud I was of him and saw tears slip from his eyes. Paul gave me great comfort that night, though I begged him to go home to Becky and his three children, but he stayed with me awhile, and I will never forget it. I felt so lucky to have such a wonderful son.

I felt very frail now – I had had three operations in the space of five and a half months – but was able to be sent home the following week to recuperate at home. Paul and Brogan, his eldest daughter, visited me at home and I showed them my back and legs, where I was black-and-blue from my upper back all the way down to the backs of my legs.

It took me a long time to recuperate. I was so weak I had to be taken out in a wheelchair, much to my disgust. It was all very dramatic at the time and I was emotionally very traumatised by it, but with the support of our doctor and his wife, Jeremy and Hazel, as well as all my family, I did eventually recover. The year 2002 had been another eventful year.

TWENTY-SEVEN

In early 2003, we had another blow. Richard's mam Dot was taken into hospital. She was there for three weeks and we visited her constantly. She had a virus infection. She seemed to be making no progress, though they talked of sending her home after some rehabilitation. We could see she wasn't well enough to be sent home and sadly she died on a Saturday morning in March 2003. She was 88 years old, yet we were unprepared for her passing and it still came as a shock to us all.

Richard had to arrange everything and I helped him as best as I could. We arranged a quiet funeral, attended by only family and a few close friends of hers. After the funeral, Richard and I had the job of having his mam's flat cleared out and her affairs put into order. That was another chapter of Richard's life over and was a very sad time for us. We had to try and show brave faces for the family's sake, but we both felt deep sorrow at the loss of Richard's mam.

Later in 2003, we had some good news: Ann, David, Angela, Joshua and their two boys, Jake and Kye, were to make another visit to the UK in the summer. They were all to stay with Molly and Jack but had arranged a week to come and stay with us in Leicester. It was Joshua's first visit to England and he was keen to see as much of our country as possible. While they were up North David took them to Gretna Green, Scotland, the Lake District and many other places of interest.

Richard and I went up to see them all before they were to come down to Leicester, staying with Betty and Eric for the weekend. Molly and Jack were in their element at having them all stay with them, especially young Jake and Kye, their great-grandchildren.

When we got to see them all we were in for another surprise. Our Angela gave us her news that she was pregnant again. I was overjoyed for her. She had suffered a recent miscarriage so this new baby would be especially precious.

We returned home after the weekend away and awaited their visit to Leicester. All our family were excited at the prospect of seeing them all.

We knew that David and Joshua are not ones for just sitting around indoors, they like to get out and about, so Richard had prepared a rough itinerary of things for us all to do. Joshua was keen to see all the sights in London, but Jake and Kye were a bit too young to be trailing around there yet. So Joshua and Angela set off early one morning on their own to catch a train to London, leaving the little ones with Ann and David. We all went down to Abbey Park with the boys and took Nicola and baby Jake with us too. We had a lovely day down there with the children. When Angela and Joshua got back from London late that night, Kye and Jake were fast asleep in bed; they had been no trouble.

Another good day out we had was when we took them all to Cadbury World. Again, we took Nicola and Jake with us and also Gemma and James. All the kids loved that day out, you could see that by the amount of chocolate around their faces. We all piled back to our house afterwards for tea. We still have a basketball hoop on the side of our house, which Paul used to use when he was younger and practising. Wayne had used the basketball hoop when he was younger too. After our day out at Cadbury World, all the children wanted to try their hands at the basketball hoop, even the grownups joined in. Angela's son, Jake, tried and tried relentlessly and finally managed to get the ball through the hoop, his little face shone with pride.

We took them all to Foxton Locks on the nearby Grand Union Canal on another occasion. David had already been there with us on one of their earlier stays in the UK, but they thought Joshua might find it interesting to see how the locks worked on the canals. Indeed he did, but Jake and Kye loved it too, especially seeing all the barges pass through the locks. The man operating the locks let them help him ease the lock gates open and they were thrilled at this and laughed excitably.

Before they left Leicester to go back up North, we all went out for a big family meal at a local pub. Afterwards, when Jake and Kye had been put to bed, Richard got out his bottle of whisky for him and David. As they got quite merry together, the jokes flew between the two of them and the night became hilarious. It was all good fun. Richard and David share the same dry humour. David likes to tease our Ann and always has. When he does this, she gets on her high horse and gets huffy with him, which David knows and he will then tease her all the more. The banter between them has been a great source of amusement to us over the years. Whenever they have played games with any of the children over the years, be it Scrabble, Monopoly or whatever, David tends to deliberately cheat and Ann would then end up getting all irate as she always took the games so seriously. Ann, like myself, is a sore loser, though she will not admit to this.

Ann also loves her game of bingo, as does Richard, whereas both David and myself find the game totally boring. When they are back home in Australia, Ann has her regular days out at her bingo sessions, while David is at work. Now, as Richard and David enjoyed their whisky, David took huge delight at regaling us with Ann's bingo days out and how she is so serious about them. I think Ann tends to feel a bit guilty over her love of the game, and becomes defensive over it. The more defensive Ann got, the more David teased her, and all the while Ann looked to Richard for his support. As he chose to back her up, David teased the two of them.

Ann told me she had visited her doctor in Australia, complaining of the severe headaches she got after having sex. 'Do you get them, Lyn, when you and Richard have sex?'

'No,' I told her. 'What did your doctor say it was?'

'Well, it was Barney, our doctor, and he said to me, "I don't know what that can be, Ann, why don't you get your husband to give you a neck massage after making love to see if that will help." I told him, well, I could try that, Barney, but I will have to wake him up first.'

She said he nearly fell off his chair laughing.

As the drinks flowed, so did the banter that night, and although I was only drinking tea, I could see the funny side to it all and was in stitches of laughter. It wound up the evening extremely well. As I remember the times we have shared together with Ann and David I feel so lucky to have such a wonderful husband and family, and I know Richard and David are two of the good guys. Before coming over to England, Ann had asked Richard, during a phone conversation, if he would take her to a bingo session in Leicester once they got down to our home, and Richard had promised her he would. It had been on the plane journey from Australia to England that Ann had suddenly remembered she had forgotten to pack her bingo dabber. Just as David had closed his eyes starting to doze off, Ann had startled him awake, crying, 'Oh no, guess what I have forgotten to pack?' David had thought it must be something like her medication or her purse, so was none too pleased to find out it was only her dabber. When we found out about this, Richard had a good idea! He bought her a new dabber and we put a label on it stating it was Ann's pommie dabber. We had then packed it up in tissue paper and had packed it in several boxes, each box bigger than the next, so it ended up a sizable package, which we then wrapped in gold paper. Richard presented Ann with her gift and told her to handle it very carefully, as it was fragile. Her face was a picture when she found out what it was and the amusement it caused had been well worth the effort.

So they travelled back up North to spend a few more days with Molly and Jack, but we managed to get another weekend up there just before they left for Australia and went to Newcastle Airport to see them off on their connecting flight down to London.

In hindsight, maybe we should not have gone, as most of David's family, including his mam and dad, all turned up at the airport to say their goodbyes. Molly and Jack were well into their eighties by then and it turned out to be a very emotional day for all concerned. Angela gave me a gift at the airport, a little gold heart on a chain. I never take it off. I think we must have made it all the harder for Ann and David, Angela and Joshua, to have to finally leave. It was extremely hard for us to see them go and we were all very emotional.

Some weeks later, David sent us a DVD he had put together on his computer. Ann sent a letter with it and warned me to have a box of tissues handy for when we watched it. On the disc, as we played it, David had put lots of still photos of them, and of us all. He had put a musical background to it; all the different songs he had chosen were so fitting. Towards the end of the DVD we got to the photographs taken at the airport and the music that David applied to this was 'Time to Say Goodbye' by Sarah Brightman and Andrea Bocelli. It brought all the memories flooding back to when we did have to say goodbye. As the music built up to the final crescendo, the DVD ended with a photograph of Ann and I together. It's a wonderful disc, brilliantly put together, but Ann had been right to warn me about the tissues. I certainly needed them, as I must have wept for England when we watched it.

When my granddaughter Gemma came round to our house to see us, we told her about the DVD and she wanted to watch it as well. I warned her that she might find it sad at the end but I was determined I wouldn't cry again. Richard, Gemma and I watched it together and sure enough, at the end of it, as much as I steeled myself up for it, as soon as Gemma started weeping, so did I, much to Richard's amusement. Credit to David though, it was all very cleverly put together, he must have given it a lot of thought. We have watched that DVD now many times, and it never fails to move me to tears. Memories!

We took Gemma and James with us to stay with Betty and Eric for a weekend and went to visit Molly and Jack, who were very pleased to see us. They were delighted to see the children as they had not seen them since they were very young and had sat on Jack's lap. As Betty and Eric had only a two-bedroomed bungalow, my niece Sharon let Gemma and James sleep at her house with her children, Ross and Tamsyn. Her children were also growing up fast. Ross was sixteen years old and in college. Tamsyn was a little beauty who was very close to her Uncle Richard. She was a tomboy just like our Ann used to be and was into football and all sporty things at school. Our Betty would have liked Tamsyn to act and dress like a proper young lady, but Tamsyn was happiest in jeans and tracksuits, she had a mind of her own. Ross had grown up a very tall and handsome young man and, like our James, was also showing an interest in girls.

The children all got on so well together. It was the first time they had been reunited since Wayne and Nicola's wedding.

We took Gemma and James to see Durham, and visited the cathedral, where I lit a candle for our Stuart and said a little prayer for him. Then we all went on to Beamish Museum. We had been there several times but it was nice being able to show Gemma and James how things had been years ago. The sight of the old houses and cottages with their open fireplaces instilled memories of how it used to be when I stayed so many times with my Aunt Kitty and Uncle Joe when I was a young child. When we reached the mine, Gemma wouldn't go down it but I managed the tour with the help of my grandson, James. When we got down the drift shaft as far as we could go, the guide turned off his lamp for a few minutes so everyone could feel how it must have been working deep underground in total blackness. James and I clung tightly together as I remembered my dad and how it used to be when he had shown me a drift mine once in Dipton. I didn't know who was trembling the most, me or James. I was glad I had been able to take a step back in time with my grandchildren by my side.

Wayne and Nicola are still devoted to each other. Their son, Jake, looks so much like Wayne when he was the same age, four years old, about the time when Richard and I first met. Jake is a very loving child and is bright and intelligent. He spends a lot of his time at our house and Richard and I both adore him. We are honoured that we've been given so much time to spend with him.

We now tease Jake in the same way we once teased his daddy and now Jake feels for *his* invisible whiskers when we have him out in the car. He also believes I have eyes that can see around corners and feels for the eyes that I tell him 'I have in the back of my head'.

When Richard tells him, 'I know what you need, I can see it on your forehead,' Jake will lift up his fringe for his granddad to have a better view of his needs, whether it be the toilet, a drink or his dinner. He is his granddad's boy and the two of them gain hours of pleasure from each other's company.

I am also blessed to have been given the chance to enjoy Jake's company. He loves listening to my stories and I make sure to lavish him with love and praise. Never would I tell him he's a bad boy, even if he can be naughty sometimes, as all children can be. I would never be responsible for making him, or any of our children and grandchildren, feel anything less than worthy. I firmly believe all children are a blessing and should be treated as such. The love and care we give them today are the foundations that we lay down for their future happiness and self-confidence.

When Jake says, 'I love you, Grandma,' with his arms around my neck, his words are pure magic and worth more to me than all the money in the world. I tell him I love him too, and he will say, 'I know, Grandma, all the world and a pound of sugar, but I love Granddad as well and I am Granddad's boy!'

My niece, Angela, gave birth to another son, baby Ben. She sent us photos of him and he looked gorgeous. He had the same red hair and vivid blue eyes as Angela and looked just like her when she was a baby. I doubt I'll ever be able to make that long haul flight to go back to Australia. Richard would love to return but I don't feel my health is up to it – but you never know, where there is life, there is hope. We tend only to travel to Tenerife these days, as it's not so far. We love it there and are frequent guests in the Hotel Noelia Sur, the one they put us into after having my operation in Hospiten Sur. The first time we returned to it following that episode we went up to the roof of the hotel. It looks out to the sea on one side and the other side includes a view of Hospiten Sur. That first return visit there we stood on the roof and I said a silent prayer of thanks, to God and the skills of Dr Cherubino and all his staff, that I had been spared to witness being back in Tenerife.

In the summer of 2005 we received word from my sister Betty that poor old Jack's health was failing, so we went up to see him in early July. We were in for a shock though: Jack was deaf and almost blind and was so frail he could barely shuffle his feet.

Ann and David knew Jack's health was deteriorating and had already arranged a trip over, but were not due until 16 July. When Richard and I went to see Jack and saw how poorly he was, Molly told me that she did not think Jack would last long enough to be able to see Ann and David again. Molly knew I was to phone David and asked me to tell him this – she felt they needed to come earlier. David's sister, Jean, and her husband, Clifford, were helping to look after Jack and Jean herself did not feel her dad would last to see his son David again. She too wanted me to tell David of the situation.

They were all doing their best trying to cope and helping out as much as they could, but Jack was nearly 89 now and Molly herself a frail 87.

When we returned home after our weekend, Richard phoned David and we both spoke to him and Ann and let them know of his mam and dad's situation. David was under enormous pressure at his work so we left the decision up to him.

Not many days afterwards, they phoned us to let us know they had managed to get their flights rearranged and would be in the UK sooner than expected. They got to England on 7 July and were both distressed to see how much Jack had deteriorated. They stayed with Betty and Eric for their visit as Jack was sleeping downstairs by then and there were carers going in as well as Jean and Clifford.

We gave them time to get over their jet lag and settle in before we once again travelled up North to see them. We went on 15 July, and my daughter-in-law Becky had gone into labour that day, so I felt torn between Leicester and County Durham. We had not been up there long when I got the phone call from Paul to give me the news of the birth of Tate, their fourth child, and I was relieved to hear mother and baby were well.

After our weekend away we drove straight back to Paul and Becky's house to see them all and see our latest grandson, who was beautiful, so placid in nature. Ann and David did as much as they possibly could for his mam and dad while they stayed up North, but eventually managed to come down to our house at the end of the month for a few days.

When we took them to see Paul, Becky and their four children, complete with new baby, Ann was overwhelmed to get to hold Tate. She laughed and cried at the same time as she held him in her arms. She had missed so many of my grandchildren's births and being able to hold them as babies, it was all too emotional for her and she was overcome.

On Monday 1 August, Ann and David packed up their suitcases, as did Richard and I – we were flying out to Spain for a four-day break together. They were under considerable strain during this stay in England with the worry over David's mam and dad, and it had been decided months ago that we would go away with them for a short break. Richard had booked all the flights and the hotel on the Internet so off we set for Fuengirola.

It had been decided that we would do our own thing in Spain, as Ann and David wanted to sightsee more, while we were quite happy to relax by the side of the pool. Richard suggested a coach trip to Gibraltar, as Ann and David had not been there before, so we decided to go there together. I was quite excited as we got on the coach and set off on the two-hour journey. It was a Wednesday and the busiest day of the week for going to Gibraltar, as most of the other tour operators did their trips on Wednesdays. Consequently, when we arrived at the customs barrier, there was a huge delay and tailback of traffic. Our tour operator advised us on the coach that it would be much quicker if we all got off the coach and walked through the frontier.

We did as advised, but I was cramped and stiff with sitting so long on the coach. We had just cleared through immigration when I felt a huge blow to my head. I thought someone had hit me with a shovel. Apparently, I had been so busy watching where I was going with my feet, I had failed to see a huge, cast-iron taxi sign and had walked straight into it. Ann and David were way ahead of us and did not see what had happened. As Richard stopped to check I wasn't bleeding, he had me pulled close to him as I suddenly felt all my senses receding and I passed clean out. I don't remember much else then until I woke up in Gibraltar Hospital with a huge bump on my head. They wanted to keep me in, in case I got a small bleed inside my head, but I was determined to get out as we were due to fly back home next day. Ann and David came to see how I was; they were anxious but could see the funny side of it too.

We had missed the minibus that was to take us up the rock of Gibraltar and never did get to see the Barbary apes that day. Ann and David went to do some shopping and we said we would meet them back at the coach for our trip back. We barely had time to get a cup of tea before getting back to the coach in time, but at least we made it.

I was both aghast and embarrassed about the situation and felt I had let them all down by missing our trip up the rock to see the apes. Richard and David teased me relentlessly about it; it was one quip after another. They will never let me live it down. They took great delight at rubbing it in and telling anyone who would listen about it. I'm sure all of David's friends in Australia got to hear of our tale of Gibraltar. David later told me it gave him a chance to practise his first-aid skills.

We were on the plane on our way home. David sat by the window doing puzzles, Ann was next to him in the middle and I had the aisle seat next to her. Richard was in the other aisle seat directly opposite me, reading his newspaper. Ann was sat quietly reading her book, and I had a magazine in front of me but was distracted. I kept looking at our Ann as she read her book. I knew it was going to be hard to let them leave once again the next day – they were returning up North the following morning, as they were anxious to see Molly and Jack again – especially as I knew that we would not be going to see them again before they flew back to Australia on 20 August.

They needed the rest of their stay in England to spend time with David's mam and dad. I realised how hard it was going to be for them to leave this time, with David's parents being so old and frail. I could sense David's pain, though he tried not to show it.

I kept sneaking little looks at Ann as she read, noticing the fine blonde hairs on her arms. I watched her hands holding her book; they were disfigured by scars from the many operations she has had on them, one finger missing where she had to have it amputated. I looked at her poor hands and thought how much suffering she had gone through in past years. Both the pain of ill health and the tremendous pain she must have suffered at losing her beloved son.

I wondered how she had managed to keep going bravely on. I knew they had to go home, they had Angela, Joshua and three lovely grandchildren to go home to. They must have been missing them so much by now. They also had many friends in Australia, and David had his work there. That was now their home and I knew I had to try and keep strong for their sakes. I realised that they also worried about me, even though they could see how good Richard was to me and the love that we shared was obvious.

Australia is their home, as Leicester now is mine. I could not help but remember the times when Ann was just a little toddler and followed me everywhere. I tried to be a good sister to her and like to think perhaps I was like a second mother to her during her younger years. I secretly watched her on the plane, I felt her nearness and didn't want to ever let her go, but I knew I must. My heart was full of love for her and I promised myself I would try and stay strong for her sake until they had left. Inside of me I felt I could quite easily have fallen to pieces, but I wouldn't, not yet.

I was startled when Ann put her book down, turned to me with her vivid blue eyes and told me, 'You must be strong.' She went on to tell me how hard it was going to be for them to leave but said, 'You have to keep going.' I had to pull myself together quickly; our flight was already into its descent to England. There was no more time to reminisce.

My precious baby sister, with whom I had shared so much over the years, had to leave me yet again. They had stayed a total of seven weeks that time in England.

David had warned me that they might be unable to return for some time. It was, once again, time to say goodbye.

EPILOGUE

During the time I have been writing, I have been on autopilot.

I have neglected my husband, children and grandchildren as I have trawled through the corridors of my mind to recall my memories.

I apologise to my two sisters, Betty and Ann, if my memories of events differ from theirs. As individual beings, we often recall things in a light we need to remember them. I tell my story as accurately and truthfully as I remember things.

Some events of my life have proved extremely painful to recall, but at last I can exorcise old ghosts. I regret not being able to write more kindly of my mother, especially as she is no longer here to defend herself. I am sure she tried her best to be a good mother to us all. Perhaps she lacked the ability to let herself get too close to me. She kept our clothes clean, managed to feed us and looked after us materially, yet I cannot recall one instance of my mother ever telling me she loved me.

I never felt I came up to my mother's standards of what she needed from me. She always seemed to be disappointed in me, however hard I tried to please her. I cannot remember ever having sat on her lap or felt a mother's loving arms around me, yet surely that must have happened at some point in my life. The only instance I recall of Mam putting her arms around me is the day she came to me to apologise for the time she had tried to get Helen and Paul put into temporary care.

It does not matter now.

I remember my dad's love, though he was not a demonstrative man. His love shone through during all of my life, especially my childhood years when I trailed through fields, scrap yards and pit heads with him. I would happily sit for hours with my father on the back steps of our home as he worked on one thing or another. I was always eager to watch and learn from him. He taught me to change electrical plugs, put new washers onto taps and a host of other things. These things he taught me came in very useful during the times I was left alone with two young children to bring up on my own. Dad was strict with us as children and his word was law, but he was protective of us all and I know for sure he loved me and was proud of me.

I like to think that I gave him some comfort during his illness and the last few years of his life. Our father worked down the mines for forty years, sometimes in terrible conditions. It was working down the mines all those years that caused his terrible illness that led to his death at the age of 62. He did this for us, his family, and always managed to provide for us.

I remember him with love and will never forget him.

I must also apologise to my eldest children, Helen and Paul, for any painful memories they may still have of the times we spent with Jim, my second husband. I bitterly regret that they may have suffered because of mistakes I made during my life and I pray they won't blame me too much. Times were hard when I was on my own with Helen and Paul, especially during the times I struggled to feed and clothe them and keep them warm when they were so young and I barely had two pennies to rub together. Ann and David would vouch for the hard times we had when they stayed with me in Wolverton that summer in the 1960s.

I have made a lot of mistakes along the way during my sixty years. I cannot change the mistakes now. We got through it all, however, and I like to think that Helen, Paul and Wayne will remember the love that I always tried to show them. We may have been dirt poor, yet I always felt truly blessed at having such wonderful children whom I loved with all my heart and always will.

My children have been a great source of comfort and pride to me, and I could not have wished for better. I hope they realise what joy they have given me. I hope they realise how deeply I love them all.

I am lucky to have two wonderful daughters-in-law. They are so close to me and I love them as daughters. I am extremely proud of Becky and Nicola, they are both wonderful mothers – my two sons chose wisely.

The grandchildren they have given me have also been a great source of joy to me and I love them all dearly. They are very special to me in their own unique ways. They too will always hold a special place in my heart.

I think they will remember me. I hope they remember my 'magic bag'. It's an old black shopping bag I keep constantly filled with chocolate and sweet treats. They had to believe it was magic or they did not get their treats. Treats had been very scarce in the old days when Helen and Paul were very young. It had been a daily, perpetual struggle to provide basic food for them, never mind anything else. The constant worry of where the next meal was coming from kept me awake so many nights, nights when I myself had been too hungry to sleep. Is it any wonder that I get so much pleasure to be able to treat my grandchildren now, in my latter years? Surely, that is a grandmother's prerogative?

One of the happiest days in my life was when I met my husband, Richard. Richard turned my life around and has been the most caring, loving husband I could have ever wished for. He has remained steadfastly devoted to me during all of our years together.

Any unhappy years of my past have been made up for with the wonderful love we have shared together for the past 23 years. He truly is an amazing man with a calm, laid-back way of looking at life. He has a wonderful sense of humour, and always makes me laugh. Sometimes I will ask him how he feels and he says, 'I usually use my hands.' If I have had a bad night's sleep, I will ask him how he slept last night, and inevitably his reply will be, 'Well, I got into bed, put my head on the pillow and closed my eyes.'

Richard has seen me at my best and also at my worst. I believe he knows me better than I know myself. He has been behind me in everything I've ever done during our marriage and has always been a great source of comfort and support. He is solid, reliable and dependable. His total love and devotion has helped me over many hurdles.

Richard has been a good father, not only to his own three daughters but to my children also. He has been a wonderful granddad to all of our grandchildren. He has always been protective of me, sometimes overly protective, yet I realise this is only because he loves me.

I thank Richard for all the love and happiness he has given me over our years together, as well as all his endless support in everything I have ever done. He knows how much I love him. He is my best friend.

He is the one who restored my self-confidence. He is the person who has comforted me so many times during the nights when I suffered nightmares over my traumatic past life spent with a violent alcoholic. I've woken him in the night so many times over the years, he is used to it now.

In times of insecurity I have said to Richard, 'You would never forget me, ducky, would you?'

His reply has always been the same: 'Who could forget you?' he will say.

Sometimes I wonder how he's been able to cope with me all of these years, but I am glad that he has. That's the sort of man that Richard is. He has been my rock and my salvation.

I am now classified as an old-aged pensioner, yet I do not feel old in my mind. My body may be letting me down, yet still my mind remains young. As far as I am concerned, I shall keep plodding onwards as long as I have Richard, my beloved husband, by my side.

As my dad would have said . . .

'There is life in the old dog yet.'

A lot of water has run under the bridge since I first sat down to write my story. There have been many changes, some of them very sad, and we've lost dear friends along the way. We've experienced events that have nearly shattered us, but not quite.

My spirit is strong and I'm happy.

We've also had changes that have been extremely happy and we now excitedly await the birth of Wayne and Nicola's new baby – it will be our twelfth grandchild.

I've forged new friendships and met wonderful people along the way. I've shared wonderful experiences with some special people, which I will share another time.

We all have a story inside of us to tell. I am proof that dreams really can come true . . .

Dreams can come true; miracles sometimes take a little longer . . .

ACKNOWLEDGEMENTS

To my father, George William Bennett. He guided me during my early years. To Michael Kenneth Jack and George Basten. Two great friends. Their friendship enriched our lives.

This book is for my husband, Richard, my children, Helen, Paul and Wayne and all of my family, without whom the story would not have been possible.

My children understood when I had to take time out to write it.

My special thanks to Richard, who stayed faithfully by my side, through each step of the writing process. He encouraged me to keep going when I felt ready to give up. He inspired me when my spirits flagged. His help with computer skills was tremendous and he devoted endless hours of his time to help me. Without his dedication and support, it would not have been possible.

Thanks also to Ann and David who offered their encouragement from afar.

Thanks to Denise, Simon and Rachel Jack. Denise is a special friend and gave me a shoulder to cry on. She gave me strength when I needed it most.

Thanks to Juliet Martin of JAM Secretarial Services. Juliet was the first person to give me a positive response to the story, my apologies to her husband Kevin, who had to bear her tears as she worked on the manuscript.

Thanks to John Welford as he proofread my work, and offered words of wisdom.

A huge thanks to another knight in shining armour, he knows who he is! A chance letter to him started the ball rolling. Without him, it would never have become possible. He passed the letter on to KT Forster, who astonished me by having faith in my work and she kept the ball going, she deserves a big thanks. KT is a very special person with whom I share a great affinity. I owe her a huge debt. Her friendship is special and she has proved to me that dreams can come true. Thanks to KT and Sir Richard Branson.

Thanks also to all of the dedicated doctors and nurses of Glenfield General Hospital, especially Dr Peak's team of respiratory nurses, the REDS team, including Karen, Sue, Chrissy and Claire – they're all so dedicated, they kept me going.

Many thanks to Natalie, Edward and Davina, for their editorial supervision, and all the rest of the team at Virgin for all of their hard work.

To Moly and Jack Douglas, never to be forgotten.